REWRITING
HISTORY

Dick Morris

Compliments of
THE PRESIDENTIAL COALITION

REWRITING HISTORY

DICK MORRIS

with

Eileen McGann

1● ReganBooks
Celebrating Ten Bestselling Years
An Imprint of HarperCollins*Publishers*

The Library of Congress has catalogued the hardcover edition as follows:

Morris, Dick.
  Rewriting history / Dick Morris with Eileen McGann.—1st ed.
    304 p. ; 24 cm.
0-06-073668-2 (acid-free paper)
Includes bibliographical references (p. 267–290) and index.
1. Clinton, Hillary Rodham– 2. Clinton, Bill, 1946– United States—Politics and government—1993–2001. 3. United States—Politics and government—2001–.
E887.C55M67 2004
328.73/092 22

ISBN 0-06-073669-0 (pbk.)

06 07 08 09 PDC/RRD 10 9 8 7 6 5 4 3

To the brave men and women who
defend our liberty and fight against terrorism

CONTENTS

REWRITING HISTORY

1

DECONSTRUCTING HILLARY

Like the moon, she shows us the same face each time we see her. Sometimes she displays more, sometimes less of her visage, but always it is the same carefully presented persona: friendly, open, giggly, practical, family-oriented, caring, thoughtful, unflappable, serious, balanced, and moderate. Just like the moon, though, Hillary Rodham Clinton has a face she never shows us, a side that is never visible, never on display.

This book is a voyage around that side of Hillary—the parts of her personality and history that have been rewritten, reinvented, or omitted from her memoir *Living History* and her other writings or public statements. Senator Clinton's book is no more revealing of her hidden side than is a telescopic view of the moon seen from Earth. Her book simply presents, in one volume and in greater detail, all the pretense and pretend that dominates the Hillary we are allowed to see. *Rewriting History* offers a kind of annotation of Hillary's memoir, to tell more of the story she hides and the facts she omits. For much of *Living History* is not history, and much of Hillary's history is not in her book.

Some of what Hillary conceals is not dark, only unseen. Not sinister, just covered-up, protected from our gaze. Parts of it, although not always flattering, would be quite acceptable if she were to expose it to full public view. With incredible discipline, however, she conceals this side of herself in order to create the idealized portrait of Hillary that's on display in *Living History.*

But some of Hillary's hidden side is indeed dark. Like the moon, she has been scarred by the constant pounding of political meteorites. Under their battering, she has developed a sinister side, which is chilling even to those who know her well. Some of her reinventions are defensive, a form of protective coloration to minimize her potential vulnerability and maximize her capacity to deny what she must to survive politically.

This secretiveness about who she really is creates a puzzle for onlookers. Just as we are curious about the dark side of the moon—and spend billions to fly there to have a look—so the missing parts of Hillary's public image drive us to speculation, myth, and rumor about the real person underneath.

Both of the Clintons are masters of subterfuge. But Hillary's deceptions and disguises are very different from Bill's. Bill Clinton deceives himself, and fools us in the process. He pretends, even when he is alone, that he is not doing what he knows he is doing. He never tells his right hand what his left hand is up to.

By contrast, Hillary knows full well who she is and what parts of her must never be exposed to public view. She reminds herself consciously, day after day, which parts of herself to hide and which to expose. Where Bill's instinct for deception is neurotic, Hillary's is opportunistic. He wants to hide his private life from our eyes; Hillary seeks to conceal her character from our view. But the things that Hillary hides are integral to her political essence. They are who she is and what makes her tick. Her trickery is designed to hide her most basic character and instincts from all of us.

Covering up one's flaws is certainly not unusual—especially in politics. All politicians have done things they would rather not see broadcast to their constituents. Everyone in the public spotlight has private issues he or she would like to keep hidden. JFK did not want us to see his illness or promiscuity. FDR disguised his paralysis. Bill Clinton pretended to be a faithful husband. But what makes Hillary's unseen side unique is that, for the most part, it represents her real personality, her true self, far more than the person who smiles and giggles at us day and night. All public figures use makeup to cover a blemish or two. But only Hillary wears a mask of so many layers, one that hides her true face altogether.

Who *is* Hillary? We need to know. In fact, it's become critical that we do so.

After all, John Kerry is the Democratic Party's candidate in 2004, but Hillary is still its most popular politician. Unless Kerry beats Bush, she can have the nomination for the asking in 2008. And even if Kerry wins and runs for a second term, it will probably be Hillary's turn in 2012. She could even run for vice president in 2004. But would such a public step forward show us the real Hillary Rodham Clinton? It's hard to believe it would. Even after all the media coverage of the past twelve years—after we've read the interviews, reflected on the editorials, and absorbed the analyses—she still remains a mystery.

Is Hillary a dedicated public servant, or an unabashed self-promoter? The victim of a vast right-wing conspiracy, or a shrewd operator who often gets caught in her own devious schemes? An innate politician, or a reinvention of herself refined by her ghostwriters and handlers? A sincere advocate for women and children, or an opportunist out for power? A New Democrat, or an old-fashioned liberal?

More than a million people bought Hillary's book hoping to get the answers. But, instead, all they got was a flattering self-portrait of an earnest, talented, devoted daughter, mother, and wife. Her rewrite of her own history reflects only the thoroughly reinvented Hillary she wants us to know—a softer image, a kind of Hillary Lite, but also an incomplete portrait. After reading it, we still don't know what makes her tick. We still don't have the answers. Once more, we see only what she wants us to see.

Yet the answers to our questions become more important as the possibility of a Hillary Clinton presidency becomes more and more real. After thirty years of political consulting, I know that long-range forecasts of political climate are dangerous. Even so, we should not ignore what the coming alignment of demographic and circumstantial forces means for Hillary and her ambitions. Like the weather systems in the book and movie of the same name, they seem to be gathering into a political "perfect storm" that Hillary Clinton plans to ride all the way to the White House.

Consider the omens:

- The population of African and Hispanic Americans is rapidly rising.
- Voters are drifting to the left.
- The Republican Party is low on future presidential candidates, and Hillary's strongest potential rivals there are the ones most likely to sow division within the party.
- Likewise, no major Democratic alternative stands in her way.
- Democratic fund-raisers are setting new records for an out-of-power party.
- The Clinton machine is strengthening its control over the party.
- Bereft of winning issues beyond terrorism, Republicans are still groping for a theme to replace welfare and crime, which Bill Clinton stole away from them—and George W. Bush seems destined to leave huge deficits as a negative part of his legacy.

So things look pretty good for Hillary. She could be the first female president of the United States. But should she?

The list of biographers of this would-be president is extensive. Dozens of books have been written to chronicle Hillary's development and probe her character. Unlike these other authors, though, I worked closely with her for two decades.

And that firsthand experience tells me that the person Hillary's supporters want to see in the White House is a fiction—a character carefully and assiduously cultivated for decades to mask the real Hillary.

The mask is imperfect, of course. Its gaps are revealed in the questions raised frequently, by the press and the public, about the junior senator from New York—questions that remain unanswered. We'd better answer them before she gets to be president. After that, it will be too late.

The presidency magnifies the personal qualities and character—good or bad—of the chief executive and projects them onto our nation. In the 1960s, John F. Kennedy's dynamism electrified an entire generation. Lyndon B. Johnson's obsessiveness led us into massive trauma. Nixon's paranoia plunged the country into a spasm of recrimination and reform. Jimmy Carter's naiveté triggered what even he termed a national "malaise." And the joy and optimism of Ronald Wilson Reagan animated the world.

What qualities of Hillary Clinton's personality would characterize her presidency? And how would they influence us all?

Every man or woman who morphs from private citizen into public figure is changed forever by the journey. As the personalities of these figures are inevitably simplified into caricature by the media, the relationship between their public personas and private selves becomes especially complicated. A public figure's image begins to look like a cartoonist's drawing of his face, exaggerating certain qualities and omitting others from the cartoon entirely.

But Hillary's transition—perhaps the word should be "transitions"—has been unusual, and not merely because it has taken place on the most public stage imaginable. As she journeyed from campus activist to lawyer to governor's wife to first lady, and finally to United States senator, Hillary has changed just about everything about herself—her politics, her physical appearance, even her life story. In the process, she became not only the candidate but the cartoonist, deciding what features to emphasize and which to sublimate.

Think about it. As we all know, Hillary has changed her hair, her eye color, her dress, and her face more frequently than a professional model. But the changes run far deeper. In her decades of public life, she has adjusted her opinions, modified her ideology, altered her priorities, and revised her rhetoric. Her marriage is different from what it once was; her tax bracket has shifted nicely upward. Those who knew her before all this could be forgiven for asking for DNA evidence that she is, in fact, the same human being they used to know.

Hillary might like to describe this wholesale alteration as a product of growth or maturity. But most of it is the result of simple calculation. Hillary Clinton's image became what it needed to become in order to maximize the chances of election to high public office and to minimize the odds that her hidden side would come into public view.

So, again, we ask the question: Does Hillary Clinton have the character and personality to be president?

Many people seem to assume that, since we know one Clinton, America must know them both. We are, after all, living in what author Kevin Phillips has described as an era of "dynastic politics"; by that token it's tempting to treat the Clintons as a unit, and put great stock in Bill's 1992 offer of two Clintons for the price of one. Likewise, we assume that Bill Clinton's political talents have rubbed off on Hillary. Some have even characterized a prospective Hillary presidency as a third and fourth term for her husband.

But *should* we assume that Hillary is just like Bill? The natural human tendency to expect a similarity between namesakes has led good people astray before—look at the spotty record of the British monarchy to fathom the limits of inheritance. How much of the increasingly dismal and undistinguished record of the United States Senate is due to the presence of eleven members—more than a tenth of the body—who hold their seats as a sort of legacy from their famous relatives? These derivative senators won their seats mainly because their brothers, fathers, or husbands made their name in politics before they came along. Just call the roll of these hereditary senators: Ted Kennedy of Massachusetts, Lincoln Chafee of Rhode Island, Chris Dodd of Connecticut, Hillary Clinton of New York, Evan Bayh of Indiana, Elizabeth Dole of North Carolina, Mary

Landrieu of Louisiana, David Pryor of Arkansas, Lisa Murkowski of Alaska, and both John Sununu and Judd Gregg, the two senators from New Hampshire.

In 2000, we watched two sons of political fathers—Bush and Gore—battle it out for the presidency.

Not only are the sons and daughters of famous politicians ascending with ease into national office; now the wives of presidential candidates are themselves running, propelled by the names of their famous husbands. As Phillips points out, Hillary Clinton and Elizabeth Dole—the spouses of the two 1996 adversaries—sit together in the Senate. In 2001, Tipper Gore was mentioned as a possible candidate for a Senate seat in Tennessee. Will we see Mrs. Heinz Kerry or Mrs. Lieberman on the ballot next year?

Where shared DNA is part of the inheritance of these second generation politicians, there is some logic, however strained, to the equation. But there is no shared genetic talent for politics between husband and wife. Whether one likes Bill Clinton or not, his towering brains and political magnetism cannot be denied. But these traits are uniquely his, not transferable by marriage license. Like most other people, Hillary Clinton is in a totally different category from her husband, Bill, when it comes to political skills.

Somehow, though, in the past year or two, a political consensus has emerged that Hillary could easily step into his shoes and become the first woman president. Most who think that way believe that she would prove a virtual female carbon copy of Bill Clinton. This new conventional wisdom allows for no differentiation between the two Clintons. And, more and more, Hillary has begun to adopt this mantra for her own purposes, appropriating the successes of the Clinton administration as her own.

As much as Bill and Hillary would like to morph into one political being, however, they are separate people with different skills and flaws. Hillary Clinton is a highly focused, hard-working, and effective advocate for women and children. But she no more possesses the political strengths of Bill Clinton than she does his personal weaknesses.

To paraphrase Senator Lloyd Bentsen's famous gibe at Dan Quayle in the 1988 vice presidential debate: I know Bill Clinton. Bill Clinton was a client of mine. And Hillary, you're no Bill Clinton.

She lacks his instincts, his empathy, his political savvy, his creativity, his subtlety, his antennae, his ostensible earnestness. Bill Clinton is flexible, charming, charismatic, and solicitous; Hillary, to put it mildly, is not. Bill Clinton has a rags-to-riches story and a down-homey warmth; Hillary has neither. And while Hillary is certainly bright and book-smart, she lacks his creativity and intellect. Hillary is robotic, where Bill is as human as they get. He is spontaneous; she is packaged. Hillary is a memorizer, sometimes a plodder; where her husband wanders, ponders, prowls, explores, weighs options, and circles around a problem, she moves straight ahead. Where Bill loves nothing more than to dance lightly over his policy options, never getting nailed to a firm position until it is the perfect one, she promotes her chosen policies and programs with dogmatic assertiveness. To warm up his audience, Bill needs only uncork the bottle and let the charm flow. Hillary must resort to contrivance and pretense to try to connect with her audience.

He can be friends with anyone. She keeps a mental enemies list.

He's a natural. She's not.

Hillary Clinton, in plain fact, is a student of Bill Clinton. She is not his clone.

When Bill Clinton speaks to an audience, he famously taps into the emotions of each and every listener. Hillary, on the other hand, never seems to live up to her billing. After the excitement of her dramatic arrival by motorcade has passed, her speech itself is usually a disappointment. With a speaking style that ranges from flat to shrill—and that sometimes ascends to a shriek in high E—she rarely gets an emotional response from a crowd. Her speeches routinely echo the cadences of an old-fashioned political rally, punctuated with designated pauses for partisan applause. She may get a rise out of the faithful, but that is very different from the emotions Bill evokes.

Once, when I was at the White House, President Clinton called me to ask that I tune in and watch a speech he was giving at Georgetown University. He told me it would be a "conversation" with the student audience. *Some conversation,* I thought, *he'll be doing all the talking.* As I watched him speak, though, I understood what he meant. He watched the faces in the crowd, picking up their reactions on his well-tuned personal radar, and adjusted his tone, delivery, content, emphasis— even his arguments—to take their emotional responses into account.

Hillary Clinton, on the other hand, never talks with her audience on such occasions. She only talks at them.

Hillary, in turn, has many strengths that Bill himself lacks.

Bill Clinton's convictions are always open for discussion; he seems to tailor his ideology to the political needs of the moment. Hillary's political orientation, on the other hand, is fixed, her opinions ardent. Americans always had difficulty explaining what Bill Clinton stood for. No one has any difficulty identifying Hillary's signature cause: the needs of women, children, and the Democratic Party base. Where Bill tended to be accommodating to the views of others, Hillary has a fierce faith in the justice of her own convictions. She is moved by a commendable desire to spare other children the pain her own mother suffered as the child of an irresponsible teenager without the skills or desire to nurture her child. She is passionate about these issues because they are a part of her. She owns them. Bill Clinton's emotional elusiveness has always made such conviction impossible for him.

Where Bill brings only empathy to his favorite issues, Hillary brings passion. Her agenda has a moral tone that Bill's lacks. The pledges on which he was elected—to focus "like a laser beam" on the economy, to "end welfare as we know it"—are scarcely rallying cries for those who would storm barricades. But Hillary's determination to end injustice against single mothers, working women, babies in day care, foster children, adoptive parents, teachers, students, and those who go without adequate health care stems from a moral, not an intellectual, calculus. His memorable appearances at the National Prayer Breakfasts notwithstanding, Bill Clinton in almost every respect is about as secular a candidate as America has seen in recent years. It's Hillary who wears the religious fervor in the family.

Yet Hillary's passion about political issues is both her strength and her weakness. It often leads her into inflexibility, and traps her within moralistic requisites that distort her political compass. Her health care reform program, which began as a way to lower health care spending, became an almost theological crusade to make health benefits a universal right and entitlement. She moved fearlessly—but also heedlessly—into the teeth of strident opposition—and in the end her failed efforts only contributed to her party's loss of Congress in the ensuing election, almost toppling her husband from office.

Hillary's tendency to treat political questions as moral issues also makes her susceptible to the lure of gurus who eagerly try to sell her on their omnibus programs or ideological utopias. Would she be vulnerable to new Ira Magaziners—the Rasputin who got her to embrace a complicated and crazy holistic approach to health care reform? Would her apparent credulity give rise to a presidency entirely subsumed by an ideological construct?

Hillary Clinton is passionate and, by her lights, honorable. But can she be trusted?

We have seen time and again that the most fundamental element of a good presidency is the trust of the electorate. When a Johnson, Nixon, or Clinton lies to the voters, he soon finds it impossible to govern. Bush Sr. was doomed to a one-term presidency when he broke his "read my lips" promise not to raise taxes. If voters decide that George W. Bush's claims about Iraq's weapons of mass destruction were not a mistake but a fabrication, he may face similar problems in the 2004 election.

The yawning credibility gap that separates *Living History* and Hillary's other public pronouncements from actual history point ominously to the difficulties that could cripple her presidency. *Between Hope and History* was the title of President Clinton's 1996 campaign book, but it would have been a better fit for his wife's autobiography. *Living History* is, in fact, a mélange of hope and history—Hillary's hopes for how we will perceive her, mingled with the history of what she actually did and who she really is.

Throughout the Clintons' White House years, Hillary's constant physical transformations—represented most dramatically in her ever-changing hairdos—offered an almost-too-easy metaphor for her awkward efforts to reinvent herself as first lady. But her personal reinventions are more than a cosmetic matter. She has a disturbing tendency to concoct carefully revised "facts" about her past, her persona, her circumstances, and her experiences—in other words, she has a real problem telling the truth. Sometimes her deceptions are silly. At other times, they are deeply pernicious. But even the fluffier fabrications send us a warning not to trust her.

Take an apparently innocuous example: her nutty claim that her mother named her after Sir Edmund Hillary, the first man to climb Mount Everest. Meeting Sir Edmund by chance at the Katmandu airport, Hillary apparently made up the story on the spot, telling reporters she was named after the intrepid explorer. To bolster her claim, she piled on the details: While her mother was pregnant, Hillary extemporized, she had read an article about Sir Edmund and noticed that he spelled his name with two l's—"which," the first lady said, is how her mother "thought she was supposed to spell Hillary." She continued: "So when I was born, she called me Hillary, and she always told me it's because of Sir Edmund Hillary."

But Sir Edmund didn't climb Everest until May 29, 1953—five and a half years *after* Hillary was born. In fact, until 1951 Sir Edmund Hillary hadn't even left New Zealand for his first climb in the Himalayas. Before that, he was an unknown beekeeper.

Why would Hillary make up such a silly and unnecessary story? To give the press good copy? To try to glamorize her family history by connecting it with the heroic mountaineer? The reporters covering her trip would have written favorably about a simple meeting with Sir Edmund, but Hillary had to make it into something bigger—something up front and personal, something that made her different. She wasn't named Hillary just because her mother liked the name. No, the real story was much more important than that: She was named after a world-famous explorer. It's as if Hillary was trying to absorb his aura by osmosis.

Is Hillary charismatic? Her circumstances are: She is a United States senator, a former first lady, and likely to become the first serious woman candidate for president. Her ideology is: She is a strong advocate for the rights of women and children. Her past is: She is married to the former president of the United States. And, unquestionably, there have been times when she has made all of that work for her—when she has seemed to exude a certain *je ne sais quoi*. But the crowds that throng her book signings and speeches seem more driven by curiosity than drawn by whatever personal charisma she may radiate—by what she stands for, rather than what she *is*. So she reaches for more.

Sometimes, though, Hillary's inventions have been more than simple Walter Mitty fantasizing—as when she invented a story about 9/11 on the *Today* show, implying to Katie Couric that her daughter, Chelsea, had narrowly missed being on the grounds of the Twin Towers at the time of the attacks. Hillary told a national television audience that Chelsea had "gone on what she thought would be a great jog. . . . She was going to go around the [World Trade Center] towers. She went to get a cup of coffee and—that's when the plane hit. . . . She did hear it. She did." Couric told NBC's viewers that Hillary, "at that moment . . . was not just a senator, but a concerned parent."

Chelsea herself, though, flatly contradicted her mother's account in an article for *Talk* magazine, which she apparently had not cleared with Hillary. As Chelsea revealed, she "was alone at a friend's Union Square apartment in Manhattan that morning" when her host phoned to tell her what had happened.

Instead of being anywhere near the World Trade Center, she was three miles northeast of Ground Zero—clear on the other side of town. Chelsea wrote that she "stared senselessly at the television" as she saw the terrorist plane strike the Towers. No mention of a jog, of a coffee shop, of hearing the planes hit.

Hillary had lied. Effortlessly, spontaneously, chillingly, Hillary simply invented the tale. Why? It was a week after 9/11. She was under no pressure to come up with a story. And she could not have been confused about the facts. What would make a person try to capitalize on a tragedy—and insult by implication all those who truly were killed or imperiled on that dreadful day?

Why did she do it? Was she trying to make herself a victim, one of the people who had been personally seared by the tragedy to get a warmer reception from the families, firefighters, and police at Ground Zero? Was she trying to one-up Chuck Schumer, New York's other senator, whose daughter *had* been in danger, attending classes at Stuyvesant High School, adjacent to Ground Zero? Was she trying to share the limelight with her erstwhile political rival, Rudy Giuliani? Did she feel the need to bond more closely with her newly adopted state at the moment of its greatest catastrophe? Whatever it was, to lie in this way at that time suggests a serious character flaw.

It's worth noting that neither this tall tale nor the story of how she came to be named is repeated in *Living History.* Of her daughter's experience on 9/11, Hillary merely expresses gratitude for Secret Service agent Steve Ricciardi's "calm presence" when he reached Chelsea by phone in "lower Manhattan."

When Al Gore claimed to be the father of the Internet, or that his marriage was the basis for *Love Story,* his exaggerations tripped him up. Would a Hillary candidacy—or presidency—be constantly embroiled in similar controversy?

If her history is any guide, this might be an area of great difficulty for Hillary given the harsh and unrelenting media spotlight placed on presidents and presidential candidates. For if Hillary exaggerates and fabricates stories on the national campaign trail, or in the White House, an attentive press corps will pierce her mask, damaging a president's most important asset: her credibility.

The chapters that follow will take you behind each of the layers of Hillary's mask. One layer hides the canny political tactician, another the ideologically doctrinaire zealot, a third layer draws a self-serving veil over Hillary's long history of dubious financial transactions, and a fourth covers up her streak of ferocity, even viciousness.

It is vitally important that we peel back these layers of Hillary's mask—before she becomes our president.

2

HILLARY AS PRESIDENT

So what kind of president would Hillary Rodham Clinton be? It's tempting to answer the question by examining her years as Bill Clinton's assistant president. But the presidency is not a collective responsibility. No matter how influential an advisor—or a spouse—may be, the chief executive must lead alone. If Hillary were president and Bill in the shadows—a reversal of their roles in the 1990s—their two presidencies would be as different as the two Clintons themselves.

But such a forecast, using the 1990s as a guide to the future, also assumes that Hillary won't grow. Will she? That is the real question. The Hillary we have come to know through her public and private dealings to date most closely resembles two political figures from our recent past. Each of these men grew to political maturity right outside the Oval Office, just like Hillary. Like her, each of them held passionately to his strong convictions, and grew certain that anyone who was not utterly for him was completely against him. They shared with Hillary Clinton what Richard Hofstadter has called "the paranoid style of politics"—ruthless, angry, moralistic, and dogmatic. Each began his career as an investigator, dogging those they felt had betrayed the nation. And, like the former first lady, each had to work hard to conceal scandal—one to protect his president, the other to save himself. And after a time on top, each suffered a loss of power and then came back on his own to try to regain the heights from which he had fallen.

And yet, while one of these men became the idol of millions of idealists, the other descended deep into scandal. One emerged as a national hero, the other as the greatest villain in American politics. One conquered his shortcomings; the other succumbed to them.

So which will Hillary Clinton be? Robert Francis Kennedy or Richard Milhous Nixon?

The similarities between Hillary and RFK are almost eerie to contemplate.

Both were elected to the same Senate seat, each a carpetbagger basking in the afterglow of the tenure of their popular presidential namesake.

And both shared more than a president's name; each was his campaign manager, first as he ran for statewide office and then as he sought the presidency.

At 1600 Pennsylvania Avenue, each occupied the historically unique role of alter ego to the president. Neither was limited by clear job descriptions or administrative boundaries; the bureaucrats of the White House cleared a wide path whenever they chose to make their influence felt.

Both found their years in the White House tainted by the need to shelter their respective presidents from personal scandals of his own making. Hillary had Monica Lewinsky and Paula Jones; Bobby Kennedy had Marilyn Monroe and Judith Exner (a girlfriend JFK shared with Sam Giancana, the leading mob boss of his day), among many others.

Each worked to expand his president's vision. As JFK focused on the Cold War, Bobby Kennedy dragged him reluctantly to confront the evils of racial discrimination. And as Bill Clinton worked on the economic issues with which he was most comfortable, Hillary induced him to work harder on the needs of women and children.

But even as each served his president loyally, they disgraced themselves with unbecoming conduct. As attorney general, Robert

Kennedy approved wiretaps on Dr. Martin Luther King Jr.; Hillary's enlistment of private detectives to dig up dirt on Bill's women and the Clintons' political opponents is a play from the same book.

After JFK's assassination and Bobby Kennedy's subsequent fall from power, however, Bobby—who had hunted out supposed communists at Joseph McCarthy's behest—came to personify tolerance and respect for the views of others. This inveterate cold warrior came to oppose American involvement in Vietnam, and to embrace global initiatives for peace. This supreme pragmatist gambled his political career on a frank challenge to the racism that dominated the South, and the complacency about poverty that characterized the North.

Will Hillary rise above her past and embrace the sincere idealism, respect for civil liberties, and understanding of other views that characterized the latter-day Robert Kennedy?

Or will she descend into the pit of scandal, like Richard Nixon?

Hillary, as we will trace in *Rewriting History,* has an unsettling amount in common with the man she investigated during Watergate. For Hillary, as for Nixon, all politics is personal. Like him, she ruthlessly opposes those who disagree with her. Like him, she sees her opponents as evil, and spots them behind every tree. Like him, she harbors a deep suspicion of the motives of her political opponents and believes the press and media to be arrayed against her.

And each was mired in financial scandal. Nixon's desperate effort to collect campaign cash in 1972—right up to the hour when the first disclosure law would take effect—is a first cousin to Hillary's mad dash to collect gifts and donations before joining the Senate.

To conceal their fierce political instincts, Nixon and Hillary each cultivated a false façade of homey, small-town virtue. And a "new Nixon" showed up almost as often as a new Hillary coiffure.

Will Hillary decline like Nixon or grow like Kennedy? Like archaeologists, this book will sift through her record for clues, always aware that the future may be nothing like the past.

THE POSITIVE INDICATIONS

Hillary's Belief Structure

Where Bill Clinton is a pragmatist, always willing to adapt his ideas to changing situations, Hillary enters politics with an ideological compass fixed on the needs of women, children, and the Democratic base. President Clinton's issues have no faces; he articulates his goals in statistics and policies. Hillary's ideology, on the other hand, is motivated by the real, everyday problems she has seen and the horror stories she has heard.

Bill Clinton lives in a world of numbers. He wants to reduce the unemployment rate, narrow the gap between the rich and the poor, raise student test scores, increase exports, and lower the index of violent crimes.

Hillary Clinton's priorities all have faces, and most have names. She wants to help working women juggle career and family, to end gender discrimination and shatter the glass ceiling, to help pregnant teenagers learn to be mothers and give them the prenatal care their babies need, and to end the unfathomable cruelties to which women and girls are subjected abroad—genital mutilation, bride-burning, stoning for adultery.

During his presidency, there were always those who wondered whether Bill Clinton truly believed in anything. Those same critics would find no shortage of conviction in his wife. President Clinton sees himself as a keen policy analyst, able to get to the root of social problems. He takes issues as they arise and tries to solve them. But Senator Clinton marches with determination toward her private vision of utopia, an idealized world of gender equality and childhood opportunity. Bill is a troubleshooter. Hillary is an idealist.

Hillary's Management Style

Bill and Hillary march to the beat of their own individual drummers—and their manner of marching is very different.

Hillary is a manager, seeking order and discipline. Bill is a wanderer, exploring options, sowing chaos with his unregulated mind.

So many American presidents have failed because they proved unable to manage the vast bureaucracy at their command. Jimmy Carter found himself enveloped in minutiae, unable to delegate or even to recognize the shape of his self-created trap. Carter's memoir *Keeping Faith* opens with the scene of the president of the United States personally orchestrating the flow of cash to Iran necessary to spring the hostages from captivity on the eve of Reagan's inauguration. Like a bank teller, he frantically phones financial institutions to be sure that the transfers go off without a hitch. And he's proud of the achievement.

The Iran-Contra scandal showed the danger of the other extreme—leaving the details to subordinates. While Ronald Reagan spoke broadly of freeing American hostages and backing anti-communists in Nicaragua, his White House staff broke the law, consummating an arms-for-hostages trade involving the Iranian ayatollahs and the Central American *contras* that almost brought down his presidency.

President Clinton's management style was maddening. Unable—and unwilling—to establish clear lines of authority, he found duplication empowering and political infighting amusing. Leaking in the Clinton White House was so pervasive that the president once chided me for telling his two top aides—George Stephanopoulos and Rahm Emanuel—about our polling data. When the information ended up in the *Washington Post,* he shouted into the phone at me: "Who did you tell?" Learning that I had merely briefed his two staffers, he yelled: "You only told George and Rahm? You only told George and Rahm? Why didn't you issue a fucking press release?"

Hillary Clinton, on the other hand, knows how to run a presidency. On her staff there are no leaks, no disloyalty, no infighting. She inspires a level of commitment from subordinates that Bill can only dream about.

Hillary's priorities are rigid, and she imparts the same discipline to her staff that she imposes upon herself. First things come first;

others come later. She cannot be distracted from her appointed tasks. She follows through on her directives to ensure that they are implemented and punishes disloyalty with swift and sure political decapitation. No member of Hillary's staff leaks twice.

Where President Clinton procrastinated, delaying appointments until the media forced his hand, Senator Clinton makes quick decisions and rarely reverses them. She hates to leave issues hanging. Bill Clinton can be pressured, advised, cajoled, and even threatened into changing his position or decision. Once Hillary has made up her mind, there is no stopping her.

Anyone who found the Bill Clinton presidency frustratingly ad hoc, inefficiently organized, and chaotic to the point of entropy, would find Hillary's management style a distinct and welcome contrast.

THE NEGATIVE INDICATIONS

But Hillary's skill at managing, and her dedication to the needs of women and children, do not overshadow or excuse her many, many defects. One can only hope that before she decides to run for president she can grow, as Robert Kennedy did, and avoid slipping deeper into a swamp of paranoia, phony branding, and greed.

Hillary's Gurus

Some of Hillary's shortcomings are the flip sides of her virtues. The fact that she feels so deeply about the plight of her young and female constituents, for example, makes Hillary susceptible to a brittle, self-involved, dogmatic moralism that is anathema to the give-and-take of Washington politics.

Where others see half-measures and compromises as steps toward an ultimate goal, Hillary is inclined to dismiss them as palliatives that lull people into a numb sense of complacency when they should be galvanized into action.

Most successful politicians are pragmatists, experimenting here, running pilot programs there, to see what works while testing public reaction. But trial and error just isn't Hillary's style. As she did with health care reform, she begins with a grand theory, develops and designs omnibus solutions and comprehensive programs, and then seeks to implement her blueprint in toto, redesigning everything according to her predetermined theoretical parameters. Where most great cities grow organically, one building at a time over many years, she draws up her plans from scratch, then tries to will her perfect vision into being—regardless of practical considerations.

Even with the best intentions, though, anyone who depends so thoroughly on grand theories will inevitably find herself in thrall to grand theoreticians—gurus, in common parlance. Fundamentally insecure in just this way, Hillary latches onto advisors and follows them onward. Vince Foster, Ira Magaziner, media creator Mandy Grunwald, former chief of staff Maggie Williams, and I have all served as her pathfinders at various times in her life. And Bill Clinton, her supreme guru, is always at the ready when all the others have fallen away.

In this respect, she would be very different from virtually every other American president. Roosevelt would never trust one person enough to hand over such power. His staff—from Louis Howe and Harry Hopkins on down—were his servants, not his leaders. Truman listened to all his advisors, but never delegated his power. Each policy discussion was unique unto itself, and the best argument carried the day, regardless of who offered it. Eisenhower and Kennedy held their cards too close to their vests to permit advisors (except for Bobby) a peek. Each supremely self-confident in his own judgment, Ike and JFK had operatives more than advisors. Lyndon Johnson and Richard Nixon rarely listened to anyone other than themselves; their advisors served as sounding boards for their own thinking. Reagan conducted an orchestra of his advisors, tapping out the beat and laying down the theme, trusting to each instrument to pick up the melody in its own voice.

And Bill Clinton? His advisors were really his tutors, acclimating him to new situations until he could take over himself, learn what they had to teach, and then dispense with them like oranges that have surrendered their juice. Clinton had his gurus, but their life expectancy was short.

Hillary, though, is an advice addict. As she confronts each new situation, she seeks out a supplier to dole out the answers each day. Unlike Bill, she never fully internalizes their advice or develops insights that make their contribution redundant. Rather, she shows up for a new shot as soon as the last one runs out.

Which leaves open a dangerous prospect: If we vote Hillary into office, we may find that we have actually elected her latest guru.

The Enemies List

Hillary has a Manichean view of issues, splitting the political world into dueling forces of good and evil. There is very little space in such a universe for honest disagreement. She sees herself as idealistic, moral, and righteous, and can only conclude that those with opposing views must have opposite motives.

The opponents of health care reform are self-interested profit-hungry insurance companies, brokers, and health care providers. The adversaries of her views on education don't care about the needs of children, secure in the private schools their money can buy. Those who back tax cuts are greedy Scrooges hoarding every last dollar of profit, unwilling to pay for their fair share of the public good.

Behind every disagreement lurks an enemy. And not just an enemy, but the embodiment of evil. It is this Hillary who once wondered, incredibly, "if a person could be both a Republican and a Christian."

A focus on good and evil, of course, is not unique to Hillary. As Sean Hannity notes in *Deliver Us from Evil*, both George W. Bush and Ronald Reagan famously saw the world as polarized into good and bad. What makes Hillary's perspective more dangerous is that neither Bush nor Reagan ever saw their fellow Americans as the enemy. While each viewed issues from a moral perspective, neither took political disagreements personally. Perhaps tellingly, both Reagan and Bush delighted equally in the company of their supporters and their political adversaries. The fundamental optimism of each man lent him a generosity toward his political opponents that Hillary's paranoia, like Nixon's, doesn't allow.

Presidents who see the world through the prism of paranoia, enemies, and political threats do not have happy administrations. In his landmark work *Presidential Character,* historian David James Barber discusses these questions with particular insight. Writing in 1972, Barber grouped all presidents into four categories, based on whether they were active or passive in their personalities, positive or negative in their self-image.

Hillary would clearly be an active president. No question there.

But would she likely be active-negative or active-positive?

An active-positive president enjoys his work. He shows an "ability to use his styles flexibly, adaptively, suiting the dance to the music." FDR, JFK, and Truman were among America's active-positive chief executives.

But an active-negative president "seems ambitious, striving upward, power seeking. His stance toward his environment is aggressive and he has a persistent problem managing his aggressive feelings. . . . Life is a hard struggle to achieve and hold power, hampered by the condemnations of a perfectionistic conscience. Active-negative types pour energy into the political system but it is an energy distorted from within."

Sound familiar?

Barber notes that active-negative presidents have a tendency toward "rigidification." Read his description of how it works, and think of Hillary's health care fiasco:

Adhering rigidly to a line of policy long after it had proved itself a failure . . . each of these presidents had in his mind a theory, a conception of reality, of causation, a set of principles which came to guide his action. These principles . . . [were] shared by a great many thoughtful people. . . . They were "wrong" in terms of logic and evidence but they were widely accepted.

So why did these active-negative presidents (he cites Wilson, Hoover, and Johnson as examples) cling to their failed policies?

The president appears as a man unable to see what, eventually, nearly everyone else around him sees; that the line of action is simply not working. That, for whatever reason, the costs of persevering in it are far too high. . . . In each of these cases, the president did, in fact, freeze onto a line of action and stick to it long after it began to produce terrible trouble for the country and the man.

As Barber notes, an active-negative president sees:

himself as having begun with a high purpose, but as being continually forced to compromise. . . . Battered from all sides with demands that he yield yard after yard of his territory, that he conform to ignorant and selfish demands, he begins to feel his integrity slipping away from him. . . . At the same time, he is being harassed by critics who . . . attribute his actions to low motives, adding insult to injury. . . . At long last . . . he rebels and stands his ground. Masking his decision in whatever rhetoric is necessary, he rides the tiger to the end.

Has Hillary changed? Has she grown? Will she still ride the tiger to the end? It's important, and perhaps heartening, to remember that not since the days of her health care fiasco has Hillary identified herself rigidly with a major policy initiative. Her foreign travel and writings yielded philosophical insights more than legislative programs. And yet, when the chips are down, it's not hard to imagine that the active-negative profile might re-emerge and consume a Hillary Clinton presidency.

THE PARANOID STYLE IN
HILLARY'S POLITICS

Among our post–World War II presidents, Nixon and Johnson were most famously negative in their outlooks, seeing adversaries at every turn, convinced of the evil motives of those with whom they disagreed.

The White House can sometimes resemble a greenhouse in which the warmth of sincere admiration and opportunistic flattery surrounds a president. But out there among grassroots Americans— and likewise in Washington, D.C.—the air of judgment can get very cold indeed. And, as anyone who has ever watched a TV weatherman knows, the border where hot and cold fronts meet produces fog. A president needs, as much as anything else, the ability to see through the fog. Hillary's record here is not encouraging.

Hillary gives every indication of an inability to see political opponents as good men and women who hold different opinions. Her tactics, when confronted with opposition, lead one to doubt whether she can ever learn to take disagreement in stride.

In the essay "The Paranoid Style in American Politics," published in 1964, Richard Hofstadter observed that while class divisions have played little role in the polarization of public opinion in America, paranoia has often dominated the public discussion. Defending his use of the word "paranoid," Hofstadter writes: "No other word adequately evokes the qualities of heated exaggeration, suspiciousness, and conspiratorial fantasy that I have in mind." Citing examples such as the McCarthy hunt for domestic communists and the Populist condemnation of Eastern bankers in the 1890s, Hofstadter discusses how Americans often tend to base their political ideologies on opposition to a list of enemies.

Hillary's record would suggest that her tendency to formulate her ideas based on the groups she opposes taps into this paranoid heritage. During the health care debacle, as we'll see, she demonized nearly an entire industry in an attempt to further her own agenda. And when it comes to personal political combat, the dimensions of Hillary's paranoid style—hiring detectives, exploiting wealth-creating loopholes, hiding (literally and figuratively) behind the trappings of the White House—are downright alarming.

A Hillary presidency would risk combining Clintonian ends with Nixonian means. Would Hillary order the payment of hush money as Nixon did? Some questioned whether payments made to Webb Hubbell that were arranged for by close Clinton associates were actually meant to keep him quiet. Would she form a plumbers' unit, as Nixon did, to hunt down opponents? How else to describe Hillary's hiring of private eyes to dig up dirt on Bill's enemies and erstwhile paramours? Would she erase taped records of incriminating Oval Office conversations? Her list of shredded Whitewater documents and missing billing records is not encouraging.

In the end, it seems fair to ask: Has she learned anything at all? Will she grow out of this style of politics? For readers looking for any indication of growth, *Living History* is a gigantic disappointment. The same lies and distortions that served her well in the White House are all repeated here with, if anything, more enthusiasm and polish. *Living History* makes a strong case that the paranoid style is alive and dominant in Hillary's thinking.

THE POTENTIAL FOR FINANCIAL SCANDAL

If Bill Clinton's presidency came to be defined by his reckless personal life, Hillary's tenure as first lady was dominated by financial scandal. From Travelgate to Whitewater and well beyond, she brought the smell of scandal closer to 1600 Pennsylvania Avenue than it had been in years.

If Hillary's time as first lady offers any insight at all into the possible pitfalls of a Hillary presidency, we must seriously examine the risk of financial scandal in a Hillary administration.

The administration of Ulysses S. Grant (1869–1877) ranks as one of the most corrupt in American history. Ominously, many of

Hillary's scandals bear a remarkable resemblance to those that ruined the reputation of the man who won the Civil War.

Grant himself, it should be noted, was scrupulously honest.
But until he became president he had never had much money.
Born without wealth, he married well, but soon found himself the
victim of repeated business failures. His particular gifts for leading
men in America's most deadly war brought him fame, the adula-
tion of millions, and finally the presidency. When he became president, though, his head was turned by the luxury showered upon
him by a grateful people in general, and by rich businessmen in
particular.

Cultivating their company, Grant accepted as his due the favors
they bestowed upon him. Without asking enough questions, he accepted the friendship of these barons of industry at face value and
never probed too deeply into their motives or ambitions.

And, like Hillary, Grant's family led him into scandal. The general's brother-in-law, Abel Rathbone Corbin, was bribed by finan-
ciers Jay Gould and Jim Fisk to help them monopolize the private
sector gold market. Charged with warning Wall Street sharks Gould
and Fisk when the Treasury Department was about to sell gold on the
market, Corbin used his close relationship with Grant to get and pass
on inside information to his co-conspirators. Grant, "delighted that
his [thirty-seven-year-old] sister had found so agreeable a partner" as
Corbin, "made a point of staying with the newlyweds in the Corbin
town house" whenever he visited New York.

Gould and Fisk, meanwhile, used Corbin's access to Grant as evidence that they had inside information about the Treasury's plans,
helping them drive the price of gold up to unsustainable heights. Was
Grant at fault? Biographer Jean Edward Smith writes that "Grant was
not averse to accepting the hospitality of rich men, and that may
have been a personal failing, but he was not about to give them an
unfair advantage as a result. Nevertheless, the fact that Grant was
often seen in the company of Gould and Fisk legitimized the pair
and led credence to the belief that the government supported their

economic views. That in itself gave them enormous clout on Wall Street and to that extent Grant was culpable."

When the scandal was eventually exposed, the resulting shock sent the financial markets into a tailspin for months.

As Smith writes, "the fact is Grant rarely met a businessman he did not trust."

Hillary's acceptance of gifts from rich friends, and her willingness to open her White House and Camp David homes to them, parallels Grant's infatuation with the wealthy. Her willingness to do lucrative business deals with friends—like her investments in the commodities markets and in Whitewater—even when a potential conflict of interest was an obvious risk shows a difficulty in setting up boundaries with friends.

Hillary's tenure in Little Rock and Washington shows the same carelessness, attraction to wealth, acceptance of gifts, and undisciplined family interactions that brought down Grant. Just as General Grant was intoxicated by wealth, so Hillary seems driven to seek out the famous and the rich as friends. How does her solicitation of gifts from America's multimillionaires differ from Grant's acceptance of their favors? Is Grant's brother-in-law's involvement in the sale of Treasury gold all that different from Hugh and Tony Rodham's representation of clients seeking presidential pardons? Does General Grant's desire to reward friends like Fisk and Gould bear no resemblance to Hillary's desire to steer business and consulting fees to friends like Webb Hubbell?

President Grant was personally a model of integrity. When one of the richest men in America, Cornelius Vanderbilt, lent him $150,000 to start a brokerage business, and the ex-president was then defrauded by a partner who fled with the money, Grant insisted—over Vanderbilt's objections—on repaying every penny.

Apart from a taste for exploiting loopholes, Hillary has shown no actual evidence of personal financial dishonesty except for her commodities trading. As Grant's sorry record shows, though, it's not just the president's character that counts, but his judgment and attention to friends, supporters, and family whose own scruples might not be as strict. The people who surround Hillary Clinton have exhibited far too much lassitude in this respect for the voters to be sure she would avoid serious trouble in the White House.

HILLARY'S CREDIBILITY GAP

If *Living History* proves anything, it establishes how willing Hillary is to distort, exaggerate, falsify, fabricate, invent, omit, or obfuscate facts to suit her political ends. She misrepresents even when she doesn't need to, and she bends and twists the facts—or rewrites them altogether—to prove her virtue and innocence in all things.

While tens of millions of Americans look to Hillary Clinton for leadership in the battle to help children and protect women's rights, very few people really trust her to tell the truth.

From 1963 until 1974, America was governed by two presidents—Johnson and Nixon—to whom the truth was often a stranger. Cynical in the extreme about politics, both men saw lying as an integral part of what a politician, and a president, must do. While each showed at least some allegiance to a principle larger than electoral success—Nixon to a middle American patriotism, Johnson to a liberal compassion for the poor—both deeply believed that their ends justified their means.

And both presidencies ended in disaster. Johnson was forced to abandon his race for re-election; Nixon remains the only president who ever had to resign from office.

But in neither case was it a matter of public policy that caused the president's downfall. Johnson's War on Poverty and embrace of strong civil rights legislation is enduringly popular. Even the misguided war in Vietnam still enjoyed majority support in March 1968, when he pulled out of the presidential race. Nixon ended the war, opened the door to dealings with China, capped the arms race, and passed the first serious environmental legislation in seventy years.

It was not the ends that brought down these men, in other words, but the means each chose to further their goals. By their last years in office, Americans determined that neither one could be trusted. Falsehood piled upon spin, deception followed prevarication, promises were broken, and the government privately pursued policies it publicly disavowed. In each case, the American people were outraged when the truth became plain: Their president was a liar.

Has Hillary learned her lesson? Did the web of falsehoods that underpinned her husband's presidency teach how ensnaring public misrepresentation can be? The disappearing billing records, the insider futures market trading, the nefarious discrediting of women like Gennifer Flowers, Kathleen Willey (and likely Paula Jones) who were simply telling the truth, the denial of the Lewinsky relationship—did these all leave their mark? Would a President Hillary stop lying?

Or would she just get worse?

We can't expect to judge safely from appearances alone. After all, such politicians have a way of projecting an image fundamentally at variance with who they really are.

Johnson, in reality a cunning, ruthless, profane, obsessive wheeler-dealer, pretended to be a solemn-faced Solomon, sitting in impartial judgment and offering wise and knowing leadership to his nation.

Nixon, a backroom wire-puller, compulsive drinker, coarse and bitter man, came across as a holier-than-thou apostle of middle American values and decency.

And then there is Hillary—whose public face is so contrived and calculated that each year it becomes more difficult to remember the far more complex and mercurial person behind the façade.

When the mask slips and the public catches a glimpse of the man or woman behind it, a president can never regain his credibility. The peek behind the image leaves us feeling as though we've just seen the real Wizard of Oz, the fabricator of a fantasy to which we once subscribed but in which we can no longer invest.

Hillary Clinton stands a good chance of returning to the White House for another four years—eight if she's lucky. Either way, that's a long time for the American people not to trust the person in the Oval Office. To understand what sits behind the mask that Hillary Clinton has built between her real self and the American people, we should begin with her very successful transformation from first lady to United States senator—from Hillary the woman to HILLARY the brand.

3

THE HILLARY BRAND

In the Spring of 2000, a new brand was subtly introduced to the people of New York State. As with the launch of any new product, this fresh brand was likely based on highly tailored market research that dictated the selling strategy. The fact that the "brand" was a new-and-improved version of the country's most written-about woman—and that the success of the product would be decided in voting booths rather than supermarket checkout lines—didn't really change the nature of the task. The existing brand had been familiar and well-known to the public, but its appeal had declined precipitously. It needed a complete makeover. Just as "low-fat" products have been magically transforming into "low-carb" in the past two years, Hillary Clinton's campaign for the United States Senate presented their new "HILLARY" as an independent, stable, serious, steady, mature professional, who could think and act separately from Bill. Forget "two for one"; forget the co-presidency. From then on, it was all HILLARY all the time.

Ever since Bill Clinton's first campaign for the Arkansas governorship in 1978, polling data has provided the blueprint for the strategy of every one of Clinton's campaigns. Market and survey research was the hallmark of the Clinton presidency. We polled everything—even where to go on vacations. As their pollster, I discovered that the public hated seeing the Clintons hobnobbing with celebrities in Martha's Vineyard; the polls told us to head west. The voters, it turned out, *loved* the Rockies—and they loved the idea of watching their president hiking, camping, fishing, and enjoying the wonders of nature. Dutifully, the Clintons packed up and vacationed at Jackson Hole, Wyoming. Instead of having cocktails with Jackie O, it was hiking, camping, and horseback riding. Once the 1996 election was over, they went happily back to Martha's Vineyard.

Hillary's campaign was driven just as surely by polls. Focus groups as well as traditional polling obviously only confirmed what common sense dictated: that voters felt Hillary was too aligned with Bill Clinton's political problems, and that even a minor issue like her constantly changing appearance was a looming negative.

Hillary needed rebranding.

First, she needed a new name. As we'll see, surnames have always carried great political weight with Hillary. A feminist out of Wellesley College and Yale Law School, when she first married Bill Clinton she kept her own name: Hillary Rodham. After Bill was defeated for re-election as governor in 1980, in part because of voter hostility to her refusal to take the Clinton name, she became Hillary Clinton. Shortly after Bill was elected president, she actually made a formal announcement that she was now to be called Hillary Rodham Clinton.

When she began her Senate candidacy, however, Hillary Rodham *and* Hillary Clinton *and* Hillary Rodham Clinton all vanished overnight. Now it was just plain HILLARY, the name of the new product—symbolically independent of Bill and the tarnished Clinton name. Why rub the swing voters the wrong way by reminding them of Bill Clinton? HILLARY was all they needed to know. (Still, Hillary knew enough not to distance herself *too* thoroughly from her husband: Too many Democrats—voters and fund-raisers alike— still loved him. She pushed herself away from the nest gently as she prepared to fly off on her own.)

As she announced her candidacy at the Purchase campus of the State University of New York in her waning months as first lady, the banners above the crowd read simply HILLARY. The message was clear: She was her own person, unconnected to his misdeeds. When it was opportune—at White House fund-raisers, for example—she could easily reassume her Hillary Clinton identity. Out on the stump, though, she was just HILLARY.

But it wasn't enough to change the name. The packaging needed still more alteration: She needed to look the part—and to look like she knew what she was doing. During the White House years, Hillary had changed her appearance constantly. Reveling in her new access to the top hair stylists and makeup artists, she sported every conceivable hair style: up, down, short, long, straight, curly, flip, bob, French twist, French braids, ponytail. As she admits—how could she not?—she tried everything. One week she looked like Betty White of *The Golden Girls;* the next she might emerge looking like Sharon Stone—or, even stranger, Gennifer Flowers.

Before long, her relentlessly changing look had become a running joke for late-night comedians; it suggested a flighty image—unstable and insecure. By the time of her Senate run, it was impossible to watch a video retrospective of her husband's presidency without seeing a different, sometimes unrecognizable, Hillary in each frame. It was a branding disaster: Voters were left without a core image, a fixed mental picture they could summon when thinking of her.

We'd wrestled with this in the White House. In 1996, as Bill's re-election campaign began kicking into high gear, author Naomi Wolf suggested to me that Hillary looked artificial in her strong "synthetic colors"—the hot pinks, yellows, and bright blues of her first lady wardrobe. Anticipating Hillary's later media advisors—and advice Al Gore would receive during his presidential race—Wolf suggested that the first lady should dress in softer, natural earth tones: browns, beiges, and blacks. She also suggested that open-necked blouses would help Hillary come across as more relaxed, open, and trustworthy than the buttoned-up ensembles she'd been wearing.

At my next meeting with the first lady, I relayed Wolf's ideas. It drove her up a wall. "I get *colds* when my top button is open and my neck is exposed," she screamed, "and I don't intend to get a cold just to get my husband a few extra votes. If the way I dress and the colors I choose cost him the election, that's just too bad. That's the way it's going to have to be!"

But that was when Bill was running. Once Hillary put herself on the line, though, she was ready to listen—and her media advisors were only too happy to talk. From now on, she would sport a consistent look every single day. A signature style, always the same, no deviation. Suddenly, the threat of catching a cold seemed to disappear: Her blouses were *always* open at the neck. It was out with the embossed opera coats, double-breasted jackets, gold lamé sweater sets. Out with bright blue, green, yellow, orange, or plaid suits. No more pastels or big scarves; no more giant eagle pins. No more hats, capes, or baseball caps (even for the Yankees!). And no more of those deadly bad hair days. She finally found a short blonde look that worked, and stuck with it for good. And also a signature daytime uniform that worked equally well: a single-breasted black pantsuit, with a salmon pink or turquoise open-necked blouse. In a lighthearted mood, she might tie a blue sweater around her neck; for evenings or special occasions, she might break out a turquoise pantsuit (open-necked, no blouse), or a salmon-colored suit (perfect for book signings). Otherwise, though, nothing would change. The new package projected strength, dignity, and professionalism—and, most of all, constancy.

No more heavy makeup, either: only softly flattering tones, highlighted with a little inconspicuous jewelry. Even her eyes were transformed, courtesy of brilliant turquoise contact lenses.

And *voilà!* HILLARY.

This new HILLARY brand was quite a change from the Hillary Rodham I first met in 1978, when Bill was preparing his first race for governor. The Hillary of that time had dark brown curly hair, often unkempt. She wore big, thick, dark eyeglasses, their lenses tinted deep brown. Without the colored contact lenses, her eyes were much darker than the sparkling turquoise we see today.

On the first day I met her, she wore a nondescript tan suit, with a weird-looking, oversized pin on the lapel. And—always—she wore very thick, opaque black stockings, the kind a nun might wear. Despite her peculiar affect, though, she had a presence. She was extremely articulate, and though she was clearly serious-minded, she laughed easily.

Over the next few years, though, Hillary would change her appearance dramatically. When my wife, Eileen, and I met her and Bill and little Chelsea for lunch at Manhattan's Stanhope Hotel in the mid-1980s, I almost didn't recognize her. The thick dark glasses were gone and her brown, curly hair had gone blonde and straight.

This kind of makeover by a female public figure is unusual. Indeed, among the major women politicians of the world, Hillary is the only one who has so dramatically changed her personal appearance. Golda Meir, Indira Gandhi, Margaret Thatcher—none of these prominent female foreign leaders has troubled with her looks in this way. In America, consider Elizabeth Dole, Tipper Gore, Barbara Boxer, Dianne Feinstein, Patty Murray, Barbara Mikulski, Nancy Pelosi, Condoleezza Rice, Donna Shalala, Janet Reno, Sandra Day O'Connor, Ruth Bader Ginsburg, Olympia Snowe: Every other prominent female political figure looks more or less the way she did when she first entered our consciousness. Hillary alone has found it necessary to undergo makeover after makeover.

But these alterations—and the many others that would follow during the Clinton presidency and after—were not just skin deep. They simply mirrored the equally dramatic changes in her public personality and image. Along with the cosmetic changes, there emerged a new persona, the transformation of Hillary into HILLARY, blending artifice, carefully studied conduct, concealed records, conveniently invented life experiences, and fabricated achievements, into one suspiciously coherent surface. It reached its apogee in *Living History*, where it graces almost every page, but the strategy precedes the book . . . and will long outlast it.

The HILLARY brand is based on the following tenets:

- Use, recycle, remake everything you have—no matter how trivial—for maximum political advantage, regardless of its true meaning.
- But never *appear* political. Every practical, pragmatic move must be couched as idealistic.
- Align yourself with celebrities—that makes you, too, a celebrity.
- Use stories to make yourself seem relevant and interesting—regardless of whether they're true.
- Present yourself as normal, just like everyone else; emphasize the domestic.
- Toss out carefully conjured little domestic vignettes to suggest how intimate and cozy you are with your husband, the former president.
- Giggle and laugh, loudly and often, during interviews to suggest that you have a softer side.
- Repress any outward signs of interest in material things; emphasize your frugality.
- Deflect criticism by accusing your critics of attacking your archetype (women; working women; outspoken women) rather than yourself.
- Insulate your political ambition and raw political gamesmanship with a layer of chatty, domestic camouflage.
- Adapt, adapt, adapt!

This strategy proved an effective one. And it scarcely mattered that the image was almost entirely manufactured. Because with Hillary, all is malleable. Everything can be changed to conform to the HILLARY brand. In a letter to the House Committee on Un-American Activities, author Lillian Hellmann famously wrote, "I cannot and will not cut my conscience to fit this year's fashions." But Hillary will cut, trim, dice, slice, sew, alter, or otherwise conform any aspect of her persona, record, personality, and rhetoric to fit this year's political imperatives. In the Darwinian world of electoral politics, where survival goes to the most adaptable, Hillary is a true survivor.

Nothing about HILLARY is spontaneous. Everything is calculated. Nothing is simply a reflection of who she really is. All her words and gestures, the accounts and anecdotes through which she offers us her past, the positions she takes and partisanship she shows (or conceals), even the flinty sparks of forced laughter, are part of the ongoing display. For HILLARY, even spontaneity is a contrivance.

To some extent, of course, Hillary has constructed this elaborate mask to cover up inappropriate conduct—her role in the Travel Office debacle, for example, or the disappearance of her billing records from the Rose Law Firm. But often its primary purpose is to present an acceptable pretense for petty and spiteful conduct—or merely to make herself look more attractive and talented. Many of her re-inventions are simply transparent attempts to make herself relevant, to bond with the viewers, to evoke sympathy or admiration.

Whether hiding her misbehavior or feeding her vanity, though, the ultimate function of the HILLARY brand is twofold: to hide who she is, and to project what she isn't.

In this, as in so much else, she is very different from Bill. He's never spent much time worrying over his appearance or biography or personality or manner. He knows he doesn't need to. He relies on his natural ability to seem to be what people want or need. Whether real or contrived, he gives off such intensely empathetic vibes that he doesn't need to establish a false persona to connect with people. In a room or a crowd, his radar picks up the signals of anyone who doesn't like him, and instantly grasps why they don't and what he has to do to win them over. His manner, charm, affect, humor, seductiveness, intellect, and feel for people help him actually *become* all things to all people—his perpetual political goal. He doesn't need to change his body or personality or record. He just adapts what he has to the task at hand.

What Bill achieves through instinct, Hillary can do only by using great discipline to make whatever personal alterations are necessary to achieve her goals. He exists, she changes—over and over again.

That, in fact, is one reason for Hillary's constant rebranding. Hillary Clinton learned her politics from the master himself. For decades, she watched her husband do the things she didn't know how to do. She could follow his moves, but she never really heard the music, so her dancing was stiff and awkward. Through all the years he spent as a candidate, ironically, she gave off the distinct impression that she thought she could be doing a better job. She was always prepared, always on time, always under control.

It wasn't until she entered politics in her own right that she learned the truth: Being on time isn't enough.

To find another pair of politicians of such dissimilar natural talent who are joined in the history books, we must look back to the odd-couple rivalry of John F. Kennedy and Richard Nixon. Bill Clinton, of course, is like Kennedy, endlessly charming anyone he needs, effortlessly projecting a charisma he uses with devastating effectiveness. Hillary, on the other hand, is a latter-day Nixon. Instead of stepping forward with natural confidence, she works assiduously to prepare her image. She *decides* what she must become, whom she must be, and then goes about it methodically and ploddingly. While Clinton projects his personality with a glance or a comment, Hillary must fabricate stories from her past, adopt myths about the present, and cloak her ambitions and insecurities behind a righteous façade in order to accomplish her political goals.

Hillary needs a crutch to do what Bill has no trouble doing. And the crutch includes distorting, fabricating, imagining, spinning, and re-inventing her life, her personality, and her past.

Take, for example, Hillary's attempt to empathize with victims of prejudice. At a 1997 race-relations forum for teenagers in Boston, Hillary recalled the "pain" of a "childhood encounter" that helped her to grasp the injury suffered by the victims of bigotry. "During a junior high school soccer game" on a cold day, Hillary claimed, "a goalie told her 'I wish people like you would freeze.' Stunned, the future first lady asked how she could feel that way when she did not even know her. 'I don't have to know you,' the goalie shot back, 'to know I hate you.'"

Nice story. But it probably never happened. Title IX of the Civil Rights Act, which mandated that girls' sports be treated equally with boys' in public education, did not pass until 1972. As a sport, girls' soccer did not exist when Hillary went to middle or high school. The athletic director for the South Main High School in Park Ridge—and a thirty-four-year veteran of the school system—confirmed that there were no girls' soccer teams in the 1960s. The first lady seems to have conjured up the tale to appear more relevant to her listeners and to establish a bond of empathy with them. (And, not surprisingly, the episode never made it into *Living History*.)

Can Americans trust a president who so carefully concocts her image to suit the needs of the moment? As much as we like to say that spin or political pandering is part of the normal politician's skill set, the fact is that our presidents have been remarkably candid in the personas they projected to the American people—at least since the television age began.

Harry Truman made no secret of his earthy disregard for society manners, projecting instead the man he was: a human being without artifice or polish, who told it like it was. While Eisenhower hid his tough managerial side and salty army vocabulary behind a façade of grandfatherliness, his image—simple, direct, straightforward, and modest—accurately reflected his character. We knew nothing at the time of John Kennedy's promiscuity, but his fierce intellect, aggressive energy, and patrician bearing all were obvious to his adoring public. Lyndon Johnson, try as he might, was unable to hide his earthiness. The person who showed reporters his appendectomy scar and lifted his beagle up by the ears was both the inner man and his outer image. Gerald Ford was what he appeared to be: too plain-spoken and down to earth to be manipulative. Jimmy Carter's sincerity was apparent to everyone and Ronald Reagan's sunny disposition was no put-on. George H. W. Bush's geeky inarticulateness in public and his eastern preppy bearing were evident. While Bill Clinton hid his recklessness from our view and tried to be all things to all people, his essential personality never changed and accurately projected the kind of undisciplined, humble, anxious-to-please, restlessly intelligent person that he really is. Likewise, George W. Bush is the macho Texan he appears to be.

We are accustomed to presidents who really are very much as they seem. We are as unused to one who projects a made-up personality as we are to one who changes his hair color. Americans may well elect a President Hillary who projects a chatty, gregarious, light-hearted everyday image in public but hides a vicious streak in private, but history argues that such a presidency is a risky one for the nation. The only real model for a Hillary presidency is that of Richard Nixon. Like Nixon, Hillary hides a personality driven by paranoia, fear, and hatred for enemies, and a willingness to get even and do what it takes to prevail, behind a façade of sincerity and good nature.

The only real difference between them, in fact, is Hillary's self-perception. Where Nixon never pretended to any particular virtue or goodness, Hillary believes that her motives, aspirations, positions, and priorities are uniquely good, even holy. Nixon saw himself as a regular politician trying to get ahead, no better or worse than the rest of the breed. But Hillary finds herself distinctly above the rest and, as a result, sanctions conduct that is below that to which most regular politicians will stoop. Nixon defended his actions, from Oval Office taping to slush funds, by arguing that everyone else—not least JFK—did the same thing. Hillary's defense is actually more frightening; because she believes she is acting through genuinely pure motives and sincere beliefs in good causes, to her, the ends do, indeed, justify the means.

So we need to probe the HILLARY brand and consider its variations: friend of celebrities, unpretentious housewife, sacrifice on the altar of anti-feminism, independent professional, and (apologies to Billy Joel) a woman with a "New York State of Mind."

THE CELEBRITY GAME

The HILLARY brand markets itself with celebrity endorsements, just like a box of Wheaties. These testimonials, compiled and proudly displayed in *Living History* and elsewhere, give HILLARY a hip, glamorous, and charismatic image. If the celebrities and famous political figures like her, then she is like them!

- Why did she become a blonde? She once told me that she changed her hair color because she read that Margaret Thatcher had said that "at a certain age," every woman should.
- Why did she want to make sure that Chelsea would lead as normal a life as possible, would not be spoiled, and would respect the Secret Service agents? Not because of what she knew from her own practical midwestern upbringing and twelve years of parenting in the Governor's Mansion. No, in *Living History,* she says it was because Jacqueline Onassis suggested it to her.
- Why did she choose certain foods to serve at the White House? Because Julia Child wrote asking her to "showcase American culinary arts."
- Who boosted her spirits during the Monica scandal? No less than Walter Cronkite, whom she quotes in *Living History* as saying, "Why don't these people get a life? . . . None of us is perfect. Let's go sailing."
- How did she keep her emotional equilibrium amid the turmoil of possible impeachment and scandal after scandal? With the help of the Dalai Lama, who counseled her "to be strong and not give in to bitterness and anger in the face of pain and injustice."
- How did she decide what to wear to Bill's second inauguration? On Oscar de la Renta's "strong advice, I ditched the hat."
- What gave her strength to survive controversy in Washington? It was Nelson Mandela who inspired her.
- Why did she decide, when she became first lady in 1993, against a complete makeover? In *Living History,* she writes that Jacqueline Onassis said, "You have to be you." (And yet it wasn't long before she did indeed begin changing her wardrobe and paying attention to her hair and appearance—in part because TV producer Linda Bloodworth-Thomason convinced her to do so.)
- The need to have quiet time at Camp David? Jackie O, again, "encouraged me to shelter my intimate family life in this protected retreat."

And the list goes on. Why did she change her name to Clinton after Bill was defeated for governor in 1980? Not, she pretends, to help her husband win the next election; not even because she knew that many Arkansans were appalled when she sent out Chelsea's birth announcement from "Governor Bill Clinton and Hillary Rodham." No, in *Living History,* she claims she changed her name because Vernon Jordan told her she should.

Hillary has been playing this celebrity game for decades. In *Living History* she tells us how in 1974, Barbara Pryor, the incoming first lady of Arkansas, was under attack for her "newly permed short hairdo." So, Hillary describes how she permed her own hair "in a show of solidarity." How weird is that? She actually permed her hair *as a political statement?* I'm not sure which is nuttier—the idea that Hillary actually made the change "in solidarity" with Barbara Pryor, or that she expects us to believe that she did. After all, Hillary had only just moved to Arkansas in late August 1974. As a new and inexperienced law professor in Fayetteville, she was hardly a statewide public figure; no one was paying the least attention to what she did with her hair or why. So what was this supposed to be—a silent political act? I doubt it. The truth is, Hillary evidently won't acknowledge that she changed her hairstyle, like millions of other people, to look better. Why does she find concern about her appearance so hard to admit? For HILLARY, even the most trivial choice must have a political purpose—even a hairstyle. And no personal choice can ever be attributed to a moment of vanity. Everything must be in pursuit of a higher purpose.

Why this desperate reliance on guidance from celebrity role models—even so small-time a celebrity as a future first lady of Arkansas? Naturally the first lady of the United States has spent much of her public life rubbing shoulders with famous people. But her compulsion to tell us all about it speaks volumes about her insecurity, and about her need for props to help convince us of who she really is.

Is Hillary so unsure of herself on the public stage that she needs to embrace those who preceded her there and look to them for constant reinforcement? I don't believe so. On the contrary, in person it's clear that she knows exactly who she is: an aggressive, brainy, substantive, policy-wonkish lawyer with a serious ideology and commitment to social causes and core Democratic Party ideals.

Her problem seems to be that, on some level, she believes we won't like who she is.

ACTING NORMAL

Bill Clinton doesn't need sham or artifice to bond with people. He can eat hamburgers and swap sports stories all day at the local McDonald's if he wants to. It's a part of him, of who he is. Bill Clinton never has to make up stories to show that he's unpretentious. He *is* unpretentious. For all of his deceits and cover-ups, you'll never find him posing as a devotee of art or classical music or *haute cuisine*. He golfs. He's a basketball fanatic. He loves pizza. When Clinton doesn't like something other people enjoy, he's not afraid to say so. He doesn't pretend. He is what he is.

Hillary, on the other hand, is *not* unpretentious. She is too elitist, feminist, substantive, serious, driven, focused, and careerist to relate easily to average people. It's not that she's always arrogant, or actually considers other people beneath her. It's that there is no part of her that's sufficiently "normal" to find common ground with others, to get in sync with those who genuinely *are* normal. Bill Clinton may be part everyman, but Hillary is by no means everywoman.

But she's certainly trying. One goal of the new HILLARY brand was to offer a new image of the candidate as a normal housewife and mother. *Living History* is filled with folksy stories that are ridiculous coming from the first lady of Arkansas, let alone of the United States.

This *Good Housekeeping* makeover was a long time coming. From the very moment she stepped onto the national stage, Hillary had shown a tin ear for everyday life, outraging stay-at-home moms by saying "You know, I suppose I could have stayed home and baked cookies and had teas, but what I decided to do was fulfill my profession, which I entered before my husband was in public life."

The avalanche of negative publicity that followed taught her a lesson: In order to succeed in public life, she realized that she would have to *identify* with the stay-at-home mom, rather than scorn her. She never made the same mistake again. Ever since, she has constantly invoked homey and folksy expressions, in an effort to paint herself as just another housewife, facing the same juggling act—husband, home, career, and children—that bedevils so many modern women. No mention of the chauffeurs, government-paid nannies, servants, and administrative help that have been available to her since the 1970s. Indeed, the happy-homemaker pose soon provided a kind of helpful camouflage: Whenever her ambition or financial avarice reared their ugly heads, she took cover by disguising herself as a typical, even normal, housewife.

Early in the first Clinton administration, when Hillary's efforts to reform health care created such intense controversy and strong reactions, she found that she needed to tone down the harshness and soften her image. So she scheduled an interview with *House Beautiful* magazine; in the resulting article, which appeared under the headline "Home in the White House," she painted an irresistible picture of her domestic life with Bill:

> I wanted a kitchen [in the Residence] because I knew we needed a
> private place to have our meals. Even though the [White House]
> dining room is lovely, it's a big, formal space. We use the kitchen
> for breakfast every day and for lots of dinners when we are not en-
> tertaining. We heat up lots of leftovers. My husband might come
> home from a golf game and I throw something together for him . . .

"Throw something together for him?" With a White House staff of hundreds guarding the kitchen like their fortress? That's not exactly how it was. I remember one occasion, when my niece and I were visiting the White House Residence. Hillary sent her off to play with Chelsea, who was two years older. They had both gotten bread machines for Christmas. But when Chelsea wanted to make bread, the White House usher showed up with a gigantic silver tray, loaded with neat little piles of each ingredient.

"Cooking" in the White House is different, as Hillary herself hinted in *Living History*. "Chelsea was not feeling well and I wanted to make her soft scrambled eggs and applesauce," she writes. "I looked in the small kitchen for utensils and then called downstairs and asked the chef if he could provide me with what I needed. He and the kitchen staff were completely undone at the thought of a first lady wielding a frying pan with no supervision! They even called my staff to ask if I was cooking myself because I was unhappy with their food."

No one expects any first lady to cook and prepare meals. With a staff of hundreds in the Residence and a schedule packed with events, it is neither feasible nor necessary. So why does Hillary insist on portraying herself as a genuinely domestic animal, as anxious as any other housewife to make a good home for her husband and daughter? Because it's part of the HILLARY brand.

The truth, of course, is quite different. Since the age of thirty-two—with only a brief interregnum in the early 1980s—Hillary has lived in either the Governor's Mansion in Little Rock or the White House, surrounded by a massive staff of domestics, cooks, cleaning people, waiters, babysitters, and personal assistants. Only the richest and most privileged women in the nation can boast of having had less exposure to the daily realities of homemaking than she.

During her twelve years in the Governor's Mansion, a few seasoned experts handled all aspects of the governor's limited social schedule; Hillary let herself be guided by their knowledge and cared little about developing her own independent tastes or judgment.

In the Governor's Mansion, social life was run by the staff, as it had always been. Downstairs, in public, the Clintons lived a civilized life as the state's chief officer and first lady. Dinner was served on blue and white china, left over from Winthrop Rockefeller's years as governor. The first couple and their guests were waited on by uniformed butlers (many of them felons serving long sentences, who were eager to impress the governor in hopes of securing early release). There was no need for Hillary to pretend to any serious involvement in cooking or decorating.

Her lack of interest in domestic skills was painfully apparent in the only private house the Clintons have ever lived in before Chappaqua—the yellow house they had for two years after Clinton lost the governorship. After Bill's defeat, he and Hillary were forced to leave the Governor's Mansion and set up housekeeping on their own.

The results were really something. The living room was overwhelmed by a set of red velvet Victorian furniture with dark wood carving; it looked like the lobby of a hotel in an old western movie. Hillary herself might have been aware of how bizarre it looked; at the time, she explained to me that Bill had gone out and bought the pieces on his own.

Nothing in the house was either warm or comfortable. Though the furniture was big and ungainly, it was also austere. There was no warmth, no texture.

In *Living History*, Hillary speaks fondly of an old red Victorian "courting couch" that Bill's mother gave them, and describes shopping together for antiques to fill their new home.

That's not how I remember their house. Whenever I went into the kitchen, I was amazed by the college-dorm feeling. The glasses and plates looked like they came from a gas station or supermarket—mismatched, in clashing sizes and designs. I'm no expert on tableware, but it all reminded me of the kitchen supplies I'd had in my days as a student at Columbia. I still remember wondering why such a prominent couple—a former governor and a prominent lawyer—would choose to live that way.

Years later, when they lived in the White House, the Clintons had one room redone in a style not unlike their old Little Rock living room, although much gaudier and grander, filled with gold velvet furniture and oversized crystal lamps festooning all the tables. This room, which was right next to the Lincoln Bedroom, stood in sharp contrast to the elegance of the rest of the White House. Apparently, everything in the room—the furniture, fabrics, wallpaper, lamps, pillows—had been used in a room in an Arkansas show house designed by Kaki Hockersmith, the Clintons' decorator. The room was reassembled in the White House, right down to the wallpapered ceiling, patterned carpet, and garish lighting. As Yogi Berra would say, it was déjà vu all over again.

Hillary says she was surprised by charges that she might not be able to handle the social aspect of the job of first lady. In *Living History,* she writes of her amazement "that people could perceive me only as one thing or the other—*either* a hardworking professional woman *or* a conscientious and caring hostess." In her defense, she cites the conclusions of Kathleen Hall Jamieson, dean of the Annenberg School for Communications at the University of Pennsylvania that "gender stereotypes . . . trap women by categorizing them in ways that don't reflect the true complexities of their lives." That wasn't the problem. The difficulty was that anybody acquainted with Hillary understood that she knew little about anything having to do with domesticity, and cared even less. Of course, in and of itself that's hardly a problem. Plenty of women—and most men—are in the same category. The problem was that her feelings went beyond a lack of interest to true contempt—as her 1992 jibe about baking cookies made painfully apparent. As usual, such public missteps—rare as they may be—tell us more about her real attitudes than her carefully scripted interviews and memoirs.

When she became first lady, though, Hillary realized that there was, indeed, a use for domesticity—to provide political cover as she pursued her real interest: becoming a policy-oriented, politically savvy, activist first lady. If she were seen to be doing a good job at the tasks she had never valued, she realized, she would be far less likely to attract criticism for doing what she really wanted to do. Seeking the tacit immunity from political criticism traditionally enjoyed by First Ladies, she began to emphasize the social side of the job—hoping, no doubt, that Republicans who laced into her would look like bullies attacking a woman. She was hiding behind her own apron strings.

I know this firsthand: Indeed, I bear some responsibility for Hillary's choice of tactics.

As she points out proudly in *Living History*, Hillary was unique among first ladies in having offices on each side of the White House. In the East Wing, where the first family lives and conducts its social schedule, her staff handled her social duties as chief hostess. But she also had an office in the West Wing, where the substantive work of the presidency is done—and she had a full staff there as well. Together with a second group in the Old Executive Office Building next door, Hillary's West Wing team dealt with public policy, including her work on health care reform.

In a memo I sent her early in her husband's first term, I compared the East and West Wings of the White House to two barbells she could use to steady herself as she walked the tightrope of public life. "The East Wing (social) barbell is what gives you protection in the West Wing political life," I wrote. "By going in and out of your traditional role as first lady, you insulate yourself against criticism for your public role and acquire political traction that you'll need for your West Wing activities."

I alluded to the president's ceremonial role as his equivalent of the East Wing/West Wing barbells. "When Bill pins a medal on a boy scout, he's buying political credibility to use in passing his legislative agenda. He derives authority and aura from his ceremonial functions. It's the same with a first lady, only your activities are not just ceremonial but social as well."

Hillary's memoir is replete with tales of just this kind of barbell balancing. Since social activities consumed a large and vital part of her life in the White House, she now pretends that she was interested in them for their own sake. "In my own mind, I was traditional in some ways and not in others. I cared about the food I served our guests, and I also wanted to improve the delivery of health care for all

Americans. To me, there was nothing incongruous about my interests and activities."

Not incongruous, just politically motivated. Hillary really didn't care about making sure that everything on the social side of the White House was elegantly presented or particularly sophisticated. She involved herself largely so that she could beef up the East Wing barbell to offset her West Wing activities. And eventually, later in the administration, she came to recognize the power of patronage that could be wielded through invitations to the White House.

In *Living History,* Hillary alludes briefly—if unpersuasively—to how she used the media to help burnish her image as first lady. In the first days of the administration, she notes, she "granted an exclusive interview to a reporter whose beat was not White House politics. . . . Some critics suggested that the story was contrived to 'soften' my image and portray me as a traditional woman in a traditional role."

Such coy denials notwithstanding, the interview was contrived for exactly that purpose. As Hillary's media consultant, Mandy Grunwald, told Bob Woodward, "The photos were intended to soften her image." It was the barbell theory in action: Like nearly every one of Hillary's interviews during her tenure as first lady, this was carefully arranged and orchestrated; in most cases, guidelines were established as to what questions reporters could or could not ask.

Since Hillary was actually a substantive policy advisor to the president, she was, in effect, conducting West Wing business by East Wing rules. She used the traditional guidelines for interviewing First Ladies as protection against questions that honed in on her various functions and scandals.

A first lady can limit her media interviews to a select few. So can a senator. A president cannot. Only a president has to endure the 360-degree media coverage that surrounds the office. A president's staff must have daily interactions with the national press corps. A president must stand in front of the national media, and the American people, for each new press conference, and face questions with no holds barred.

For all her time in the public eye, though, Hillary Clinton is not used to that level of scrutiny. In the White House, she hid behind the pink shield of those traditional first lady press ground rules, warding off unwanted media attention. Only certain reporters from certain publications could ask certain questions on certain topics.

In the Senate, despite Hillary's high profile, media interest in her day-to-day activities is nowhere near what it would be if she were president. She doesn't have that many opportunities to make news in any given week, and what attention she does attract is almost always at her own behest, and therefore under her control. Once that control lapses—as it inevitably will should she occupy the Oval Office— the real Hillary is likely to seep out from behind the façade. Then the contrast between the reality and the mask—between Hillary and HILLARY—will become dangerously stark. Again, the lesson of the second Nixon administration is instructive: Once we learned of the break-ins, wiretaps, payoffs, and skullduggery of Richard Nixon's presidency, no one believed that the Nixon we were watching on television was the real man telling the real truth. If she isn't careful, HILLARY could suffer a similar fate.

In the late 1990s, as the Clinton administration descended more deeply into scandal and the spears and arrows grew sharper, Hillary depended on the protective camouflage of domesticity more than ever. She never required it as much as she did on the weekend of January 16–18, 1998, a three-day period that must rank as one of the worst in Hillary Clinton's life. Saturday, January 17, was the day her husband had to testify at a deposition in the Paula Jones lawsuit and answer questions posed by Jones's attorneys. It was there that he lied about his relationship with Monica Lewinsky, which led directly to his impeachment one year later. And it was there that he finally admitted he had had an affair with Gennifer Flowers, after six years of disparagement and denial. Despite weeks of preparation by the best lawyers in the capital, the deposition went badly. Very badly.

Gail Sheehy, author of the penetrating and insightful book *Hillary's Choice,* writes that after the deposition "the first couple had planned to take [Chief of Staff] Erskine Bowles and his wife out for a celebratory dinner . . . to counter-act any impression that the President's forced deposition had shaken their lives." But the Clintons canceled. "Except for a visit to church on Sunday, they remained in seclusion until Monday. The wind had been knocked out of Bill Clinton."

According to Joyce Milton, the deposition "proved to be a lot tougher than the President had expected. . . . The Clintons did not dine out on Saturday evening. And by the time they retired for the night, there was more bad news. The Drudge Report, the Internet gossip sheet loathed but avidly followed at the Clinton White House, was reporting that *Newsweek* had the intern story but had decided to spike it just minutes before its deadline. Drudge did not disclose Lewinsky's name, but he mentioned the existence of tapes of 'intimate phone conversations.' This can only have sent a shudder through Bill Clinton," who knew only too well the content of his late night phone calls with Lewinsky.

Hillary must have wanted to hide under the bed after this beastly weekend. Instead, though, she wrapped herself in a politically savvy image of domesticity. When reporter Peter Mayer asked her "how difficult a day Saturday was for you and your family?" Hillary shrugged the question off. "It 'wasn't difficult for me,' she said. 'I just kind of hunkered down and went through my household tasks. Then my husband came home and we watched a movie and we had a'—a pregnant pause ensued while she seemed to grope for the words 'good time that evening.'"

"And Sunday?" Mayer followed up.

"Oh, we just stayed home and cleaned closets."

Gail Sheehy adds: "Another folksy image: Hillary as the dutiful homemaker whose husband comes home on a Saturday night wanting nothing more than a good video. In fact, that was the Saturday night Hillary Clinton cleaned his closets."

How could Hillary have expected the press to believe such a quaint little domestic portrait? Especially on a weekend when she must have wanted to kill Bill? Not only was he betraying her, he was endangering the positions both of them had worked their entire lives to achieve.

The answer was simple: self-preservation. As mad as Hillary must have been, HILLARY still realized it was vital to convey certain impressions:

First, she had to make it seem that all was at peace in the Clinton household that weekend. To indicate otherwise would have been to admit that there was reason for Bill to be troubled about the Jones deposition—that there was some real basis for their questions about his affairs with Flowers and Lewinsky.

Second, Hillary also had to leave the impression that Bill told her nothing to make her angry. She had to show the world that she was calm, even as she was seething inside. Revealing her anger would mean revealing that she knew about his affairs—and it was crucial to maintain the impression that she *didn't* know, if she were going to stand by Bill during the battle that was likely to ensue. If she *knew* and stood by him, it would mean she valued power over her marriage. But if she did *not* know, she could defend her power by standing up for her marriage.

Third, she needed, at that moment, to seem like any wife confronted by a wild and unbelievable charge of her husband's adultery. To conceal the political calculation that was undoubtedly going on beneath her real pain and sense of betrayal, she grasped at these pseudo-domesticity straws to bolster the impression that she was just like any other wife. To act like a politician now would be a disaster. She needed to pretend to be unpretentious— to be "normal"—so that her unflappability would indicate her husband's innocence. The reality was, of course, quite different.

Finally, she seems to have thought it a good idea to hint at intimacy with her husband, even as they were entering the most difficult period of their relationship. After all, if she was still intimate with him, how bad could his offense have been?

Her choices, of course, were limited. Other women could kick their husbands out of the house. She couldn't. Other women could walk away from such a situation. She couldn't. Leaving Bill would not only expand the scandal exponentially—it would also mean leaving the office of first lady. And there's no power in being a president's ex-wife.

Hillary had been mounting this domestic-bliss campaign for some time. Weeks earlier, to reinforce further the notion that they were a close-knit couple, the Clintons had made sure they were photographed dancing on the beach in St. Thomas in the Virgin Islands during their 1997 Christmas vacation, two weeks before the Paula Jones deposition.

In *Living History,* Hillary scoffs at "speculation by some journalists that we had 'posed' for the photo in hopes that our embrace would be captured on film."

And here comes the nondenial denial: "Hello? As I told a radio interviewer a few weeks later, 'Just name me any fifty-year-old woman who would knowingly pose in her bathing suit—with her back pointed toward the camera.' Well, maybe people who look good from any angle, like Cher or Jane Fonda or Tina Turner. But not me."

Not her. But the woman dancing on the beach already knew that her husband had been subpoenaed to testify by Paula Jones's lawyers. I suppose it's *possible* she was simply enjoying a carefree moment. But knowing Hillary as I do, I believe it's far more likely that she was very careful indeed, laying the groundwork for her defense of her husband. Dancing on the beach, knowing the media couldn't resist the shot, reinforced the impression that there was nothing wrong in their marriage. She knew it would be crucial to appear relaxed and in love if she wanted to defend her husband's presidency—and her first ladyship—once the charges of the affair with Lewinsky came out two weeks hence.

But the most astonishing trial balloon was Hillary's claim in August 1996, three months before her husband's re-election, that she and the president had "talked about" adopting a baby. Barbara Olson relates how she "let it slip that they were 'talking about it more now.' She added 'I must say we're hoping to have another child.'" Hillary was forty-nine at the time. She never mentions the idea in *Living History*. And after the election, the Clintons never talked again in public about pursuing adoption. Perhaps the idea of adopting a child was sincere. Or maybe the entire thing was created as the election approached so Hillary and Bill could adopt—not a child, but the protective coloration of a normal family.

Though they never adopted a child, they did eventually get a dog. There's nothing to warm up your life—and your image—like a dog. In *Living History*, Hillary lovingly tells the story of how they came to buy Buddy. After Chelsea left for college, she writes, she and Bill felt acute empty-nest syndrome; "it was time to get a dog." She noted that "Bill wanted a big dog he could run with," and that they "finally decided that a Labrador would be just the right size and temperament for our family and the White House."

Eileen and I have had golden retrievers for the past twenty years, and now have three: Dizzy, Daisy, and Dubs. When Hillary came to visit us in 1994, she admired our herd. I suggested that she get a golden, and offered a golden puppy from a friend of ours whose female was about to give birth.

But Hillary was way ahead of us. "If we get a dog, it's got to be from a pound or the ASPCA. We'd get criticized if we ever bought a pedigree." Nothing went without calculation: That's just the way they worked. When Buddy arrived in the White House in 1997, it was no simple attempt to assuage the Clintons' empty-nest feelings. It was a public relations move.

There's no crime in this, particularly. Every president uses his family and home life to attract political support, particularly when the going gets rough. Nixon delighted in his daughter Julie's marriage to David Eisenhower at the White House just when Watergate was heating up. Gerald Ford had himself photographed toasting his own English muffin. John Kennedy played touch football with his entire clan.

But Hillary's domestic-charm offensives are nevertheless cause for concern, because they suggest a crisis-management approach that simply won't fly if she ever returns to the White House in her own right. Once she makes the move from the East to the West Wing of the White House, it'll take more than a half-credible story about cleaning out closets to deflect the penetrating questions of the Washington press.

HIDING WITHIN THE HERD

When Hillary is attacked, she frequently parries the charges by arguing that it is all women who are under attack, rather than just one in particular. Like a water buffalo stalked by a lion, she gathers the herd around her for protection, defending the entire class under attack rather than just herself. At times like these, she drops all semblance of individuality.

Criticized for her business dealings as a lawyer, she treats it as an attack on all professional women. Knocked for tolerating her husband's adultery in her bid to hold on to political power, she gathers around her all women who want to protect their privacy. Slammed with allegations of insider trading in commodities, she cloaks herself in the garb of every woman seeking financial security for her family. This "class action" defense is designed to win sympathy from other career women and to attribute sexism to the person raising questions about her. Hillary's imputation that anyone who criticizes her is attacking her entire gender—rather than just her—works to insulate her from much disapproval.

Often, she seems deliberately to overlook what people are saying about *her* in order to discuss what some say about *people like her*. In her memoir, she has a deft way of describing the strategy. "I adopted my own mantra: Take criticism seriously but not personally." In other words, *disassociate yourself from any and all criticism.* The attacks are never about *her;* there's no need to take them personally, because there's nothing wrong with her. They're criticisms of *all* women, or working women, or women in politics, or women in professions, or women in public life, or Democrats, or liberals, or supporters of the Clinton administration in general. They're never critiques of Hillary Rodham Clinton in particular. And, because all criticism is about her class, not her, she neither listens to it nor learns from it.

Living History is full of examples:

- Commenting on the reaction to her 1992 remark about not "staying home and baking cookies," she says: "Some of the attacks . . . may have reflected the extent to which our society was still adjusting to the changing roles of women. . . . While Bill talked about social change, I embodied it. I had my own opinions, interests, and profession. For better or worse, I was outspoken. I represented a fundamental change in the way women functioned in our society. . . . I had been turned into a symbol for women of my generation."

But the backlash after Hillary's remark had nothing to do with society's maladjustment to "the changing roles of women" or Hillary's own "opinions, interests and profession." It was a clear and simple reaction to the insult and arrogance she had directed toward stay-at-home women. The only "opinions and interests" that got her in trouble were her own insensitivity and elitism:

- Deflecting the attacks directed at her for doing legal work for the state of Arkansas while her husband was governor, she said: "this is the sort of thing that happens to . . . women who have their own careers and their own lives. And I think it's a shame, but I guess it's something that we're going to have to live with. Those of us who have tried and have a career—tried to have an independent life and to make a difference—and certainly like myself who has children . . . you know I've done the best I can to lead my life . . ."

But the criticism she attracted had nothing to do with the inherent problems of juggling career and family. They had to do with a clear conflict of interest.

■ Dismissing criticism of her role in Whitewater, she claimed that it was "about undermining the progressive agenda by any means."

But Hillary wasn't being attacked because she was a "progressive." She was being attacked because of her questionable conduct in a real estate deal:

■ Tarring the investigations of her White House years with a broad brush, she writes: "the purpose of the investigations was to discredit the President and the Administration and slow down its momentum. It didn't matter what the investigations were about; it only mattered that there were investigations. It didn't matter that we had done nothing wrong; it only mattered that the public was given the impression that we had. . . . Whitewater signaled a new tactic in political warfare: investigation as a weapon for political destruction."

The Republicans obviously pursued Whitewater to "slow down" Clinton's "momentum." That's what opposition parties are supposed to do. But they never would have had the chance had the Clintons not entered into a shady real estate deal in the first place . . .

■ Citing Richard Nixon's paraphrase of Cardinal de Richelieu's famous quotation, Hillary accused her attackers of harboring the prejudice that "Intellect in a woman is unbecoming."

But it wasn't Hillary's brains—or, as she hinted, the brains of every other intelligent woman in America—that were unbecoming. It was her conduct:

- And, most famously, days after the Lewinsky story broke, Hillary told the *Today* show's Matt Lauer that the attacks on Bill were the product of a "vast right-wing conspiracy."

But the nationwide outrage over her husband's behavior was no mere partisan flare-up. It was the natural result of the shock of discovering that our president had had a reckless affair with a young intern right in the Oval Office, and lied to cover it up.

Nor is Hillary above ascribing attacks to pure jealousy. In early 1994, she, the president, and I were discussing accusations against her former law partner Bill Kennedy for his handling of the Travel Office investigation, and Deputy Treasury Secretary Roger Altman for his role in the Madison Bank investigation.

"Do you know why these reporters keep attacking us? Keep investigating us?" Hillary asked angrily, "Because they're jealous. We are the same age as they are. We're all boomers. They don't have to get jealous of Bush or Reagan. They're too old. But we are the same age as they are and they can't get over the fact that we're here [in the White House] and they're not."

(And some of these problems run in the family. In that same conversation, Bill complained that he was being attacked on the editorial pages of the *New York Times* by editor Howell Raines, a former Alabama reporter, because "I'm a southerner who didn't have to leave to make good.")

Hillary's defenses do have a certain consistency. People attack her and Bill, she claims, because the Clintons are southerners, baby boomers, smart, or hold coveted positions. They go after Hillary because she's an outspoken professional woman who embodies social change, who pursues her own ideas instead of staying home and baking cookies. It's a classic syllogism: *Critique me and you critique the*

*modern woman. But the modern woman is beyond reproach. And therefore
so am I.*

On occasion, Hillary's ability to see herself as a martyr sacrificed
for the greater good rises to the sublime. In *Living History,* Hillary
actually compares herself with Nelson Mandela, somehow finding a
moral equivalence between the Whitewater investigations and the
decades of persecution Mandela suffered because of apartheid. During
her May 1994 visit to South Africa, she describes how Mandela, at a
speech, singled out "three of his former jailers . . . who had treated
him with respect during his imprisonment. He asked them to stand so
he could introduce them to the crowd."

Then Hillary adds: "His generosity of spirit was inspiring and
humbling. For months I had been preoccupied with the hostility in
Washington and the mean-spirited attacks connected to Whitewater,
Vince Foster, and the travel office. But here was Mandela, honoring
three men who had held him prisoner."

Now, let's get some perspective here: Nelson Mandela endured
decades in jail for the crime of trying to free his people. Hillary Clinton endured the scolding of the *Wall Street Journal* editorial page for
her role in the White House Travel Office debacle. Hillary subsequently noted that if Mandela could forgive, then she could at least
try to. So refined a sense of victimization is rare indeed.

But no rarer than Hillary's sense of self-worth. As we began to
work together during Hillary's early White House years, I suggested
that she presented too perfect an image to be believable. "You come
across as fully formed, with no doubts, faults, or shortcomings," I told
her. "People can't trust your presentation of yourself. Nobody's perfect and when you act as if you are, people don't believe you."

"So what do you suggest?" she asked.

"Let people know about some imperfections—put the story out
there. Eleanor Roosevelt let people know that she was insecure about
her appearance and felt awkward about public speaking. It made her
more believable. More human."

"I'll think about it," she promised.

A few days later, I asked her about it again.

"I really can't think of anything," she told me.

Even when Hillary came upon real adversity, she has shown little inclination to reckon frankly with it and reveal how such experiences have helped her learn and grow. Indeed, in all of *Living History* there is almost no suggestion of personal growth. She gives no indication of having learned from the fiasco of health care reform, from her husband's defeat for governor, from the Gennifer Flowers affair, from her various Whitewater problems, her husband's impeachment, or any of the other tempests that tossed her during her career. She seems unable to admit to anything short of consistent perfection.

And yet an essential feature of any successful presidency is the growth of the person who holds the job. The demands of the office are entirely unique; no new president arrives in the White House fully prepared for its trials, difficulties, and stresses. Each new tenant must either rise to the occasion, or fall short.

The examples are legion: Who could compare the John F. Kennedy of the Bay of Pigs—dominated by his elders and the military—with the savvy, take-charge leader of the Cuban Missile Crisis one short year later? The callow George W. Bush who took office in 2001 after a disputed election was a far cry from the figure who mobilized America in the aftermath of 9/11. The boy became a man before our eyes.

How do presidents grow? John Kennedy is often quoted as saying that good judgment comes from experience, which, in turn, often comes from bad judgment.

But there's serious reason to doubt Hillary's willingness to learn from her bad judgments. After all, if she dismisses all criticism as a class action, how can she even recognize her own mistakes, never mind learn from them? Hillary has, at times, shown signs of growth: After the health care fiasco, for example, she backed away from further attempts at broad-scale, utopian reforms. But she appears to have learned little from the pounding she took in defending her own finances, or Bill's impeachment and its causes. Would a President Hillary Clinton show the same obtuse inability to mature or grow or learn from adversity?

FEIGNING PROFESSIONAL INDEPENDENCE

One hallmark of the HILLARY brand is that she is an independent, professional woman, admirably credentialed and accomplished, who gave up a blue chip career to serve the public in politics.

To substantiate her independence, in *Living History* Hillary makes no connection between her husband's political successes (and failures) and her legal career. But the HILLARY brand's image of professional autonomy is an illusion. Her career advances were a direct consequence of the success and political power of her husband. When he advanced, she advanced. From the day she moved to Arkansas in 1974, Hillary Clinton derived her political power and professional opportunities from Bill Clinton's career.

Hillary's account, in *Living History,* of her meteoric rise in the ranks of the Arkansas legal community makes no mention of the relationship between her husband's political prominence and her consequent access to professional opportunities. Could she really believe that there was no connection?

Part of the mythology of the HILLARY brand is that Hillary sacrificed a brilliant legal career in the corridors of Wall Street or K Street to go to Arkansas to work for her husband. The myth persists despite a few inconvenient truths—such as the fact that she failed the Washington, D.C., bar examination and could not have practiced there if she had tried to. She does her best to put a positive spin on the failure: "I had taken both the Arkansas and Washington D.C. bar exams during the summer [of 1972]," she relates, "but my heart was pulling me toward Arkansas. When I learned that I had passed in Arkansas but failed in D.C., I thought that maybe my test scores were telling me something." Apparently they were telling her just how welcoming Arkansas could be.

Despite a complete lack of courtroom experience, Hillary began her legal career in 1974 teaching criminal law and trial advocacy at the University of Arkansas Law School. At the time, Bill was already a member of the faculty and a Democratic candidate for Congress. Criminal law is generally taught by former prosecutors, trial advocacy by experienced attorneys; Hillary was unquestionably bright, but she was no kind of experienced attorney. Yet she was even put in charge of the legal clinic and prison project, which actually permitted students to represent indigent clients and prisoners in court—a responsibility generally handled only by experienced attorneys.

At the age of thirty, Hillary's husband became the attorney general of Arkansas—an achievement strangely downplayed in her book: "Bill Clinton's first election victory as Attorney General of Arkansas in 1976 was anticlimactic. . . . The big show that year was the Presidential contest between Jimmy Carter and Gerald Ford."

While Hillary claims to have paid scant attention to his victory, the Rose Law Firm was watching Bill's trajectory closely. Almost immediately, they offered Hillary a job as the first female associate at what Mrs. Clinton calls "the most venerable firm in Arkansas." She recounts her moment of triumph: "Vince [Foster] and another Rose Firm partner, Herbert C. Rule III, came to see me with a job offer." Although Hillary did not seem to associate the offer with her husband's new influence in the legal community as the attorney general and lawyer for the State of Arkansas, the Rose Law Firm was not as naive. Even before they spoke to her, Rule had "already obtained an opinion from the American Bar Association that approved the employment by a law firm of a lawyer married to a state's Attorney General." In other words, they knew exactly what they were doing.

Later, in 1979, Hillary was made the first woman partner at the Rose Law Firm, the same year her husband took office as governor of Arkansas. Every step Bill took up his ladder allowed her to advance another rung up her own.

And advance she did, even though her actual legal experience at the Rose Law Firm was sharply limited. She was never the great trial lawyer the HILLARY brand promotes. Gail Sheehy quotes Rose Law Firm partner Joe Giroir saying "I was always mad at [Hillary] for not doing more [legal work]." Sheehy notes that "She tried only five cases in her career at [the] Rose [Law Firm]."

Indeed, there's also an argument that Hillary owes even her election to the Senate to her husband. Her access to Bill Clinton's donors, political consultants, policy staff, image-makers, and even private detectives gave her a critical head start in the campaign. Her many White House perks didn't hurt either: Free government jets, White House events like state dinners and the Millennium celebration to charm donors, overnights for contributors in the Lincoln Bedroom and at Camp David, and the White House staff to do her research, all helped to give Hillary Clinton the edge that elected her to the Senate. And the newfound popularity and heightened status she acquired as the wronged first lady who acted with grace and dignity during the Lewinsky scandal didn't hurt either. Once more, her success and his marched in tandem.

BECOMING A NEW YORKER

The HILLARY brand is "Made in New York." Though Hillary was born in Illinois, spent childhood vacations in Pennsylvania, attended college in Massachusetts, graduated from law school in Connecticut, moved to Arkansas, and lived in Washington, HILLARY is a New Yorker.

The greatest challenge in launching the HILLARY brand was convincing people that she was now, suddenly, a citizen of the state she had asked to make her a senator.

And she tried hard. Her campaign started with a "listening tour" in which she visited every county of her new state. In her speeches, she spoke constantly of "we New Yorkers." After she and Bill bought their new home in Chappaqua, she relished dropping in-the-know references to Con Ed, the New York utility.

Even baseball couldn't escape her grasp. "I've always been a Yankees fan," she told Katie Couric on the *Today* show. "I am a Cubs fan, but I needed an American league team . . . so as a young girl, I became very interested and enamored of the Yankees." (Not to leave basketball out of it, Hillary identified with the New York Knicks' star player: "I've always been a Patrick Ewing fan because you know he went to Georgetown.")

Now, maybe this is all on the level. But as a lifelong New Yorker— and obsessive Yankees fan—myself, I know this much: In the hundreds of conversations I had with Bill and Hillary Clinton during our years working together, she never showed the slightest interest in what I now learn was our mutually favorite team. Though I never passed the time chatting baseball with Hillary—somehow it just didn't seem appropriate—I frequently used stories from Yankee history to illustrate the political points I was making. I remember one incident, when Hillary entered the room as I was studying the local Arkansas sports pages. Why was I so interested in Arkansas sports, she asked. I needed to find out if the Yankees had beaten the Red Sox last night, I explained—"you know, like you want to beat the Republicans." Funny— I don't remember her asking how her beloved Yanks had done.

The HILLARY brand couldn't *really* be Jewish but in 1999, just as she was getting serious about her Senate race, Hillary suddenly discovered a hint of Judaism in her background: Her grandmother's second husband, Max Rosenberg, was Jewish. Even though he was no blood relation, Hillary's discovery helped smooth her path to run for office in her highly Jewish adopted state.

And yet, in my experience, Hillary didn't always seem comfortable around Jews in her days as the first lady of Arkansas. In 1985, in the midst of a difficult negotiation with the Clintons over my fees, I saw a disturbing example of her tendency to stereotype us in a negative light.

Bill, Hillary, and I were gathered around the table in the breakfast room of the Governor's Mansion to negotiate my consulting contract. I quoted a fee that made Bill's hackles rise. (He always thought I should love him enough to work for free.) I told him I didn't have to work for him if he felt I'd become too expensive.

Bill took that as a threat to leave. "I can't stand when you do that," he said. "You know I need you, and you negotiate by threatening me. Don't Mau Mau me." (He was referring to the Kenyan nationalist group that attacked white colonialists in the 1950s with threats, violent rhetoric, and terrorist raids.)

Hillary chimed in with an ethnic remark of her own. "That's all you people care about is money!"

Stiffening at the implied slur, I gave her an escape hatch: "Hillary, I assume by 'you people' that you mean political consultants?"

"Yeah, yeah," she said, with apparent relief. "That's what I meant, political consultants."

It wasn't the only time she skirted around the subject of my Jewish heritage. When I dined at the Governor's Mansion with the Clintons, the staff would often serve pork or ham, which I happen to enjoy. Invariably, Hillary would anxiously pull me aside and ask if the food was all right with me. When she asked for the fifth time, I began to bristle at the question: She was being solicitous, but she couldn't let it go. Finally, I told her that I *loved* pork—bacon in particular. The Mansion's wonderful cook overheard the comment, and from then on she had a heaping portion of bacon ready for me whenever I dined there—even when I came for dinner!

I always told Eileen that whenever Hillary started with the pork questions, I felt like Woody Allen in *Annie Hall*. I couldn't help thinking she must see me with a prayer shawl around my neck and yarmulke on my head as I swayed back and forth praying. I don't think Hillary was anti-Semitic, but I believe she did stereotype Jews.

As first lady of the Clinton White House, of course, Hillary always basked in the glow of her husband's genuine lack of ethnic or racial prejudice. On her own, however, she periodically loses strict control over her tongue, revealing hints of a darker, less enlightened racial consciousness. Hillary blurts: When angry or pressed, words can come out of her mouth that sound very, very bad. While speaking at a January 3, 2004, fund-raiser in St. Louis, Missouri, for example, Hillary invoked the great Indian civil rights leader, Mahatma Gandhi—and then stunned the Democratic audience (and the press) with her bizarre attempt at a joke: "Mahatma Gandhi—he ran a gas station down in St. Louis for a couple of years. Mr. Gandhi, you still go to the gas station? A lot of wisdom comes out of that gas station."

As a senator who's endured far greater scandals, Hillary managed to walk away from that moment of madness largely unscathed by the press. But as president, she would be faced with a near-constant pressure to respond to questions—and her answers would be subjected to the unforgiving scrutiny of both the media and the American people. Senator Clinton has been able to dodge a few such bullets along the way, but President Hillary would have a far harder time explaining away such insensitive missteps.

The HILLARY brand depends on an element of mystery; her political machine cultivates a certain inscrutability that lends the senator an undeniable allure.

But Hillary is really one of the least mysterious people in politics. Bill Clinton is complicated. Hillary is simple. She is a professional politician, through and through. More ruthless—without question. Less subtle, certainly. More ideological, obviously. And probably more ambitious, though very much in the mold of the classic politico. She thinks like a politician, acts like one, climbs the ladder as they all do, uses her family to project an image, and shapes her positions on issues with an eye on the polls, like any other politician in our midst.

But what is odd to observers and maddening to those who have known her well is that she tries so desperately to hide what she is behind the HILLARY brand. She conceals her motives and ambitions beneath a mask that bares no real resemblance to how she acts when the cameras are off.

Take the small matter of revenge. Of course, such a base motive would have no place in the HILLARY brand. But in the actions of the woman herself, it has been known to rear its head. As senator, Hillary voted twice against the confirmation of Michael Chertoff—once as chief of the Justice Department's Criminal Division, then on his appointment to the Third Circuit Court of Appeals in Washington, D.C. Each time, Chertoff's nomination was confirmed by a margin of 99 to 1. Hillary cast the only Nay.

What has she got against Chertoff? He served as special counsel to the Republicans on the Senate Whitewater Committee. He was the enemy; her vote against him was pure retaliation.

Fair enough—how human! Who wouldn't bristle at voting to reward a former foe with a plum appointment? But the problem wasn't with the vote she cast: It was with the way she chose to cloak her spitefulness. Appearing on the *Today* show, she told Katie Couric that she made her decision because some young White House staff members felt Chertoff had mistreated them. HILLARY, of course, would never stoop to revenge—but apparently the complaints of a group of poor, young, impressionable (and notably anonymous) staffers were just too poignant to resist.

The worst thing about the HILLARY brand is that it obscures the real person beneath the façade; instead of an intelligent, strong woman who makes no apologies for her actions, we get only the carefully coiffed, ultra-sensitive, hyper-programmed media package. In this, of course, she once again calls to mind Richard Nixon.

In 1960, during his first run for president, Nixon debated golden boy John F. Kennedy on television—and fixed his image in the public mind as pale and haggard, shifty and sinister. Two years later, when he was defeated in his race for California governor, Nixon lashed out at the press, blurting out that they wouldn't "have Nixon to kick around anymore." And there his image stood for years: angry, paranoid, untrustworthy, and vicious.

By 1968, though, when Nixon returned to run for president again, he had been taken in hand by advertising professionals—and the result was the new NIXON brand. Gone were the sagging jowls and the glowering visage. A sunny, tanned, smiling candidate emerged from their tutelage, a man who reflected typical middle American values and a small-business, hardworking ethic. As he ran, carefully camouflaging his position on the Vietnam War to attract both doves and hawks, his exposure to the national media was doled out by the thimbleful, each interview carefully conducted along pre-established guidelines. He campaigned largely at staged town meetings, where he interacted with carefully chosen voters, and managed to replace his once-vicious image with a benign, statesmanlike new self-portrait.

The NIXON brand got elected president. And for some time, the president we saw behind the White House lectern kept up the façade. Moderate and modulated, he addressed the American people with an apparent sincerity that seemed to clear the air after the chicanery and secrecy of his predecessor, Lyndon Johnson.

But one can wear a mask only so long. By the beginning of his second term, when the name "Watergate" entered the public consciousness, the grim-faced paranoid reappeared, sending the nation into a massive constitutional crisis. As we read about the wiretaps and burglaries, the dirty tricks against opponents, and the ruthless disregard for veracity and civil liberties alike, Americans came to loathe the president we had elected.

And when the NIXON brand took to the airwaves once more, trying to salvage a doomed presidency, the American people weren't buying it. "Fool me once, shame on you," we said; "fool me twice, shame on me." The president was finished: the NIXON brand had lost its credibility.

It's a lesson that Hillary and HILLARY alike should heed.

4

HIDING HILLARY: THE POLITICIAN

Much as we may be attracted, from time to time, to outsiders and nonpoliticians who run for office—from actor Ronald Reagan to wrestler Jesse Ventura to actor Arnold Schwarzenegger—there's one fundamental fact that cannot be overlooked: The president of the United States succeeds or fails almost entirely due to political skill, that finely tuned combination of preparation and aptitude that decides how a presidency will be remembered in the history books. To understand how history would treat a Hillary Clinton presidency, we must examine her strengths and weaknesses as a politician—a practitioner of what R. A. Butler called "the art of the possible."

Hillary began her political career as a campaign manager, pressed into service after her husband's wrenching defeat for re-election as Arkansas governor. At some level, she remained a manager—and often *the* manager—of Bill's political career until the end of his second term as president.

It has been nearly two hundred years since the American people elected a former campaign manager to the presidency. (The early American voters did it twice: James Madison was Thomas Jefferson's manager, and Martin Van Buren ran Andrew Jackson's campaign.) The closest we have come in recent history is Robert F. Kennedy:

Eight years after he ran his brother's successful 1960 campaign, an assassin's bullet prevented him from securing the Democratic nomination—and very likely the presidency.

Campaign managers are just that: managers. They hire and fire staff, organize large amounts of work, allocate all-important (and all too scarce) human and financial resources, and translate plans into action. While most people understand that the profit-and-loss rules of business translate poorly into politics (despite protests that government should be "run like a business"), the importance of efficiency and streamlined decision making in politics is apparent to anyone who's ever been involved in the process.

The talents of a campaign manager are rarely found, as it happens, in politicians themselves. Candidates become candidates because of their talent for connecting with people, not just managing employees; they become successful candidates by nurturing that talent into an expertise. So we might assume that having experience as a former campaign manager would be a boon to a future president: It would help bring to the presidency the business and managerial skills that so many candidates do without.

But a campaign manager-turned-candidate will always see politics from the inside out. Where most presidents learn the skills of candidacy first and the internals of politics later, a campaign manager's education flows in the opposite direction.

Most candidates first learn to handle themselves in public, meet and court voters, give speeches, massage the media, raise money, debate with their opponents, and develop issue positions. But a campaign manager learns these skills only *after* mastering the slash-and-parry of a political campaign.

And so it was with Hillary Clinton. Hillary learned the skills of managing before she began to master those of running for office. She knew how to hire, fire, and manage Bill's staff before she learned how to appear in public. She knew the intricacies of budgeting and controlling a campaign's spending first, and only later began to grapple with how to handle the press. Her forte was applying the insider's skills of a campaign manager. Mastering the role of a candidate—an outsider's role—is a challenge that has come relatively late in her political and personal development.

I began working with Bill Clinton in 1977 as he was gearing up for his first race for governor. I was his first consultant and he was my first client. The Hillary Rodham of 1977 was no politician. Working at the Rose Law Firm, she seemed no different from dozens of wives (or husbands) of other candidates. She wished Bill well, would help him in any way she could, but gave no appearance of having a personal stake in his professional accomplishments. That came later.

Hillary was not much in evidence during the time I spent with Bill planning that first governor's race. She never attended any of our polling or strategy meetings. Indeed, I saw so little of her that I had no sense of what role she might have been playing in my client's career. She stopped by Bill's office on rare occasions while I was there, but that was it. In those days, Hillary seemed intent on maintaining her independence. Few of us around her would have predicted the key part she would come to play in furthering her husband's political fortunes.

But then the bedrock on which her legal career was built—Bill's political success—crumbled beneath her virtually overnight. A prohibitive favorite to win re-election, he lost in 1980 to Republican upstart Frank White.

Clinton had taken office in 1979 as a *wunderkind* boy governor. At thirty-one, he was filled with bright new ideas that were too big for the confines of his state budget. Since his enthusiasm for the programs he wanted to initiate was greater than his means, something had to give. So he raised taxes.

And the tax he increased, the car-licensing fee, was the worst choice possible. Arkansans don't like you to mess with their cars. Right after Clinton became governor in 1979, I conducted a survey that made it evident that any increase in car fees would be politically deadly. Clinton not only disregarded my advice, but fired me shortly after the election for having the temerity to offer it. At our last meeting, Clinton told me that I was "an assault to his vanity": As a master politician, he felt he shouldn't have to depend on someone else for political advice—least of all a pollster. (He soon changed his mind.) A few weeks later one of his aides called to tell me I was no longer needed. After working side-by-side with Bill Clinton for two years, I was suddenly gone. I heard nothing from Bill or Hillary for another year and a half—until they were in desperate political shape.

In those days Arkansas governors served two-year terms, so Clinton had to face the voters again in 1980. And they were *not* in a good mood. Angry over the increase in their car fees and annoyed that Clinton had let President Carter send thousands of Cuban refugees to Fort Chaffee, Arkansas (where they rioted, tried to escape, and generally made the surrounding state hate them), the voters had begun to turn on Clinton. His opponent, Frank White, exploited these weaknesses with sharp negative ads. It didn't take long before Bill was in serious trouble.

So Hillary reached for the phone.

One of the happier days of my professional life came in late October 1980, two weeks before the election, when my wife Eileen called me in Florida to say: "You won't believe this. Hillary just called and Bill is losing—badly—and they want you back right away."

Without apology or preface, Hillary had announced to Eileen that "Bill is in trouble. We need Dick down here to work on some ads."

I found it odd that Hillary had made the call; it was the first inkling I had that she was taking an interest in her husband's career. Though I warned her that it was probably too late to save things, I agreed to come and do what I could.

From the moment I stepped off the plane in Little Rock, it was evident that the Clinton team was under new management. Suddenly, Hillary was calling the shots. She greeted me at the airport and briefed me personally on her husband's looming defeat. She made sure I saw all the polls and the ads Bill and his opponent, Frank White, were running, and she solicited my opinion about the race.

Clinton's ads were pathetic. They were all about how Bill was making people proud to come from Arkansas again. But the voters of Arkansas weren't proud; they were furious over the tax increase. The only thing that might have put them in a mood to celebrate was retribution at the voting booth—in other words, Clinton's scalp.

I told Hillary that Bill was sure to lose unless the Clinton campaign made a sharp change of direction and started running some negative ads against Frank White. But Bill, proud to the end, refused to believe that he was losing, and would not stoop to attack ads. "It will only give White credibility," he argued. Hillary was frustrated by Bill's refusal; she fought in vain for hard-hitting commercials going after the Republican candidate. I shrugged and took the next plane home. Frank White kept up *his* attacks, and Clinton's numbers dropped by the day.

Hillary watched as White's campaign dismembered Clinton's reputation. She saw how his refusal to answer the attacks cost him the election. And from this lesson in the power of negative ads, the Hillary Doctrine emerged: Answer attacks. Always, always, always, always answer. No matter how low the blow—or, for that matter, how truthful the criticism—always answer.

Bill lost on a Tuesday. On Wednesday my phone rang—it was Hillary summoning me once again. "Bill's in terrible shape and he needs you. Right now."

"But the election isn't for two more years," I pleaded, anxious to begin my post-election hibernation.

"He needs you now!"

I went.

The Clintons' world had come crashing down. Re-election in Arkansas for a second two-year term was considered almost automatic. Voters generally believed their chief executive was entitled to four years to make his mark, and they regarded any new governor's first race for re-election as a kind of midterm exam. That they made an exception for Bill Clinton—expelling him before the final—was a testament to his poor performance, not their impatience.

In the long term, though, the most interesting by-product of Bill's defeat was Hillary's emergence as a major player in his political career. It seemed clear to me that Hillary stepped in to save Bill's career because she had come to see how intertwined her goals and life were with those of her husband. She couldn't get ahead unless he did. Her legal career was hostage to his political status. When Bill lost office, Hillary lost power.

Hillary's deep involvement in the final weeks of Bill's losing campaign—and in his successful 1982 comeback bid—signaled that she had made a fundamental decision: If she wanted Bill's career to be run right, she would have to do it herself. In a few weeks, Hillary had gone from being a self-involved lawyer with her own life and career, to becoming her hapless husband's manager, controller, director, and overseer.

In his seminal biography of Bill Clinton's prepresidential years, *First in His Class,* David Maraniss describes this transition: "During her early years in Arkansas, [Hillary] often deferred to Clinton's judgments about people; but that had changed forever after his defeat in 1980, when she thought that he had been ill served by poor advice and by his own amiability and that she needed to take a more direct role in his career."

It's easy to imagine the humiliation Hillary must have felt being dragged down by Bill's failures. Just as her legal career was on the rise, just after she'd made partner in the Rose Law Firm, she had to divert her attention from her own life and come running to save Bill. His defeat was like a sharp tug on her leash, reminding her that any sensation of independence she might have felt was illusory. In her newly adopted state of Arkansas, she was nothing if he was out of office. For the rest of his time as governor, she took regular leaves of absences from the Rose Law Firm to work for his election and his policies.

By 1982, Hillary Rodham had changed her name to Hillary Rodham Clinton—and switched careers from law to politics.

Nobody felt Bill's lapses and failures more keenly than Hillary. "He's too much of a boy scout," she told me. "He never wants to fight with anybody." She knew better. She had no illusions about human nature; from then on she was determined to hit back hard—and to strike first if possible. She liked me because I had advocated going negative while her husband plummeted, catalyzing a relationship that lasted two decades. I was the consultant who was tough enough to satisfy her—the one she felt they needed.

From Hillary's very first days in politics, I saw that toughness was the characteristic she most admired; it was welded onto her political personality by the heat of Bill's first defeat. In that moment, she had learned the importance of strength in politics. And as Bill's career eventually took flight, I watched her personal aggressive streak turn into a chilling ruthlessness. With Hillary around, Bill Clinton would never again be permitted to lose an election by being too nice.

Like boxers who never forget the times they were knocked out, politicians never forget a defeat. Only a handful of our presidents had ever lost a race before becoming president. Some recovered easily from their defeats: George H. W. Bush brushed aside his loss to Ronald Reagan in 1980 to serve loyally and happily as his vice president. Bill Clinton learned lessons from his Arkansas loss, and came to see it as a bad dream from which he had emerged stronger and wiser. But Johnson and Nixon could not get over their losses to John F. Kennedy in the 1960 election (LBJ for the Democratic nomination, Nixon in the general election). In each man, the defeat engendered a bitterness and animosity that clouded his horizons even after he had triumphed and become president.

Hillary's trauma at the loss of 1980 sank just as deeply into her psyche. The lesson she took away from the experience was Leo Durocher's: "nice guys finish last." To prevent the same mistakes from happening again, Hillary imported Betsey Wright, a Texan and close friend, to be Bill's campaign manager. She hired me back as his pollster and strategist. And through both of us, she worked her will on the campaign.

But sadly, Hillary rewrites the story of her own life in *Living History* with no mention of her transition from lawyer to campaign supervisor—one of her most important crossroads. She avoids taking the credit she is due for her pivotal and vital role in the subsequent turnaround in Bill's fortunes—and hides instead behind a façade of domesticity, downplaying her part in Bill's 1982 comeback campaign, which she describes as "a family endeavor."

Like a mother right out of the pages of *Redbook,* she writes: "we loaded Chelsea, diaper bag and all, into a big car . . . as we drove around the state." Her account of the campaign is short on strategy and long on travelogue. "We started in the South, where spring had snuck under the pine trees, and ended in Fayetteville in a snowstorm. I've always liked campaigning and traveling through Arkansas, stopping at country stores, sale barns, and barbecue joints." She seems eager to leave readers with the impression that her role in the campaign was to meet and greet people: "with Chelsea on my hip or holding my hand, I walked up and down streets meeting voters."

Of course Hillary campaigned for her husband, like all politicians' wives (and, these days, not a few husbands). Unlike those others, though, she was also the Clinton campaign's manager, advisor, co-coordinator, and everything else. Far from the campaign trial, she spent much of the 1980 campaign—and all Clinton's other Arkansas races—sitting right next to me as we worked together writing the negative ads that propelled Bill to victory.

One ad we worked on together attacked Clinton's primary opponent, Congressman Jim Guy Tucker, for his poor congressional attendance record. Tucker's slogan was that he followed "the Arkansas Way," a slap at the Georgetown- and Yale-educated Bill Clinton. Our ad featured four country boys around the breakfast table discussing how many votes Tucker missed in Congress. I remember how Hillary laughed out loud at the tagline: "The Arkansas way is to show up for work when they're payin' you."

Each time I proposed a negative ad, Bill would squirm—but Hillary would giggle. From the start, she showed a feel for attack politics equaled by few consultants I've known, let alone candidates.

The skill, energy, and dedication she devoted to her husband's campaigns were certainly unique in my experience of working with candidate spouses (who more often intrude with amateur musings while the campaign staff is trying to get work done). Hillary Clinton was a valued colleague and a collaborator.

She should be proud of her real role. And she probably is. But she hides it . . . and for a very good reason, one that goes to the heart of the difference between candidate and campaign manager. Hillary's decision to portray her part in the campaign in chatty, anecdotal terms—entirely alien to her real contribution as the mastermind of her husband's comeback—reflects the determination of the HILLARY brand to avoid being seen as what Hillary, the person, truly is: one of the best and most hard-nosed political strategists and tacticians in politics today.

Hillary did everything she could to get Bill back in power . . . which brings us back to the subject of her name. After the 1980 defeat, in the first of a long series of Darwinian adaptations—to survive as the fittest in politics—she left Hillary Rodham behind and became Hillary Clinton.

At first, Hillary had refused to change her name; she had planned to be independent of her husband's career, crafting her own way in a one-couple/two-careers world. But when Bill lost the governorship, she realized that she *needed* him to win. And so—to the relief of the tradition-minded voters of Arkansas, who had bristled at her rejection of her husband's name—she swallowed her feminist pride and became Hillary Clinton.

Those voters were probably as amused as I was to read the new account of the change offered in *Living History*. Now she claims she chose not to use the Clinton name early in her marriage in order to avoid the perception that she was trading on her husband's prominence. It was "to avoid the appearance of conflict of interest" that she never changed her name from Rodham to Clinton.

Was there anyone anywhere in Arkansas who didn't know that Hillary Rodham was married to Bill Clinton, first the state's attorney general and then its governor? Could merely using her maiden name truly mitigate the potential conflict of interest inherent in practicing law in a small state where your husband was governor?

It doesn't really matter. Upon closer examination, her story glides over one critical fact: Her decision not to change her name had been made long before her husband became a statewide elected official. She married Bill on October 11, 1975, keeping her own name from the start. At the time, he held no public office at all, much less one that would have generated conflicts of interest. He was just a defeated candidate for Congress. It was not until 1977, more than two years later, that he became state attorney general. At the time of their marriage, Bill and Hillary were both law school professors. So it's hard to know just what kind of impropriety she was trying to avoid; perhaps she was simply trying to avoid any confusion among law students during finals week.

It is to Hillary's credit that she kept up her law practice, braving the charges of conflict of interest to do so. But why must she conceal her real motivation in not taking Bill's name? What would be wrong with admitting that she liked her own name and identity and decided to keep it after her marriage? Why must she pretend that it was neither feminism nor personal preference but a desire to "avoid the appearance of conflict of interest" that impelled her to call herself Rodham after her marriage?

Whatever Hillary's reasons for keeping her own name in 1975, by 1982 she had determined to eliminate it as an issue. But it was scarcely the only issue confronting the campaign. As Bill Clinton confronted the challenge of running for the office he'd lost two years before, a key question loomed over his strategy sessions: How would he account for his failures during his first term? With stiff-necked pride, he refused to admit he'd made any mistakes, and certainly was in no mood to apologize. "I lost because Frank White ran negative ads and I didn't answer them," he insisted.

But the polls told a different story: The voters *liked* Clinton, and were shocked that he lost. They had wanted to teach the young man a lesson, not to kick him out of office. The people of Arkansas worried that this Ivy League governor, in whom they had invested such hope, couldn't appreciate their problems or understand how close to the margin so many of them lived. They wanted some indication that Bill Clinton got the message before they would forgive him and give him back the power to raise their taxes again.

It was Hillary who understood that Bill must say he was sorry. Though she was not from Arkansas, she grasped the voters' concerns in a way her husband did not. In all the strategy sessions and the seemingly interminable debates on the subject, Hillary pushed Bill to apologize. "Bill," she pleaded, "they didn't want to throw you out—they just wanted to make sure you knew how they felt. Put aside your damned pride and show them that you get it."

On a cold, snowy day in December 1981, Bill Clinton strode confidently into the office of New York media guru Tony Schwartz and announced that he was ready to film his first ad. "*Will he apologize?*" I wondered. "Can I go through the script with you?" I said out loud.

"Don't worry," he replied haughtily, "it'll have what you're looking for."

Facing the camera, Clinton began:

In a few days, I will formally announce my candidacy for governor. But before I do, I want to speak directly with you, to share some of what I've learned not only as governor but from my defeat in the last election. All across this state, many of you have told me you were proud of some things I did as governor. But you also think I made some big mistakes, especially in increasing the car-license and title-transfer fee. When I became governor we had serious problems with our streets and roads, and I did support those increases to try to solve the problems. But it was a mistake, because so many of you were hurt by it. And I'm really sorry for that. *When I was a boy growing up, my daddy never had to whip me twice for the same thing.* And now I hope you'll give me another chance to serve as governor because our state has many problems and opportunities

that demand strong leadership. If you do, I assure you I won't try
to raise the car licenses again . . . [emphasis added].

Wow, I thought. What a line: *My daddy never had to whip me twice
for the same thing.* I was amazed at the performance. It was better than
I had ever hoped, more deft and effective than if I'd tried to script it
myself. It conveyed that he was sorry, without ever quite saying the
words, and expressed his contrition in terms so folksy that no one
could doubt its veracity. It had all the elements of the mystery that
was Bill Clinton: his commitment to exculpation from blame at all
costs, his rural southern penchant for pathos, his uncanny charm.

The apology ad ran as scheduled, and it shocked the state's political establishment. Cartoonists began drawing Clinton in sackcloth
with ashes. Confident, I took a tracking poll to find out how we were
doing . . . and found that we had dropped twenty points. It looked as
though our ingenious strategy had backfired massively.

Hillary picked me up at the airport, and together we rode to a
nearby rally where Bill was speaking. "How are the numbers?" she
asked.

"Um, not quite what I had hoped," I replied trying to put the
best face on them.

"The ads didn't work?" she pressed.

"They backfired for the moment," I answered. "We dropped in
almost every category because we reminded them that Bill had raised
taxes." Then I ventured a theory I had begun to believe was true.
"It's like with an injection. You get a little sick. You get cowpox so
that you don't get smallpox later. You get inoculated. You trade off a
small short-term drop for long-term immunity to negatives."

"You think so?" she asked doubtfully.

"Absolutely," I answered, hoping my theory was as valid as I
stated it was.

As we waited in the car for Bill to finish his speech, I marveled at
his effortless, fluid delivery. "He really could be president," I mused
to Hillary.

"We have to get re-elected first," she shot back pointedly.

To my vast relief, the apology ad eventually began to work. *Really* work. It gave Clinton the immunity we had hoped for, and he bounced back. Clinton won the primary, the runoff, and the election, propelled by his mea culpa. Whenever his opponents attacked him, people would tell the pollsters it made no difference. "He already said he's sorry," they would say.

It was due to Hillary's badgering, then, that Bill took the fundamental step he had to in order to win: He apologized. How I wished that this side of Hillary Clinton—the part of her that recognized how effective an apology can be in politics—had remained dominant in her persona as first lady. Back in 1982, she grasped what eluded her in the late 1990s: that an apology can work where stonewalling and prideful refusal to admit wrongdoing does not. By the time Hillary reached the White House, the bitter partisanship of national politics had driven the idea of a mea culpa out of her playbook. In the ruthless politics of the 1990s, no quarter was asked and none was given; any apology seemed like surrender.

Looking back, it's hard not to wonder which part of her 1982 self Hillary is trying to hide in *Living History:* the emotionally perceptive human being who understood the virtue of contrition, or the savvy political mind who knew a smart campaign tactic when she saw one. But my guess is the latter. The HILLARY brand embraces a number of different personalities, but "campaign strategist" isn't among them. Whether it's her own instincts—or someone in a focus group—telling her as much, Hillary seems convinced that the American people would recoil at the prospect of voting for a professional politician. And so in *Living History* we get only HILLARY, the dutiful wife who spends two paragraphs touring rural Arkansas with her husband before his miraculous re-election.

HILLARY FOR GOVERNOR?

As the 1980s came to a close, Bill Clinton was a restless man, having decided not to run for president in 1988—out of fear that his extramarital relationships would erupt into scandal—he felt his career might be at a dead end. He was bored being governor of Arkansas, but hadn't settled on his next move.

Should he run for re-election to a job that he found repetitive and tedious? Did he need to stay in office to help bide his time until he felt he could run for president?

As his plans to run for president in 1992 grew serious, he was increasingly inclined to bow out and not seek a fifth term as governor in 1990. Haunted by the memory of Mike Dukakis, who was forced to return to Massachusetts to raise taxes right in the middle of his 1988 presidential campaign, Clinton was inclined to kiss Arkansas goodbye. He was encouraged by the example of Jimmy Carter, who had left the Georgia State House in 1974 to concentrate on campaigning for the 1976 Democratic nomination. He didn't want to be stuck governing in Arkansas when he should have been campaigning in Iowa or New Hampshire.

As it came to seem less likely that Bill was going to run for governor, another lost chapter in Hillary's life transpired: The first lady of Arkansas decided that *she* would try to become governor. Having led the state's education reform, Hillary now saw her chance to step out of her husband's shadow and become the leader she wanted to be. With a giddy expectancy, she began planning her own run for office.

The first couple summoned me to the Governor's Mansion to discuss the idea, and Bill was clearly going overboard in encouraging her to run. "She's always deferred to my career," he told me. "I don't make much money as governor and she's having to support the family while I'm out campaigning. It hasn't been fair to her, and I want to give her a shot at her own political career." They asked me to conduct a poll to assess her chances of winning, and I agreed.

But the results that came back were devastating, and they would have a crucial impact on Hillary's political development: According to the poll numbers, she couldn't win. It wasn't that people didn't like her. In fact, she was quite popular. But voters just didn't feel she could be her own person as governor. They worried that she would just be a placeholder for Bill, a warm body to keep the governorship in the family—who would step aside should her husband's presidential race fall short.

There was some precedent for the idea—but it was the wrong kind of precedent. When Alabama's term limits law had made Governor George Wallace retire in 1966, he persuaded his wife, Lurleen, to run in his place. After she died in office (and her term was completed by the state's lieutenant governor), he came back for eight more years in office. Now, as we discussed Hillary's potential candidacy, I made a big mistake: I referred to the Arkansas voters' reaction as "the Lurleen Wallace factor."

"Hillary is no Lurleen Wallace!" Bill screamed, red-faced and furious. "She has her own record, her own career, her own accomplishments." He pounded the table with his fist. "It's ridiculous for people to see her just as my placeholder." Hillary sulked in her chair and let her husband rant on. They actually insisted that I take a second poll, reminding the respondents more explicitly of her achievements (which Bill listed for me at tedious length). But it was no use. The voters just refused to see Hillary as anything but Bill's puppet.

Hillary was especially disappointed that education reform, her signature achievement in Arkansas, had redounded more to her husband's credit than to hers. The poll served to underscore that, despite all her efforts to raise educational standards, it was still *his* governorship, *his* administration, and *his* record of accomplishment. Hillary was eager to strike out on her own and seek office in her own name (sort of)—until she discovered, to her chagrin, that her legitimate slate of achievements just didn't matter to the voters. To them, she was still a subset of him.

In the short term, her rejection in those opinion polls wounded Hillary's self-image and scuttled her intentions of running for governor. But the incident also made a far deeper impression on her, one that lasted long after the initial shock wore off. In short, she resolved never to repeat the same mistake: If Bill ever got elected president, she would be her own person—and she would make sure the public knew it. Back in 1981, when she had made the crucial career move from law to politics, she had hoped that her focus on education reform would win her a constituency of her own in her adopted state. But when the poll dashed those hopes, she realized that she could only succeed in politics in her own right if she crafted a separate identity for herself, with her own agenda, supporters, and allies. It was at this moment that Hillary made the critical decision to embark on creating an independent image, with an eye toward running for public office. Of course, circumstances would prevent her from withdrawing permanently as Bill's de facto campaign manager; at critical moments in the coming years, she would be forced to step in and make sure the trains were running on time—or at all. Whenever she could, though, she gladly left administrative matters to others while she embraced a life of advocacy.

Unfortunately, *Living History* is silent on this significant chapter in Hillary's life. She seems almost afraid to tell us how she became the person she is, preferring instead that we believe that HILLARY sprang, like Athena, fully armed and clothed from the head of Zeus.

THE 1992 CAMPAIGN

When Bill decided to seek the presidency, Hillary felt that she and her husband were on their way at last.

The election campaign of 1992 was, of course, a seminal event in Hillary's emergence as a politician. On the national stage for the first time, she had to grapple with the way she would be received by a national audience. Finally able to campaign by herself—although not yet *for* herself—Hillary loved the direct thrill of adoring crowds, and the adrenaline rush that comes with personal appearances. The legendary Clinton/Gore bus tours that began immediately after the Democratic convention—featuring Bill and Hillary, Al and Tipper—gave her a taste of big-time campaigning, and the joy of it never left her.

But the 1992 campaign was also a baptism by fire for Hillary. She had assumed that the national media would be more feminist, more receptive to her as an aggressive, independent woman, than the Arkansas press had been. But she was soon disappointed. In 1992, while campaigning, she told me, "I always thought that I had to watch myself in Arkansas because it was such a male-dominated culture and outspoken women were not accepted. I assumed it would be different on the national level. But really, it's just the same. Or worse."

Not only did she discover that her abrasive feminism worked no better than it had in Arkansas; she also found herself sucked ever more into Bill's gravitational pull—and in the worst way possible. When Bill was accused of adultery by Gennifer Flowers, she had to rush to his defense, overlooking her feelings as the victim of his conduct to become, instead, his chief defender.

And soon she had a scandal of her own. Early in 1992, a detailed investigative article by Jeff Gerth in the *New York Times* laid out for the public the facts of the Clinton/McDougal Whitewater investment, and of her legal representation of Madison Guaranty Savings and Loan. Forced to defend Bill with one hand and herself with the other, Hillary was suddenly facing an inauspicious beginning for her first venture into national politics.

If defending against these charges was difficult and demeaning, Hillary found her other role even more galling: With her clumsy remarks about baking cookies and her aggressive feminism, it soon became apparent that she presented an irresistible punching bag for the Republicans. George Bush Sr. may have seemed distant and out-of-touch compared with the younger, more dynamic Bill Clinton, but Barbara Bush—a grandmotherly figure beloved by the entire nation—stood up quite well alongside Hillary Clinton. Forgetting who would eventually appear on the ballot, the GOP directed its fire, relentlessly and remorselessly, at Hillary.

But there was a utility to this new role: Hillary was serving as the classic lightning rod, drawing to herself the blows that might otherwise have landed on Bill. During the 1992 Republican National Convention, speaker after speaker lambasted Hillary, attacking her for Whitewater, her career conflicts of interest, and her seeming scorn for stay-at-home moms. The Republicans seemed to forget about Bill and zero in on Hillary instead. They ranted on, racking up points against the wrong Clinton.

In phone conversations with the Clintons during the summer of 1992, I tried to get them to see the silver lining within this new cloud. "Hillary has gotten the Republicans so nutty about her that they can't help themselves," I told Bill. "They end up attacking her and forget about you!"

"They're just vicious in the way they go after her," he agreed, genuinely angry at the attacks on his wife. "They keep hitting and hitting and hitting her. Pounding on her, day after day."

But their attacks were misdirected, I reassured him. "They have to spend four days (the length of the convention) attacking somebody," I said. "It's a lot better—"

"—if they go after her than me," Clinton interrupted, finishing my sentence.

The Republicans were falling into a trap of their own making. "They didn't gain anything from their convention," Hillary announced triumphantly in a phone call in early September 1992. Even though history suggested that the average convention catalyzed a ten-point gain for its party's candidate, the polls showed no rise in Bush's numbers after his convention.

"Because they attacked you and not Bill," I said.

"They sure did that," Hillary said ruefully.

By the time the votes were counted in 1992, Hillary had been through a campaign of humiliating experiences. Not only did she have to defend her husband against charges of adultery and herself against accusations of financial misdeeds in Whitewater, but she had to sit there taking shots until the Republicans so exhausted themselves hitting her that they had nothing left for Bill. And when the Clintons finally prevailed, it was time for Hillary's reward . . .

MAKING THE NEW ADMINISTRATION

Hillary's hand was in evidence again after the 1992 election, as she and Bill began planning their administration. It was clear that Hillary would be at the center of the action: As Bill considered his cabinet, sub-cabinet, and staff appointments, the opinion that counted most was Hillary's.

Three of her law partners made it into the administration: Vince Foster and Bill Kennedy to the White House staff, and Webster Hubbell to the Justice Department. (None of them came to a good end: Kennedy was forced out, Hubbell went to jail, and Foster committed suicide.) Her former mentor, New York lawyer Bernie Nussbaum, became counsel to the president. (Nussbaum, too, left prematurely after criticism about his handling of the Vince Foster and the travel office matters.) Moreover, Hillary had the key voice in a number of other appointments, including the embarrassingly difficult effort to find an attorney general. In succession, Zoe Baird, Kimba Wood, and finally Janet Reno were required to meet with Hillary to ensure that they passed muster with the incoming first lady. Baird and Wood were shot down. Reno, unfortunately, made it to the cabinet. Hillary made particularly sure that women would be well represented in the new cabinet—and that they would be *her* women, responsive to her political agenda and willing to defer to her when necessary.

And yet, once again, Hillary makes little mention of her critical role in the formation of the new administration. She says almost nothing about how she proposed, vetted, killed, or approved most of Bill's major appointments. Instead *Living History* describes the crucial period between the election and the inauguration in almost exclusively domestic terms—as if we cared more about the details of housekeeping than we do about how the cabinet was chosen.

Hillary adopts the perspective of a sitcom wife trying to cope with a chaotic household—as if somehow the term "cabinet" led her by free association to think about kitchens. "Within hours, the kitchen table in the Governor's Mansion became the nerve center of the Clinton transition," the harried housewife tells us. "In the next few weeks, potential cabinet nominees came in and out, phones rang around the clock, piles of food were consumed . . ." Bob Woodward has reported that it was with the help of "Hillary, [Warren] Christopher, [Al] Gore, and Bruce Lindsay [that] Clinton would pick his cabinet." In her own account, Hillary mentions Christopher, Mickey Kantor, and Vernon Jordan, but omits the key player: herself.

Instead she focuses, in excruciating detail, on the domestic challenges of moving to Washington—the housewife at work. "We were also facing the more mundane challenges of any family changing jobs and residences. In the midst of forming a new Administration, we had to pack up the Governor's Mansion, the only home Chelsea remembered. And since we didn't own a house of our own, everything would come with us to the White House. Friends pitched in to organize and sort, piling boxes in every room. Loretta Avent, a friend from Arizona who had joined me on the campaign after the convention, took charge of the thousands of gifts that arrived from all over the world, filling a huge section of the large basement. Periodically, Loretta would shriek up the stairs. . . ." And so on.

Back then, however, Hillary was not at all shy about feeding media speculation about the potential extent of her influence. First Ladies had so often been confined to the "pink ghetto" of the East Wing; Hillary welcomed coverage that suggested that she had real power and was not afraid to wield it.

Eleanor Clift and Mark Miller extolled Hillary's behind-the-scenes prominence in a *Newsweek* article shortly before the inauguration. "If another Democrat had won the White House," they wrote, "Hillary would be on his (or her) short-list for the cabinet. But in the Clinton administration, Hillary has a wider role to play. The expectation among friends and aides is that she will act as an unofficial chief of staff . . . she will find a way to oversee everything. . . . Hillary Clinton is Bill's Day-Timer, the gentle lash who keeps him focused, who doesn't mind making decisions and refereeing disputes when Clinton would rather stall."

Hillary's power and role ranged far and wide during the first years of her husband's presidency. Before her wings were clipped by her failure on health care, she worked inside the White House to shape foreign as well as domestic policy, military as well as civilian.

Hillary and I spoke frequently about various names under consideration for the cabinet. We agreed, for example, that giving Walter Mondale a cabinet appointment might trigger concern that the administration was filled with Carter retreads. I warned her that it would be a mistake to appoint Federico Peña as secretary of transportation, because of lingering controversy about his role in the construction of the Denver airport. We spoke at length about bringing in a Republican to give the administration a more bipartisan appearance, a plan that came to fruition only in Clinton's second term.

Hillary became Bill's *de facto* chief of staff. The nominal chief, Clinton boyhood buddy Mack McLarty, was a kind, dear soul who posed no threat to Hillary's power base. That attribute may, indeed, have been a key factor in his selection—otherwise one wondered why a president with no Washington experience, and his wife, whose time in the capital comprised a few months on the Watergate Committee—would choose to be guided by a chief of staff who was similarly unfamiliar with the ways of the city. It was the blind leading the blind through a maze.

I visited the Clintons in Little Rock during the first week of December 1992. Hillary was not packing, or doing the dishes, or even whipping up one of her favorite recipes. She was sitting right across the small breakfast table from Bill, focusing intently on our conversation. As we discussed his cabinet, the inaugural address, his relations with Congress, and strategies for injecting a bipartisan note into the administration, I was struck by how little had changed since the days before Clinton's election. It was the same scene I had seen a hundred times before: a strategy meeting with Bill and Hillary in which each participated equally—a scene that appears nowhere in *Living History.*

Hillary's attempt to find a place for herself in the administration had begun practically the day after Bill's victory. While I was vacationing in Paris in November, Hillary had called for my take on media speculation that she might become her husband's chief of staff—a leak she may well have orchestrated herself as a trial balloon. "What do you think of the idea?" she asked.

"You can't be chief of staff," I objected. "A president has to be able to fire his chief of staff when things go wrong. It's like a baseball owner being able to fire the manager. He can't very well fire all twenty-five players, or fire himself, so he needs to fire the manager. Bill can't fire you."

In *Living History,* Hillary does discuss the Clintons' concern over how their tradition of equal participation would travel from Little Rock to Washington, noting that Clinton couldn't name her to the cabinet because of an anti-nepotism law passed in the wake of President Kennedy's appointment of his brother Bobby as attorney general.

Before Clinton's staff came up against the anti-nepotism law, though, Hillary was hell-bent on securing a position in her husband's cabinet. At one point, she called me and asked whether she should become attorney general. I advised her to take a second-tier cabinet post, like secretary of education, during the first term, and then move up to attorney general in the second. "That way the accusations of nepotism won't be so loud," I counseled. I also warned her of the dangers of accepting any position that required Senate confirmation. Though the Democrats held the majority, I warned that the confirmation hearings wouldn't be pretty: The Republicans would be sure to rehash all the accusations about Whitewater and the Madison Bank scandals they'd been airing since the campaign. Since they had enough votes to block any attempt to shut off debate, they might even filibuster the confirmation—leaving Hillary to twist embarrassingly in the wind.

During my early December visit, Hillary told me she'd found her niche. "I am going to have the title 'counselor to the president for domestic policy,'" she told me. It would be a new position, the domestic equivalent of the national security advisor—the post made famous by the likes of Henry Kissinger and Condoleezza Rice.

Then came the shock. Dispatched to scout out any roadblocks to appointing Hillary to the cabinet, Bill's staff concluded belatedly that the law prohibited a president from appointing his wife to a position in the administration.

A few days later, Hillary was back on the phone to me asking what she should do. "I think you should figure out some sort of task force you would head on a key issue, just like you did with education in Arkansas," I suggested. "That way you will have a clear body of work of your own, which you can use as the basis for your future."

"Like what?" she prompted.

Seeking to bolster Hillary's credentials as a centrist, I suggested that she chair a commission on cutting costs in the government, akin to the Reinventing Government effort Vice President Al Gore eventually ran. "You can go around the country citing evidence of waste and mismanagement. It would be a modern variant of the old Hoover Commission that dug up examples of waste. You'd be like Eleanor Roosevelt, your husband's eyes and ears, or like Harry Truman investigating wartime cost overruns," I said, hoping the precedents would convince her of how easily such a position could be accepted by the public. As the chair of such a commission, I felt, Hillary would get a chance to flex her managerial talents before the nation. She would be leading with her strength.

When President Clinton announced that the first lady would be heading just such a task force, I was as surprised as anyone else to learn that health care, not government waste, would be her mission. It was, to put it mildly, a mistake. Her success on the health care task force would be a direct function of Congress's willingness to support her proposals. When Al Gore assumed direction of the Reinventing

Government Task Force, he faced no such obstacles: Ultimately, he was able to claim broad success in his efforts to streamline the bureaucracy. Hillary, meanwhile, had chosen a highly visible, highly accountable post—and one in which she would inevitably tack to the left when she should have been reinforcing her credentials as a middle-of-the-road politician who could work with colleagues in both parties to get the job done.

The first two years of Clinton's presidency were a disaster. With Hillary off on the sidelines running her health care initiative, the management of the White House was an administrative and political fiasco. Tripped up at the starting gate by a futile controversy over gays in the military, embarrassed by amateur-hour tactics like firing the White House Travel Office staff, pursued by the media for stonewalling the Whitewater scandal, the Clinton administration shuffled along from bad to worse.

During 1993, as the administrative mess was paralyzing the executive branch, I urged Hillary to take a more direct role in the management of the White House. Pointing out that Clinton's troubled first year as president echoed his troubled first year as Arkansas governor, I suggested that the Clintons resort to the same remedy: Hillary's management skills.

Now, however, Hillary was adamantly *against* assuming the burdens of *de facto* chief of staff. "I have to let Bill and his people work this out," she said. "I'm up to my neck in health care and I just don't have time to run the White House. I'm only one person."

But a far greater debacle lay ahead, in the realm of policy initiatives. The administration's first major legislative battle led to a resounding defeat, when Democratic majorities in both houses proved unable to pass a pork-laden economic stimulus package. Clinton was more successful in passing his budget program—but the tax increases he signed into law would ultimately prove fatal to the Democratic majority in Congress that voted for them. Despite some successes, like ratification of NAFTA and the passage of a good, strong anti-crime bill that led directly to the subsequent drop in violent crime, much of the Clinton program stalled in Congress. And the crowning failure, of course, was Hillary's own: After two years of ballyhoo and bad judgment, her health care reform initiative never made it out of committee in the Senate, leaving a deadly black mark on Hillary's resume and the opening act of the Clinton presidency.

The capstone to Hillary's and Bill's disastrous first two years in the White House was their loss of control of Congress in the midterm elections of 1994. The Democratic Party, which had held the majority in the House of Representatives for the previous forty years—twenty elections—lost not only the Senate, but the House as well.

Hillary catalogs several reasons for the 1994 defeat in *Living History:*

> Most Republican voters were intensely opposed to the upper-income tax increase for deficit reduction, the Brady bill and the assault weapons ban. . . . I also knew that some core Democratic supporters felt disillusioned by our failure to reform health care or betrayed by the Administration's successful push for NAFTA . . .
>
> Deflated and disappointed, I wondered how much I was to blame for the debacle: . . . whether I had gambled on the country's acceptance of my active role and lost . . .

Reality check: My polling at the time showed that the Democrats lost mainly because they imposed a five-cent increase in the tax on gasoline. Voters were largely willing to forgive the tax hike on upper income families, but not a gas tax that hit the blue-collar worker in his wallet. Bill and Hillary had forgotten the lesson of their 1980 defeat: Don't mess with peoples' cars! The voting public is very, very sensitive to the idea that you are charging them more to travel to work every day. While revisionist history tends to credit future House Speaker Newt Gingrich's Contract with America for the GOP's ascendancy, and to blame health care reform for the Democrats' defeat, at the time it was clear to us that health care reform was a secondary issue. Once again, it was a car tax that had brought Bill Clinton down.

Oddly, the gas tax didn't produce much money. But Clinton passed it because Alan Greenspan and the Federal Reserve Board made him do it. He had to prove that he was serious about deficit reduction. "Why don't you just increase the top bracket in the income tax a little more?" I asked Clinton over the phone in 1993 as his tax package took shape. "That's where all the revenue is."

"I'd love to," the president answered, "but I have to show the Fed and the bond market that I am willing to take a political hit to cut the deficit."

I reminded Clinton how dangerous automobile taxes were, but he plowed ahead to self-inflicted disaster.

How odd that Hillary doesn't even cite the gas tax as the reason for the 1994 defeat. Liberal Democrats always have a hard time realizing how unpopular that word is: T-A-X-E-S.

The tax increase remains the third rail of American politics. Those who touch it in their first term generally don't survive to see a second. If Hillary truly doesn't grasp that her husband's tax increases were the real cause of the Democrats' 1994 rout, it bodes poorly for a HILLARY presidency. If she takes office after years of Bush tax cuts, and then follows her instincts and raises taxes, she will fall and take her party down with her.

Whatever her blind spots, though, Hillary's instincts for political reality have usually proven sound. Before the 1994 midterms, she foresaw the Democrats' looming defeat and called to ask my advice.

In October 1994, I conducted a poll to help determine how the Clintons could best defend themselves. I found that very few Americans believed Clinton when he said he had cut the budget deficit or created lots of new jobs. But they did give him credit for some small advances: AmeriCorps, his volunteer plan; the Family and Medical Leave Act; pro-choice judicial appointments; the Brady gun control bill; and the assault rifle ban. If they could be reminded effectively of these accomplishments, my poll suggested that enough voters might come back to the Democrats to avert defeat.

But President Clinton would have none of it. "I cut the deficit by one third. I've created millions of new jobs. *I've done the big things,*" he railed over the phone in a conference call with Hillary and me. It was a throwback to the arrogance of 1980 and his refusal to admit his license-tax mistake in Arkansas.

"Bill," Hillary concurred, "of course you've done these things. But nobody believes that you have. Go with the messages they *will* believe." It was a familiar scene: Hillary trying to beat sense into Bill, despite his head-in-the-clouds, prideful refusal to embrace reality.

I accused Clinton of not just wanting to win, but wanting to do so only if he could prevail "for the right reasons." But he wouldn't budge. He ran on the big themes—and lost.

The larger lesson of the 1994 defeat was not lost on Hillary. She and the president had to move to the center. They simply could not win re-election running as the liberal Democratic standard bearers.

As I worked with Clinton to move to the middle, Hillary was helping me behind the scenes. In her memoir, she writes that "I encouraged Bill to include Dick Morris in his consultations" after the defeat. She did.

She also absorbed the lessons of my theory of triangulation, which she defines accurately in her book: "when opposing camps are in two polar positions and neither believes it can afford to be seen as moving toward the other, they can decide to move toward a third position—like the apex of the triangle—what came to be called 'triangulation.'"

By 1995, Hillary was reinventing herself as a moderate, triangulating "New" Democrat. She provided crucial help in urging the president to back a balanced budget and to sign the welfare reform bill, the two acts that came to define his move to the center. Like Bill, she showed great dexterity in shifting in such a centrist direction, a move that appealed to the great mass of American voters. Her leftward tilt in the health care reform days was a thing of the past. She seemed to have learned her lesson.

But a deeper personal adjustment lay behind her political moves. The loss of Congress had shaken Hillary to the core. She felt the defeat very, very personally, and took much of the blame on her own shoulders. And most observers in both parties agreed with her. Bewildered and assailed by atypical self-doubts, Hillary confessed to me in mid-November 1994: "Dick, I feel so lost, so confused. I don't know what's right anymore. Everything I do seems not to work. I've never felt this way before. I don't even trust my own judgment. I don't know what I should be doing."

For all her self-confidence, Hillary can lose her bearings when things don't go right. Her strong and resolute leadership has a brittle quality to it; when her basic assumptions are proven wrong, they undermine her resolve and even her self-esteem. Bill copes with adversity by showing up for work each morning and hoping things will improve. Hillary has less flexibility, less give. She is more inclined to try to ram her way through obstacles. When it works, she does very well. But when it doesn't—as in 1994—it can paralyze her.

To help get to the bottom of the Clintons' loss, I conducted a series of surveys in November and December 1994, and reported the results to the president in early January. There seemed to be two different strains of negatives that characterized the voters' attitudes toward him. "One third of the people feel you are immoral and one third think you are weak," I told the depressed president.

There was nothing we could do about his perceived moral failings—his draft avoidance, the Gennifer Flowers scandal, Travelgate, Whitewater, or the innumerable scrapes to which the first family seemed forever prone. But as I examined the reasons that people gave explaining why they thought that the president was weak, one concern kept coming up over and over again: Hillary. "She's the power," the respondents complained. "She wears the pants." "She thinks she's president." "I voted for him, but she's in charge now." I read them to Clinton one after another, letting their cumulative effect wash over him.

In these voters' eyes, the president's perceived weakness was directly proportionate to Hillary's perceived influence. To them, the first couple was in a zero sum game: The more power she had, the less power he wielded.

One of the great phobias in political history is the fear of hidden power. At the slightest indication that their rulers have come under the sway of hidden forces, the people can be expected to rebel. After rumors spread that Rasputin was dominating policy by influencing Czarina Alexandra, for example, czarist Russia was catapulted into revolution. Likewise, Hillary's power had begun to spawn fear and resentment. Voters had failed to grasp the reality of the Clintons' relationship: that they fed off one another. Power, in fact, was a nonzero game with the Clintons. The stronger each was, the more powerful they both were.

Then I turned to the bright side. It turned out that many of the very same people who complained of his wife's role behind the scenes were thrilled by her outspokenness. For all of their anger about her backstage role, they welcomed and approved of her public statements. The thought of Hillary whispering in the president's ear may have excited their anger, but making her speeches to an audience—particularly when she was battling for women and children—won widespread approval.

"Hillary needs to avoid White House meetings where word of her role will get out and focus her efforts on public advocacy," I told the president. "In fact, her outspokenness before audiences can be an antidote to the perception of hidden power. The voters know she's not sitting there doing nothing. The more they read about her public role, the less they will speculate on her private doings."

A week later, Clinton asked me to start sending Hillary memos suggesting new directions for her public advocacy, always making sure to send him copies.

Hillary's reaction was immediate. She withdrew from *all* White House strategy meetings. She just stopped coming. For a year she didn't even send a representative. She totally cut herself off from overt involvement in White House strategizing. She was less involved in decision making than she had been at any point since the early two-career couple days of the late 1970s.

And slowly but surely her withdrawal began to have an effect. Gradually the articles that spoke of her extensive influence faded. She was mentioned less and less frequently as a key White House honcho. And, predictably, Bill's strength ratings began to bounce back. It worked.

And so the HILLARY that appears in *Living History* says nothing about her behind-the-scenes influence. In its pages, she is only the chatty housewife in private, and an aggressive advocate for women and children in public. Why does she hide her skills as a strategist and campaign manager under a bushel? Why the focus on her campaigning with Chelsea "on her hip" in 1982 rather than on her critical role as her husband's campaign czar? Why does she emphasize the domestic challenges of moving to Washington from Little Rock, rather than her involvement in choosing the cabinet and the policy agenda?

Because the HILLARY brand cannot be about hidden power.

The corollary of her reduced role in private was that HILLARY became more outspoken in public. The first lady leapt at the chance. After squandering her opportunity to cut an independent figure during the health care episode, now she had a second chance to make a solo impression. And this time, instead of having to fight for congressional approval, she was able to appeal directly to the public with speeches and symbolic gestures. No bills, no deals, no obstacles, no policy hang-ups, no budgetary constraints, no competition for priority, just speechmaking and traveling. It was HILLARY Lite: at last, a chance for the moon to move out from behind the sun and shine on her own.

Hillary followed this strategy, shifting her energies to public advocacy while withdrawing from private power, from 1995 to 1997. It was only the Monica Lewinsky scandal that forced her out of this role and back into the strategy meetings at 1600 Pennsylvania Avenue. With her husband's presidency on the line, she had to get back in control. Then, after the Lewinsky storm finally passed, Hillary returned to public advocacy. As she prepared to run for the Senate, she was more and more a public figure and less a private Svengali.

Thus far, then, Hillary has remade herself successfully: After getting her political start as a manager, she changed horses midstream, developing the skills (and the look) of an advocate, then a candidate, and now a Senator. But Hillary's early experiences as a manager were imprinted deeply upon her political consciousness, and they remain crucial to understanding what kind of a president she would make.

In fact, Hillary is a great manager. She keeps her focus on the main objective, and delegates authority and power well. Her formidable self-discipline allows her to focus on her job while allowing her subordinates to do theirs. In all of this, she surpasses Bill. While he really trusts no one but himself to make decisions, she selects good people and gives them great loyalty, expecting as good in return.

At the White House, Bill Clinton saw his staff primarily as ambassadors to other wings of the Democratic Party. Nominated by his party only after the favorite, New York Governor Mario Cuomo, decided not to run, and elected with only 43 percent of the vote, he saw the need to build bridges to his own party and the Washington establishment. So he gathered around him a collection of emissaries: Deputy Chief of Staff Harold Ickes was his ambassador to labor and the left, White House advisor George Stephanopoulos to the *Washington Post* and the White House press corps, Chief of Staff Leon Panetta to the chairmen who controlled the House committees. Ron Brown and Henry Cisneros were his ambassadors to the African American and Hispanic communities. I was his link to the Republicans who ran Congress.

But Hillary's staff has always been predominantly, overwhelmingly, and totally loyal to Hillary. Longtime Hillary allies like her first chief of staff, Maggie Williams, her successor Melanne Verveer, press secretary Lisa Caputo, and speechwriter Lissa Muscatine are *her* people, first and always. With clear lines of authority and strong discipline, Hillary runs a tight ship, never weakened by leaks or infighting.

Such talent for management would be one of President Hillary's major assets, a welcome change from the floating chaos of her husband's administration.

To date, Hillary Clinton has distinguished herself as a superb manager, political tactician, and hardnosed executive. It's ironic, and rather a shame, that the HILLARY brand overlooks these real skills altogether, presenting her as the traditional first lady and *hausfrau* she never wanted to be.

5

HIDING HILLARY: THE IDEOLOGUE

One of the questions that always worried voters about Bill Clinton looms just as large with Hillary: Is she really a liberal or a moderate? A New Democrat or an old one? Is she the Hillary of health care reform—a dogmatic advocate of big government—or the moderate who urged her husband to sign the welfare reform law passed by a Republican Congress in 1996?

Living History offers no clue. Indeed, just as Bill Clinton always insisted that he had not changed from the big spender and taxer of his first two years in office to the budget balancer of the next two, so Hillary recognizes no incongruity or even dissonance between the liberalism of her health care agenda and the relative moderation of her advocacy during her husband's remaining years in office.

Yet if we examine her real history and *Living History* side by side, we can get a glimpse of the answer: She is an opportunist when she needs to be, and an ideologue whenever she can. An opportunist by necessity but an ideologue by choice.

Unlike Bill, Hillary is deeply committed to an ideological agenda. But she is like him in a different respect: She will do what she has to do in order to get elected. When the political tides are with him, Bill ultimately does what makes sense to him. When they are flowing Hillary's way, she tacks as far left as pragmatism will allow.

Hillary has a core issue: the needs of women and children. While Bill has a wide-ranging set of political values, including a general belief in social betterment, an end to racism, and a reduction in income and class disparities, there is no single constituency with which he identifies so purely as Hillary does with hers. And she deserves credit for this: While the tactics she uses to help her constituency have changed over the years—maturing from the utopian panacea of health care reform to more modest measures—her devotion has never really waned. It's not just a part of the HILLARY brand; it's Hillary herself.

In fact, the only consistent beneficiary of Hillary's loyalty other than women and children has been political opportunity itself. When the voters call for liberalism, Hillary moves left. When they want moderation, she tacks back to the center. This practical compass has proved a lifetime's work for Hillary. As a student, she was a radical. As a first lady of Arkansas, she was a moralistic reformer. In the health care debacle, she was a utopian visionary. Finally, in Bill's second term and thus far in her own Senate career, she has evolved into a center/left Democrat, liberal on some issues and moderate on others, highly attuned to the political tenor—and polls—of the moment.

Inside all this, however, is an ideologue awaiting her moment.

In this respect, Hillary's evolution is not altogether different from many who have lived in the White House. Ronald Reagan moved left to right as he matured. Bill Clinton outgrew his student radicalism. But Hillary deliberately, if ineffectually, conceals her past as a radical and spins her role on health care to avoid admitting that she has changed or even grown. There is a fragility to her pretense of consistency. If Hillary does run for president, and if she ultimately serves in the White House, the media will never allow her to skate by without a fuller reconciliation of her past and the present.

The HILLARY brand will be forced to reckon, at last, with Hillary's past.

STUDENT RADICAL

In Hillary's college and law school years, she was anything but a moderate. A dedicated leftist at left-leaning Yale Law School, she spent the summer of 1971 clerking for the Oakland, California, law firm of Treuhaft, Walker, and Burnstein—which she describes in *Living History* merely as "a small law firm."

It was a bit more than that. Its lead partner at the time, Robert Treuhaft, and his wife, Jessica Mitford, were both former active members of the American Communist Party. For years, in fact, Treuhaft was the Party's lawyer. And what loyal members Treuhaft and Mitford were, staying in the party well into the 1950s—through the show trials and purges of the 1930s, through the carving up of Poland after Stalin's nonaggression pact with Hitler in 1939, even through the Soviet occupation of Eastern Europe. It was only in 1956, long after the American left had abandoned the Party en masse, that Treuhaft and Mitford finally left it, spurred by Khrushchev's revelations of Stalin's brutality and genocide.

Hillary biographer Joyce Milton notes that Treuhaft was "long known as Oakland's Red Lawyer." As she reports, "Treuhaft had defended Harry Bridges, the Australian head of the longshoreman's union, enabling him to avoid deportation even though, as is now thoroughly documented, he was a member of the Central Committee of the Communist Party USA. Treuhaft and Mitford left the Party . . . only because their chapter had lost so many members that it was 'ineffectual.' Their views remained fixed."

Hillary was no Communist, nor should her work in the Treuhaft firm imply that she was. But the fact that she chose this job out of all the summer jobs that might have been available, traveling three thousand miles for it, tells something about her orientation at the time. Just as the fact that she does not describe the firm's work or reputation says something about her today.

During her time at Yale Law School, Hillary was especially active in defense of the Black Panthers. She treats the topic gingerly in *Living History*, describing how her quiet academic universe was invaded by political action: "That world and its realities came crashing down on Yale in April 1970 when eight Black Panthers, including party leader Bobby Seale, were put on trial for murder in New Haven. Thousands of angry protesters, convinced the Panthers had been set up by the FBI and government prosecutors, swarmed into the city. Demonstrations broke out in and around campus."

Hillary then describes how "I learned, late on the night of April 27, that the International Law Library, which was in the basement of the law school, was on fire. Horrified, I rushed to join a bucket brigade of faculty, staff, and students to put out the fire and to rescue books damaged by the flames and water."

But Hillary did a lot more than put out a fire. She actively worked in support of the Panthers' defense team.

Eight members of the extremist group had been charged with the torture and murder of Alex Rackley, whom they suspected of being a government informer. *Insight* magazine describes how Rackley was "clubbed, burned with cigarettes, doused with boiling water and stabbed with an ice pick before being taken out and shot twice in the head by his comrades."

The late Barbara Olson probed Hillary's role with the Panthers in her book *Hell to Pay:* "The evidence against the Black Panthers was overwhelming—including an audio tape of part of the 'trial' to which Rackley was subjected. Two Panthers confessed to shooting Rackley as part of a plea bargain." But Panther leader Seale fought extradition from California, and became "a rallying point for student radicals who idolized the Panthers as leaders of a necessary black insurrection against the repressive white establishment."

Former radical leader and Panther ally David Horowitz, the co-editor of the sixties leftist magazine *Ramparts,* says "The fact is that the Panthers were torturers and murderers of black people, and Hillary Clinton . . . organized . . . demonstrations to get them off."

Horowitz, who has taken a far longer road from left to right than either of the Clintons to become one of America's leading conservatives, elaborates: "It was a bunch of revolutionary law students who were trying to obstruct justice; that's what it was about. A guy was tortured and murdered; the government was trying people for the crime. . . . The Panther leaders who were on trial all thought it was okay to torture and murder somebody. That's what Hillary Clinton was defending, people who thought it was okay to torture and murder somebody."

As Olson reports, "Hillary attended Black Panther trials and put her considerable leadership and organizational skills to work in organizing shifts of fellow students to monitor the trial and report alleged civil rights abuses."

Where most law students try to work for their school's mainstream law review, Hillary served as an editor of the *Yale Review of Law and Social Action,* an alternative leftist publication whose first issue, in 1970, included this declaration: "For too long, legal issues have been defined and discussed in terms of academic doctrine rather than strategies for social change." Contributors included William Kunstler, Charles Gerry (the lawyer representing the Panthers), and Jerry Rubin, who wrote in the *Review* that parents should "get high with our seven-year-olds" and students ought to "kill our parents."

Olson reports that "The combined second and third law issues of the *Review* in the fall/winter of 1970 on which Hillary served as associate editor, centered on Bobby Seale and the Black Panthers. It included many cartoons depicting the police as hominid pigs, their snouts wet while they mutter, 'niggers, niggers, niggers, niggers.' "

If Hillary was a leftist at Yale—sympathetic to the Black Panthers, defensive of campus revolutionaries, and antagonistic toward the police—she had a lot of company. Millions of students of the era shared her views. Few would argue that the Hillary Clinton of today and the student radical of the sixties are one and the same. Times have changed; so have we, and so has she.

What is notable are the lengths to which she goes in *Living History* to avoid discussing that part of her life. Rather than frankly acknowledging the far-left positions of her twenties—or her evolution to more moderate views in her thirties and forties—she tries to conceal her radical background. Her sole mention of the Panthers in *Living History* is the harmless, even charming anecdote about the "bucket brigade" she led to put out a campus fire during the Panther riots. A past life as a campus radical doesn't fit in with the HILLARY brand.

In a presidential campaign, of course, all is fair game. During the 1992 race, photos of Bill Clinton as a long-haired teenager, taken at peace rallies during the late sixties, were broadcast around the world. His adolescent drug use became an issue ("I did not inhale"). Thus far, Hillary's involvement with the Panthers has yet to surface as a political liability—in part, perhaps, because she chose to begin her career in relatively liberal New York. But it's sure to haunt her when she runs for the top office.

EDUCATION REFORM

Hillary's first major foray into public policy came after Bill's restoration as Arkansas governor in 1982. Working day and night to re-elect her husband, she had put her own career on hold. Now she faced a decision: whether to return to her own life at the Rose Law Firm or move further down the road of politics. She chose politics.

And almost immediately Bill needed her again. Just after he returned to office, the Arkansas State Supreme Court handed him a live grenade, ruling the state's entire existing education-financing system unconstitutional. The system's dependence on property taxes to pay for schools was illegal, the court found, because it left poor communities with worse schools than wealthy ones. Clinton was presented with a sobering choice: either cut aid to wealthy neighborhoods (a political impossibility) or increase funds in poorer areas—which would necessitate a tax increase.

Clinton had just been voted out of office for raising taxes. Now he would be forced to increase them again. There seemed no way out. "I'll be a one-term governor twice," he complained.

Bill, Hillary, Betsey Wright, and I huddled for strategy sessions long into the night, trying to find a way around the problem. Clinton had calculated that he had to raise the state sales tax by one half of one cent to fund the mandates in the court decision. My polls showed that voters would resent a half-cent hike that did nothing to improve the schools, but would accept a full one-cent increase if it really helped education. The Clintons embraced the idea of the higher tax—it's never hard getting them to raise taxes—but realized that if they were going to collect more money from the voters, they had better deliver.

It was Hillary who came up with the idea of a commission that would travel around the state holding hearings and bringing attention to the low quality of Arkansas schools. The commission, which she would lead, would then recommend fundamental reforms in education standards and big raises in teacher pay. Anticipating the Bush administration's "No Child Left Behind" program by twenty years, Hillary realized that voters—and the state legislature—would be less grudging about raising teacher salaries if they felt educational standards were rising.

And yet, strangely, *Living History* completely misrepresents the origins of Hillary's education-reform initiative. Nowhere in the book does she reveal that her decision to focus on education was impelled by a court order. The court's decision goes completely unmentioned. Rather, Hillary claims that she and Bill decided to focus on the issue because they "agreed that Arkansas would never prosper without an overhaul of its education system."

Talk about revisionist history! When Clinton first came back to power in 1982, he planned to focus on lowering utility rates, not on education. Exploiting Frank White's dependence on donations from large utility companies, Clinton had campaigned for direct popular election of the state utility regulatory board, which was then appointed by the governor.

But the court decision on school finance soon eclipsed the utility rate issue. Clinton had to come up with an education program, and mobilize all his resources to get it passed.

So why does Hillary fail to mention the court decision? What would be wrong with admitting that her education campaign was born of a judicial ruling? The reason is simple: The HILLARY brand moves in response to inner conviction, not outside necessity. Hillary, the political tactician? She saw how a good public policy initiative would help her husband survive another tax increase. HILLARY, the brand? She acted only because she cared about children.

In contrast to her later failures on health care, Hillary did a fantastic job working to reform the state's backward education system . . . and backward is putting it kindly. When Arkansans of the time said "thank God for Mississippi," as they often did, everyone got the reference: Only the even more abysmal schools there spared Arkansas the indignity of being 50th in the nation in education.

It was Hillary who first introduced to Arkansas the idea of giving schools "report cards" based on their students' performance on standardized tests, a measure since adopted as the core of Bush's school reforms. If a school's students failed standardized tests in disproportionate numbers, it would get special help and extra funds. But if the school's poor performance persisted, the school itself would be decertified, closed, and the children transferred to other institutions.

The gutsiest part of Hillary's program was a decision to test teachers to see if they were sufficiently skilled, informed, and educated to teach effectively. A state with a poor education system is frequently in danger of falling into a vicious cycle: Bad schools turn out bad teachers, who are then employed by the bad schools. (One teacher famously taught her class that the conflict that engulfed the globe in the 1940s was "World War Eleven"—that's how she read World War II!)

So Hillary demanded that every teacher, tenured or not, be tested. Those who failed the examination would get remedial help. If they still failed, they would be fired. She also proposed big pay raises for the teachers who passed the test—and got them. No longer would the poorly educated products of the state's segregated school system of forty years ago teach in modern schools, perpetuating the cycle of ignorance that dogged them.

Her decision, and Bill's determination to back her up, took enormous political courage. The teachers' union was the core of the progressive wing of the state's Democratic Party. Alienated beyond imagination by the testing plan, the union's membership turned on the Clintons in a flash when they got wind of Hillary's proposal. Pickets appeared. Teachers attacked the governor, and singled out the first lady for special scorn. For years thereafter, the union refused to endorse Bill Clinton—despite its almost Siamese twin-like connection to the state Democratic Party.

Testing teachers was a bold and innovative move. Hillary describes accurately in *Living History* how the tests "enraged the teachers union, civil rights groups, and others who were vital to the Democratic Party in Arkansas."

But *Living History* does not tell the full story.

When the teacher test scores came in, Bill and Hillary were shocked. Arkansas teachers had failed miserably. Clinton complained: "I'd have to fire half the teachers if we held to the standard passing grade." Minority teachers flunked the test in especially large numbers. Clinton knew he would be in hot water if he decimated the minority teachers as a result of the test. It would have been a political disaster.

So the Clintons commissioned me to take a poll to find out what percent of the teachers the voters felt ought to fail the test. 1 percent, 5 percent, 10 percent, 20 percent, 30 percent—what would the market bear?

The poll revealed that they expected one teacher in ten to flunk. Only about one voter in twenty would find it acceptable to fail half the teachers. So what did Bill and Hillary do? They adjusted the passing grade so that only 10 percent failed the test.

In fairness to Hillary, firing 10 percent of the teachers in Arkansas was no easy task. But here the Clintons held firm. While the failing teachers got remedial courses and more chances to pass the test, eventually a lot of them lost their jobs just as Hillary had promised. But the teacher test was not the objective affair the Clintons had portrayed.

Does it detract from Hillary's laudable efforts to reform Arkansas education that they were impelled by the court? Does the Clintons' decision to adjust the passing grade on the teacher test besmirch her courage in urging the examinations in the first place? To some extent, of course, the answer to both questions is yes. A full-throated idealist would have focused on education reform without having to be driven by the courts to do so. And adjusting pass/fail scores to account for public expectations certainly reflects a level of political expedience. But neither fact diminishes Hillary's foresight and courage in her efforts to reform schools.

Obviously, however, this is a side of her education reform efforts she would rather not expose to public view. It doesn't fit the HILLARY brand.

Even so, as Hillary battled for education reform, she was never finer. In those days, I never thought of Hillary as a liberal. During this, her first foray into public policy, Hillary adopted a distinctly moderate tone, combining a liberal generosity toward education with an insistence on high standards—a foreshadowing of Clinton's "New Covenant," coupling opportunity with responsibility. During her husband's second term as governor, Hillary was very much a "New" Democrat.

It was also during these years that Hillary discovered how much she relished the chance to take the stage as a public figure in her own right, making her own proposals and developing her own ideas. It was a heady experience, and it left her with a taste for the spotlight's warm glow that never left her.

And yet, when Hillary tried to recreate the experience on the national stage, the results were a memorable disaster.

THE HEALTH CARE REFORM FIASCO

The health care reform drive that became so thoroughly associated with Hillary began in Bill Clinton's mind, as an exercise in controlling health care costs. Originally, the president saw it as more of a conservative than a liberal initiative. Worried that health care was consuming an ever-larger part of the nation's wealth and undermining our competitiveness abroad, he was determined to rein in spending. As Bob Woodward reports, Clinton felt "the explosion in the federal debt was largely attributable to skyrocketing health care costs. The health system was wasteful and irrational, and reforming it would be a priority for him as president."

In his first State of the Union Address, in 1993, Clinton made clear that cost control was his central goal: "In 1992, we spent 14 percent of our income on health care, more than 30 percent more than any other country in the world; and yet we were the only advanced nation that did not provide a basic package of health care benefits to all its citizens. Unless we change the present pattern, 50 percent of the growth in the deficit between now and the year 2000 will be in health care costs."

Hillary brought huge reservoirs of hope, enthusiasm, effort, and skill to her solo policy debut in the new Clinton Administration—and had she approached it with no preconceptions except for the need to reduce the looming deficit, she might well have succeeded. But Hillary's liberal health care gurus quickly persuaded her that health care costs could only be controlled if everybody had health insurance, as part of a managed care system structured by the government.

The reasoning went like this: To control health care costs you had to bring all Americans into managed care, where medical decisions would be checked and balanced by budgetary considerations. But you couldn't contain health costs if many people were uninsured, and therefore outside the system. When they got sick or injured, their treatment costs, which were not reimbursed by any insurer, had to be absorbed by the hospital or other health care provider, driving up the costs of medical care for everyone else.

Not only did the liberals around Hillary hijack the cost-cutting initiative and transform it into a campaign for universal health coverage; they also persuaded Hillary that incremental change was impossible. Either the entire system would be fixed, or nothing at all would be accomplished.

As Hillary once explained it to me: "If you clamp down on costs in one area and not in another, the costs in the other area will soar. If you control hospital costs, your outpatient fees will rise. If you clamp down on emergency room charges under Medicare, Medicaid costs will go up." For the system to work, you had to regulate all the health care providers and all the patients. It was like a balloon, clamp down on one area and the other just inflated more. Hillary describes this all-or-nothing approach in *Living History:* "We wanted a plan that dealt with all aspects of the health care system rather than one that tinkered on the margins."

By 1994, Hillary's reforms were being described as offering health security to all Americans.

Of course, as no one needs reminding, Hillary and Co. badly misread the historical moment. The health care system had already begun to reform itself as the competitive realities of the marketplace convinced large corporations and labor unions alike of the need for managed care. This would have happened even if Hillary had never embarked on her health care reform crusade. Furthermore, the demand for universal health insurance did not turn out to be as widespread as Hillary's liberal advisors imagined.

As a case in point, consider CHIP. In 1997, as part of his balanced budget deal with Congress, Bill Clinton established the Children's Health Insurance Program (CHIP) as a way of offering health coverage to all kids who didn't have it already. Speaking to the Democratic

National Convention in 2000, Hillary described how it worked: "Now, you may remember, I had a few ideas about health care and I've learned a few lessons since then, but I haven't given up on the goal, and that's why we kept working step-by-step to insure millions of children through the Children's Health Insurance Program."

CHIP set out to fund insurance for all uninsured children in the United States, but there was only one problem—the program couldn't find enough kids to cover. Forty of the fifty states had to admit defeat and send money back to Washington. Forty-five percent of the $4.2 billion allocated for CHIP went unused—because the states couldn't find enough noncovered kids to enroll. Either the parents didn't want to sign up their children, or there weren't that many uninsured children in the first place. Even liberal California proved unable to find children needing coverage; they were obliged to return half a billion dollars to the Feds.

Worse yet, a large proportion of the children who were signed up for CHIP turned out to be eligible for Medicaid all along. Their parents had just never bothered to enroll them. Like her original abortive attempt at reform, Hillary's latter-day health care program was based on a perceived need, deeply rooted in liberal gospel, that turned out to be largely illusory.

How did Hillary let herself be brainwashed?

When she first took control of health care policy for the administration, she admits, she had no clue where to begin. In *Living History,* she writes: "I didn't fully realize the magnitude of what we were undertaking." She was intimidated enough that she reached out for experts to guide her through the immensely complicated field of health care, with its myriad providers and multiple interest groups. Most significantly, she brought in Ira Magaziner, an Oxford college buddy of Bill's, to serve as her executive director on the health care task force. She held huge meetings and collected volumes of data. When the task force began, President Clinton had promised results after 100 days. That goal quickly became impossible, as Hillary moved from recommending improvements to calling for a total redesign of the system. The task force eventually grew to include vast numbers of people; the bill it produced ran to more than a thousand pages.

In 1993, President Clinton had asked Hillary to serve as a liaison with me to sound out my political advice. She was also anxious to discuss her health care initiatives, so we spoke a few times each month by phone. As these conversations progressed, it became clear that Hillary was unsure of herself as she traveled through the health care maze, and was slipping more and more under the influence of Magaziner and others who were pushing for total reform. It was quite a change from her confident handling of education in Arkansas. There she had focused on specific steps to improve schools, while leaving the basic system in place. Faced with the enormous health care labyrinth, however, she grew convinced that everything must be changed.

Hillary's advisors also convinced her that the key to true reform was to slay the villains who profited shamelessly from the present system. Her universe became peopled by enemies: insurance companies and brokers, the medical establishment, unscrupulous hospitals, and the like. This division into good and evil, us versus them, fit Hillary's worldview, and appealed to her increasingly partisan instincts. She became more strident in defending health care reform and attacking those who opposed her.

When I warned her about antagonizing the nation's hundreds of thousands of insurance brokers, she was unmoved by the advice.

"They are the best field force in politics," I told Hillary in a phone conversation late in 1993. "There is an insurance broker in every small town and every neighborhood in the United States. They each have their clients, all of whom are voters. If you cut them out of your system, you'll send them up and down their neighborhoods rallying support against you. It won't just be a media campaign by the insurance companies. That you can rebut. But the one-on-one attacks from brokers will be too much to handle."

"But *they* are the problem," Hillary scolded me. "It's the money they take out of the system that is driving up costs so much. We need to cut out the middlemen to keep the costs in line. We don't want to raise taxes to pay for universal health coverage, so we have to generate internal savings and this is a very good way to do it."

"But you will antagonize the hell out of them," I persisted.

"Then so be it," she answered.

The task force itself became a point of controversy, as doctors, hospitals, insurance companies, and other special interest organizations tried to disrupt the reform effort at its inception. Hillary played into their hands. The same arrogance that caused Hillary to dismiss the consequences of antagonizing the insurance brokers also led her to insist that the meetings of her task force be held in secret—a policy that led to a lawsuit. She describes the suit in *Living History* as "a blow that none of us anticipated."

Those opposing Hillary's task force contended that she was not a public employee and, hence, could not chair the task force. Hillary notes that "if I was allowed in the meetings, the lawsuit claimed, government sunshine laws required that the closed meetings be opened to outsiders, including the press."

Federal law did allow government agencies to deliberate in secret . . . providing that only public employees were involved. Once private citizens were invited to participate, the meetings must be opened to the public and the media.

Was Hillary a public employee or a private citizen? If the former, she could chair the task force. If the latter, she had to step aside.

The entire issue would have been avoided had Hillary simply agreed to open the meetings to the public. But so intense was her commitment to secrecy that she ran afoul of federal law. The entire scandal was a consequence of Hillary's fanatical need for secrecy and obsessive fear of leaks.

Worst of all, the secrecy was being enforced selectively. Ira Magaziner had to admit that many private citizens—including representatives of foundations, German health care officials, employees of California's Kaiser Permanente managed care organization, and other "outsiders"—had attended some of the task force's meetings. Angered,

U.S. District Court Judge Royce C. Lamberth ruled that Magaziner had "intended to deceive the court" when he asserted in a sworn statement that only federal government officials were members of the health care task force. Calling Magaziner's conduct "reprehensible," Judge Lamberth wrote: "The Executive Branch of the government, working in tandem, was dishonest with this court, and the government must now face the consequences of its misconduct."

The government was ordered to pay a $285,000 fine because of Magaziner's misconduct. (Those who enjoy irony will relish the way Senator Hillary Clinton has criticized Vice President Dick Cheney for refusing to open meetings of his energy task force to the public.)

Hillary's health care reform program fell under withering fire. Her proposal to hold down costs through managed care and use the savings to offer universal health insurance coverage became distorted into a plan to eliminate the right to choose our own doctors. All Hillary had really done was to anticipate the growth of private HMOs and seek to impose the new system all at once—a system to be orchestrated by Washington. But her ideas did not go down well with the American people, and not merely because of the aggressive television ad campaigns mounted by the initiative's opponents.

In a sense, Hillary had learned the wrong lessons from her successful education reform efforts in Arkansas. Consider a story Bob Woodward reports in *The Agenda*. Speaking with her husband's newly appointed cabinet and top White House staffers at Camp David shortly after the inauguration, she explained what she saw as the reasons for her education victory in Arkansas: According to Hillary, her team had succeeded because "they had devised a simple story, with characters, with an objective, with a beginning, middle, and end. And it had all come from a moral point of view."

It was her very obsession with seeing health care as a moral issue that ultimately prevented Hillary from reforming the system successfully. For while the question of health care unquestionably has a moral *dimension,* what confronted Hillary was ultimately a legislative battle, not a spiritual crusade, and her attitude did little to engender the spirit of compromise that was vital to the passage of any reform program. As Woodward writes, "a number of staffers noticed an increasing self-righteousness in Hillary. She acted as if she had seen the light." He quotes Hillary as saying "I believe in evil and I think that there are evil people in the world." And a lot of them were opposing her health care plan.

Bristling at the norms of Washington, Hillary became both defiant and arrogant. Woodward describes how she insisted on telling a group of senators that her new plan would cost $100 billion, a number sure to set off alarms throughout Capitol Hill. "I don't care how they do things here," he quotes her as saying. "If they can't take the truth, at least they're going to get it from me. . . . That [the $100 billion cost] is the truth and they'd better get used to it."

For his part, President Clinton came to take a curiously detached view of the process. The health care task force became increasingly cumbersome and unpopular. Sued to open its meetings to the public, berated by critics for taking more than a year to make recommendations, and finally derided as an effort to introduce socialized medicine and eliminate freedom of choice in medicine, the project became radioactive. What had started as a New Democratic safety net was becoming a noose around the neck of the administration. And in our conversations, I noticed, the president was becoming almost dismissive of her efforts. After a press item appeared that Clinton was planning to raise taxes to finance his wife's health care proposals, I had an Oval Office meeting with the president. He was furious. "I'm not going to raise taxes for *that*—believe me," he said contemptuously.

But as Hillary's health care proposals dropped in popularity and faded in the Congress, the common understanding that Hillary was the pragmatic one while Bill was "the boy scout" (Hillary's phrase) underwent a dramatic reversal. Hillary had always been the one who watched Bill's back, who made sure he wasn't knifed. But now the tables were turned. Bill was learning how to be president and doing an increasingly good job. He had passed his tax package, NAFTA, and his crime bill. It was Hillary who was mismanaging her assignment: Health care reform was going down in flames.

Hillary didn't know what to do. She sensed that her efforts were imploding, but the solution seemed to elude her. The key problem was that, having constructed an interlocking system of new measures, each dependent on the other, she could not deconstruct it to compromise on its component parts.

After her bill died in committee in the Senate, never to see the light of day on the floor, I suggested that she regroup in the closing days of the session and endorse another piece of health care reform legislation, known popularly as the Dole Bill. This proposal, introduced by Republican Minority Leader Bob Dole as an alternative to Hillary's reforms, closely resembled the Kennedy-Kassebaum bill that ultimately passed in 1996. It allowed insurance beneficiaries to take their policies with them when they switched jobs, and barred a patient's new insurance company or his employers from excluding as "pre-existing" those conditions that were covered under their previous employers' insurance.

Dole had sponsored the bill back in 1993, when Hillary's initiatives seemed unstoppable. Now that her bill was fading fast, Dole probably didn't really want his program to pass either. But he had introduced it, it bore his name, and, I told Hillary, he would have to let it pass. "He can't very well kill his own bill, without seeming disingenuous." Passing this incremental improvement, I told her, would avoid the sting of failure, and allow the Clintons to cite a concrete accomplishment in the realm of health care.

She rejected the idea completely. Either the entire package had to be approved at once, or nothing could—or even should—be done. "You don't understand," she lectured me. "Everything in the health care field is interrelated. If we just fix one part of the problem, we throw something else out of whack." It was like talking to a Trotskyite.

"If we pass the Dole Bill and do nothing else," she continued, "we'll drive up health insurance premiums to cover the extra cost of the new benefits. Do you want us to have to run for re-election in 1996 with a record of increases in health insurance costs?"

Her argument was identical to the specious one that would be advanced two years later by conservatives trying to kill the Kennedy-Kassebaum Bill. And it was just as wrong. "How do you know what the situation will be in 1996?" I asked, incredulous at her inability to think clearly. "There could be high inflation. There could be deflation. There could be a war. Anything can happen. Pocket this achievement now so you don't have to go away humiliated and empty handed."

No dice. Hillary had been programmed to believe that it had to be all or nothing.

In 1994, she opted for nothing. But notwithstanding her resistance to the Dole Bill, in *Living History* Hillary takes credit for the passage of the Kennedy-Kassebaum legislation two years later. But she doesn't mention that workers would have had the right to take their health benefits to their new jobs much earlier if Hillary herself hadn't been so stubborn about her own initiative—and the Democrats might well have held onto Congress in the bargain.

Hillary's liberal dogmatism—which one might have thought she'd left behind at Yale—re-emerged during the health care fiasco. I was shocked at the change. Her pragmatism of the 1980s seemed to have disappeared, along with the capacity to think for herself; instead, she followed the progressive creed wherever it led. Her innate skepticism was replaced by a blind faith in her liberal advisors. It was as if an old friend had fallen under the spell of some cult.

Hillary's eventual, inevitable defeat was a crushing blow. It cost her dearly in self-esteem, and gave even the president doubts about her political savvy. As she slowly emerged from the almost hypnotic spell Magaziner and his crew seemed to have cast upon her, it was clear that she needed deprogramming.

In her memoir, Hillary attributes the defeat of health care reform to "my own missteps and because I underestimated the resistance I would meet as a first lady with a policy mission." In truth, though, being first lady had nothing to do with it. In fact, the thing most voters liked about health care reform was that it was the product of an activist, outspoken first lady "with a policy mission." The reasons that Hillary's health care reform initiative died were many, and they were clear: It was too massive a change; it drew the opposition of most doctors; it was discredited by Hillary's attempts at secrecy; it would have forced Americans into managed care and limited their medical choices. It failed, in other words, on its merits.

Once again, though, Hillary's account in *Living History* is all about branding. Hillary may be capable of making mistakes—who isn't?—but HILLARY is incapable of admitting them. If HILLARY failed, it must not only have been in a noble cause—universal health security—but have been caused by an ignoble opposition to an activist first lady.

But the lessons Hillary did learn in the health care defeat were deep and profound. Never again would she ignore polls in public policy formulation. From now on she would confine her advocacy to the possible, and leave her idealistic friends to spin their theoretical webs. Idealism, she realized, must always be checked by practicality.

But did Hillary learn the larger lessons of the health care debacle?

Her moralistic denunciations of the special interests who opposed her health care plan were among the factors that led directly to its defeat. Has she absorbed that making enemies is no way to make public policy?

Not likely. Hillary still sees public policy in terms of friends and enemies, good and evil. She is inclined to oppose the positions held by people she thinks are ill-intentioned, reflexively embracing the other side. The idea that there are good people and bad people, not just good ideas and bad ideas, remains fundamental to her worldview. To Hillary, *who* matters more than *what*.

Bill Clinton is largely immune to this habit of thinking. At a White House strategy meeting I attended in 1996, he was considering a proposal to let employers offer their workers compensatory pay or extra vacation for overtime work. The unions opposed the idea because they felt the bosses would coerce the workers into taking the vacation days because they were cheaper. "I don't think that employers are evil," Clinton told us. "I think that they are good people and will try to do the right thing. I don't think you have to pass laws to stop people from taking vacation time if they wish because you are afraid that management will be evil and will try to game the system. It just doesn't work that way."

As dangerous as it is to let your enemies' positions define yours, it is even more hazardous to adopt the positions of your advisors uncritically. Has Hillary learned to distrust gurus? Has her experience with Magaziner and the leftists who led her astray made her more suspicious of those who have all the answers?

One wonders.

The very evolution of the HILLARY brand itself—formulated by her handlers, pollsters, market researchers, media advisors, speechwriters, makeup and hair people, and advance people—suggests that she has not lost her susceptibility to gurus. Is the woman who turned her face and image over to the experts as she ran for the Senate the same one who let Magaziner and the health care liberals throw off her political compass in 1994?

And how about her reliance on dogmatic liberals? Is she over that?

Maybe not. When Senator Clinton voted to oppose the Bush prescription drug benefit under Medicare, her position suggested that she may still be in their thrall.

After months of negotiation, Bush and the congressional Democrats had reached agreement on the scope of the benefit package. Their only disagreement was that the Republicans wanted to designate ten metropolitan areas as demonstration projects, to test whether the benefit could be better administered by private insurance companies outside of the traditional Medicare program. Ted Kennedy rose in anger, calling the plan the opening wedge to the destruction of the Medicare system. His reflexive refusal to give the experiment a trial—in which he was followed loyally by other liberal ideologues—reminded me of the conservatives' habit of invoking the bogeyman of "socialized medicine" whenever liberals tried to extend health care benefits.

The liberal orthodoxy maintained that privatizing the drug benefit would lead to the day when insurance companies would skim off the youngest, healthiest, and richest of the elderly and give them private coverage, leaving the rest to the mercy of the government. Then, their argument goes, they would cut public spending, knowing that they were punishing helpless, poor, sick, old people who weren't going to vote to protect themselves.

If that sequence of events seems a bit farfetched, even conspiratorial, the United States Senate rejected those scenarios and overwhelmingly passed the prescription drug bill. Yet Hillary thought enough of the liberal arguments to vote against giving the elderly lower cost prescription medicine, joining only thirty-four other Democrats in opposing the bill.

But at least and at last, the ideologue within Hillary *had* been shocked into remission by the 1994 congressional defeat. In 1995–1996, as her husband ran for a second term, Hillary embraced the idea of incremental policy initiatives with increasing enthusiasm. Cured of her utopian all-or-nothing approach to issues—or perhaps just scared off by her failure—she pushed hard on individual initiatives.

THE NEW STRATEGY: FOREIGN TRAVEL

As Hillary gradually recovered, and stopped dreaming of the dead Democrats who had lost their seats in Congress as a result of her miscues, she needed to figure out how to get on with her life.

In 1995, my polling had suggested that returning to her old behind-the-scenes role in the White House was not a good idea; it would only reawaken the idea that her weak husband was allowing her to "wear the pants" again.

Besides, the job of *de facto* chief of staff was no longer open. Hillary had begun to wear out her welcome with Bill, who was smarting from the first political defeat for which she bore any amount of blame. The usually infallible Hillary had proven quite fallible indeed.

In any case, Bill had replaced the kindly but ineffectual Mack McLarty with former California Congressman Leon Panetta, a savvy insider with smiling face and cutthroat moves who knew how the Washington game was played. Panetta would be his own chief of staff; Hillary would just have to settle for playing first lady.

So, after the polling confirmed that public issue advocacy would play well for her and for the administration, Hillary remade herself again, this time as an outspoken advocate for women and children.

Her decision to adopt a new role involved two changes. First, she had to move her focus from health care to education, wiping out the memory of her failure and returning to the grounds of her earlier success. The new HILLARY brand would be about women and children, not doctors and insurance companies.

But she also had to move off the news pages and into the feature section of the newspaper. No longer would she make "hard" news by proposing concrete legislation, holding hearings, writing bills, or lobbying for passage of her ideas. Instead, she would make speeches and publish articles urging greater emphasis on the needs of women and children.

But after the media got wind of the new HILLARY strategy, it stopped covering her. If she was no longer a power broker behind the scenes in the White House, or proposing specific legislation or executive action in the public sphere, she was of no further interest to them. Once the hottest story in town, suddenly she was a media afterthought. "I have to be strident or partisan or harsh to attract coverage," she complained to me during this transition time. "If I do that, they cover it in a minute. But just to go around making positive proposals on women and children doesn't bring any media coverage."

It's not that she couldn't attract local media wherever she went. If the *New York Times* and the *Washington Post* weren't going to cover her speeches, the *Jackson Clarion Ledger* or the *Memphis Commercial Appeal* would. But Hillary didn't give a damn about that kind of local coverage. She wanted the big spotlight, big coverage on the national stage.

Hillary and Bill Clinton both suffer from a variety of attention deficit disorder (ADD): When they don't get enough attention, they become disordered. Hillary seethed at the lack of coverage. So she hit on a three-part strategy—a weekly newspaper column, a best-selling book, and foreign travel.

Knowing how strongly she wanted to emulate Eleanor Roosevelt, I joined others in suggesting that Hillary write a weekly newspaper column, which could be syndicated to get her ideas into print nationwide.

The column gave Hillary visibility without having to pass through the prism of newspaper reporters and editors. It was a way of speaking directly to the people. In her columns she could focus on specific, tangible, incremental initiatives, rather than limiting herself to projects grand enough to attract national media attention. "The exercise of putting my ideas on paper," she writes in *Living History,* "gave me a clearer sense of how to recast my role as an advocate within the Administration as I began to focus on discrete domestic projects that were more achievable than massive undertakings such as health care reform. On my agenda now were children's health issues, breast cancer prevention, and protecting funding for public television, legal services, and the arts."

Hillary also authored a book entitled *It Takes a Village.* A mélange of very specific thoughts on child-rearing, education, prenatal care, preschooling, and the like, her book was an exercise in just the sort of incremental post-health care reform advocacy that the polling had indicated would be most popular. And popular it was: The book became a *New York Times* bestseller, selling hundreds of thousands of copies.

The name Barbara Feinman Todd does not appear in *Living History,* nor did it make the acknowledgments page of *It Takes a Village.* Todd had been hired as a ghostwriter to help pen Hillary's book. But she had rough sledding in getting credit for her work. Hillary may need ghostwriters, but the HILLARY brand won't permit their recognition. The weekly Washington newspaper *The Hill* reported that "[Todd's] contract to help Clinton with *It Takes a Village* called for an expression of thanks and a payment of $120,000. All went well until just before the book was published, when Todd learned her name didn't appear in the acknowledgments. Then she began hearing talk that she'd been fired from the project, which was untrue. Later, when it was time to collect the final $30,000 installment of her collaboration fee, she was told the White House didn't want her to be paid. A few phone calls to Simon & Schuster—Hillary's publisher—from powerful Washington friends . . . finally got Todd a check for her work. The publisher also agreed to pay her Clinton-related legal bills. Afterward, said Todd, she continued receiving Christmas cards from the Clintons but her name was always misspelled."

The book, and her columns, helped Hillary stake her claim on the comparatively forgiving turf of children's issues and education. Since education and child welfare policies were largely controlled by state and local governments, there was no call for her to propose specific national programs or legislation. Instead, she could simply make suggestions and hope they would be picked up by local school boards or child care agencies. When she urged funding for prenatal services or called for higher school standards, localities could implement her ideas as they saw fit. No harsh fights in Congress. No push and pull of constituency groups. And if a question was too tough politically, she could just pass on to new issues.

By writing her own book (sort of) and working with her staff on her weekly columns, Hillary was going over the heads of the media, in a sense replicating the work of Bill Clinton's paid television ads— bypassing the press and going directly to the people.

But it was the third part of the emerging post-health care reform strategy that proved the most successful: foreign travel.

Hillary was right that she could only get center stage attention at home by saying things that would get her into political trouble. Abroad, though, it was a different story. There, her every move was covered. Reporters were assigned to travel with her and had to file stories every day if only to justify the expense of sending them. Once a paper anted up the funds for a reporter to travel with the first lady, it was very likely to print the stories they had paid top dollar to get. As she writes in *Living History,* the media was "a captive audience." In foreign countries, Hillary could get the coverage she needed and avoid political risk.

As Hillary's scandals at home multiplied, and questions about her role in Whitewater, the Rose Law Firm, the disappearance of the billing records, the Webb Hubbell hush money, the FBI file scandal, and the Commodities Market trading all got louder, she adopted the patented formula of all presidents in trouble: She left the country. HILLARY was about to become a world traveler.

This is not, of course, how Hillary remembers the decision to travel. In *Living History,* she once again invokes the name of a celebrity, writing that it was Mary Catherine Bateson, the anthropologist daughter of Margaret Mead, who first explained to her how travel could have symbolic significance. As Hillary writes, "I understood her point and I soon became a convert to the view that I could advance the Clinton agenda through symbolic action."

Advance the agenda? Or dodge the negative publicity at home while having a great vacation? Likely a combination of both.

In fact, in *Living History,* Hillary usually couches her decision to travel as a response to a request. After all, HILLARY doesn't court publicity or covet exciting travel. Rather, she does her duty when asked. Her first trip after the congressional defeats of 1994, for example, came in March 1995, when "The State Department asked me to visit the subcontinent [India] . . . because neither the President nor the Vice President could make a trip soon."

She went to Bosnia in March 1996 because "The State Department asked me to go."

Why did she go to Eastern Europe in the summer of 1996? "I was asked to represent Bill . . ."

Obviously, the State Department "asked" her to go because she wanted to be asked. The Department was certainly given at least a hint that she would welcome such an invitation. The president couldn't go, to be sure. But if Gore finessed Hillary out of a trip by going himself, he'd be scalped on his return to the White House.

Her most significant trip was to China in 1995 to address the United Nations Fourth World Conference on Women, as the honorary chair of the U.S. delegation. In conversations with me at the time, she made it plain that she was very eager to go. I didn't think it was a good idea; I was worried that she would be held accountable for all the actions of the Chinese government—particularly their arrest of human rights activist and American citizen Harry Wu, who was in jail for filming the Chinese "gulag" labor camps to expose their deplorable conditions.

After Wu's arrest in July 1995, Hillary was under intense pressure to cancel her visit to China. The State Department had announced that she would not attend if Wu were still in jail. But Hillary wanted desperately to go. She craved the attention, the stage, the audience, the platform. The opportunity was too good to pass up.

In late August 1995, however, Wu was freed, even though a show trial had sentenced him to fifteen years in prison. The way was cleared for Hillary's visit.

In her memoir, Hillary says Wu gave her credit for springing him from prison. "Some media commentators, and Wu himself, were convinced that the United States had made a political deal with the Chinese: Wu would be released, but only if I agreed to come to the conference . . ."

Hillary also writes that she was anxious to free Wu because she had been moved by a personal letter from Mrs. Wu.

Harry Wu himself, though, begs to differ. He has said plainly that Hillary "overstated her role" in his release.

Did he believe Hillary made any kind of deal for his release? Wu says: "I never believed that. I never said that. I don't know why she put [those words] in my mouth. . . . I never had that kind of idea at all."

Wu also disputes whether Mrs. Wu's letter had any effect on Hillary's thinking. "When I was detained in China and facing the death penalty . . . my wife sent a letter to Mrs. Clinton. The petition was just described as a woman-to-woman, wife-to-wife [request] to help."

"But we never got any single word of response from Mrs. Clinton. [We] never [heard] anything from her."

To Wu, Mrs. Clinton's attitude seemed to suggest that "she does not care about human beings' lives, human beings' fate. She just cared about attending the women's conference as a political obligation."

Nor were there many "media observers" who claimed that her decision to go to China was instrumental in Wu's release. Most media coverage attributed it instead to the forthcoming visit of Undersecretary of State Peter Tarnoff to negotiate with the Chinese government over Taiwan, trade, and human rights.

Whatever the controversy before she went, Hillary's trip to China was her most important success of Clinton's first term. Her speech, a clarion call for justice for women throughout the world, not only electrified the conference, but it served as a broad and encompassing statement of women's rights as human rights, including a condemnation of the murder of female babies, global forced prostitution, the burning of brides because their dowries were too small, rape "as a tactic or prize of war," domestic violence, genital mutilation, and forced abortion or sterilization. Hillary was magnificent!

To come back from her own crushing personal defeat in the health care reform debacle, Hillary needed a master stroke, a moment of high drama to summon her supporters and display what she could mean to the women of the world. China did that for her. It was her moment of redemption.

The political lesson of the South Asia and China trips was that travel pays. Until Monica Lewinsky dragged her back into her husband's own particular brand of hell, Hillary would find her political role in travel abroad, where she could be a spokesperson for women—and a symbol of their potential.

In *Living History*, Hillary cites trips to seventy-eight foreign countries, saying that the travel helped "to open my mind and my heart."

She doesn't mention that when she traveled she brought with her a small army. During Hillary's second term alone, the first lady's foreign travel cost the taxpayers $12 million. Her most expensive trip—a March 1999 twelve-day tour of North Africa with Chelsea, safari included—cost $2.3 million.

HILLARY MOVES TO THE CENTER

Back home, while Hillary was traveling the globe, President Clinton was facing an increasingly acrimonious showdown with the new Republican majority in Congress. Determined to slash federal spending, the Gingrich crowd pushed for major across-the-board cuts in social programs.

Clinton decided to take them on in four areas, condemning their reductions in Medicare, Medicaid, education, and the environment. He said that the Republicans were just using the deficit as an excuse to slash programs that they had always wanted to cut anyway.

As long as the Republicans could say that their reductions in spending were vital to eliminating the deficit, though, they would win the argument. What Clinton had to show the nation was a way to balance the budget without sacrificing these vital programs.

The president's economic advisors were strong supporters of deficit reduction. But Leon Panetta and the more liberal White House staff were against Clinton preparing an alternative path to a balanced budget. They said that Clinton would have to embrace at least some cuts in vital programs in any plan he might offer, and that this would throw away the Democrats' best issue.

Which way would the president go? It was the key question throughout all of May and June 1995. The push/pull between the moderates (Vice President Gore and Deputy Chief of Staff Erskine

Bowles) and the liberals (Panetta, Deputy Chief of Staff Harold Ickes, and George Stephanopoulos) dominated every political strategy meeting.

Hillary was no stranger to the left, but in this case she went up the middle, taking the New Democrat tack and urging Bill to submit his own balanced budget plan to the Congress and the public. She also made known her opposition to the Gingrich budget priorities. To this day, Hillary is a vocal critic of the growing deficit, eager to cite the Clinton administration budget surplus at every opportunity as an eviscerated achievement of her husband's rule. On this issue, she was no liberal.

Clinton laid out his alternative plan in a nationally televised prime time speech in June 1995, taking the balanced budget issue away from the Republicans for all time. Hillary had urged him to give the speech, and cheered him on every step of the way. But she doesn't mention much about her intervention in her memoir, probably because HILLARY must tack more to the left while she's representing liberal New York. Nor does her account of her husband's strong stand against the Republican budget cuts, and the government shutdown, mention what she knows is the key point: that Bill Clinton won his face-off with the Gingrich-Dole forces in Congress through massive use of paid advertising, unique in the history of presidential politics.

As the unthinkable began to become the inevitable, it became obvious to the Clinton White House that the president was about to enter a game of chicken against the Republican leadership of Congress. They would let the government run out of money and refuse to authorize additional spending—thus closing down the government—unless Clinton accepted their draconian budget cuts.

The question we all asked was "would Clinton flinch?" If he had the public with him, I knew he wouldn't. So I proposed, again with Hillary's support, a massive program of paid advertising to bring our case directly to the voters.

But the president was afraid to advertise because he said it would look too political. No other president had ever used paid advertising in his battles with Congress eighteen months before an election. "We'll keep it secret," I said.

"How in the world do you plan to do that?" he asked. "Run ads on television and keep them secret at the same time?"

"We won't advertise in New York City or in Washington, D.C. That's where all the reporters live," I replied.

Following the plan, we advertised in half the country for six months, but never ran an ad in either of these two cities. It worked perfectly. Very few articles appeared in the media about our ads, and those that did were buried inside the newspaper. Here we were, speaking to half the nation an average of three times a week for a year, and the New York-Washington media was so introverted and elitist that it never noticed!

The most important indication of Hillary's emerging centrism was her strong support, opportunistic or not, for the historic Welfare Reform Bill of 1996, the most significant and successful piece of domestic legislation since the 1964–1965 Civil Rights and Voting Rights Acts.

Hillary proudly reports the bill's success in her memoir: It cut welfare rolls by 60 percent, and helped reduce child poverty by about one quarter during the same period. Indeed, recent indications suggest that even in the Bush recession and its aftermath welfare rolls have continued to decline.

But at the time, her support of welfare reform alienated many of her most liberal friends. In *Living History* she writes of the contrast between her pragmatism on welfare reform, and her attitude during the health care debate: "I remembered all too well the defeat of our health care reform effort, which may have happened, in part, because of a lack of give and take." Indeed.

Hillary correctly notes that Clinton had to veto two welfare reform bills that contained caps in Medicaid and cuts in food stamps and other nutrition and child safety programs. She can be forgiven some posturing here. When the Republicans passed their first welfare reform bill, she writes, "Some in the White House urged the President to sign whatever reform the Congress sent him." But "I told [the president] and his top staff that I would speak out against any bill" with these cuts, she writes, even if the president signed it.

In fact, no one in the White House wanted Clinton to sign these bills. But the third welfare reform bill Congress passed was a different story. This bill was different. Senate Majority Leader Trent Lott had compromised dramatically to try to get Clinton's signature on the legislation. He dropped the Medicaid caps, restored the food stamp entitlement, added day care and job training, and eliminated the block grants that would have capped money to fight child abuse and neglect.

But the bulk of the White House staff still wanted the president to veto the new bill. They cited the cuts in legal-immigrant aid the Republicans had included, but their real reason was more basic: None of them wanted to end the fundamental entitlement to benefits welfare recipients enjoyed.

I met with Hillary to listen to her strong objections to the immigrant aid cuts, and pointed out that these reductions could be rescinded by a Democratic Congress. Stressing the importance of the bill to Clinton's re-election, I told Hillary bluntly that I thought a veto would cost us the victory.

At the time, my house was being painted by a tribe of finicky women whose work might have qualified them for a place alongside Michelangelo and his Sistine Chapel ceiling. They inspired the metaphor I used to explain my views to Hillary.

"Hillary, we've worked together long enough so you know that I'm like a house painter," I said, making a painting motion with my hand. "Every four years the house has to be painted. So I come in and move all the furniture to the center of the room. The center. And I paint the walls. When I'm finished, I go home and you can rearrange the furniture anyway you like."

"You silver-tongued devil, you," she replied with a smile.

In *Living History,* Hillary candidly discusses the political considerations that entered into her calculus. "If he vetoed welfare reform a third time, Bill would be handing the Republicans a potential political windfall." Clinton signed the bill, and the offensive cuts in aid to legal immigrants were repealed the very next year.

When Clinton signed the Welfare Reform Law, he effectively doomed Republican attempts to oust him in the 1996 elections. Signing the centerpiece of the GOP program—albeit with Democratic alterations and additions—took away the GOP's best issue. It is a credit to Trent Lott that he acted to pass a bill so manifestly in the nation's interest, even though it pulled the rug out from under Bob Dole, the Republican candidate for president. (It also helped Lott preserve the Republican majority in the Senate.)

But the salient fact remains: Hillary backed the two measures that were most important in her husband's move to the center—the balanced budget and welfare reform. That these are his two leading achievements as president is further reason to give her credit. Hillary, no less than Bill, had learned the lessons of 1994 and moved to the center as 1996 approached.

So which is she—a liberal or a moderate? A New Democrat or an old-fashioned one? The answer is pretty easy to trace: Between 1980 and 1990 she was a moderate. From 1991 until 1994 she was a liberal. In 1995 and 1996, she moderated as Bill sought re-election. Fighting her husband's impeachment in 1997–1998, she veered left to keep the loyalty of the Senate Democrats who controlled her husband's fate. Running for the Senate in 1999–2000, Hillary moved back toward the middle to get elected.

Growth? Or opportunism? My bet is that it was just a liberal always looking for an opening.

1996: CLINTON'S RE-ELECTION

Despite Hillary's successful trip to China and the favorable coverage of *It Takes a Village,* the bad taste of health care reform lingered in the public's memory. The constant scandals whirling around Hillary made for daily negative media coverage that did nothing to improve her image.

As Bill girded for his re-election battle against Bob Dole, Hillary began to focus on the upcoming Democratic National Convention as a way to rehabilitate her image. Here she would be able to command a national television audience for an hour-long speech to the gathering—the ideal way to reposition herself.

In helping the Clintons plan the Democratic Convention, I couldn't help noticing a growing paranoia in Hillary's attitudes. She hunkered down into an us-versus-them posture that I found downright scary. I remember thinking: *This must be how it was to be around Nixon during his presidency.*

Hillary had always been partisan, and lately a little moralistic as well. Until now, though, I had never found her to be paranoid. But even paranoids have real enemies, and Hillary's had been attacking her for four years. It's not surprising that her personality showed the results. Two examples stand out in my mind, one involving the Secret Service and the other concerning tickets to the convention.

We arranged for the president to arrive at the Democratic National Convention in Chicago by train, stopping at all the swing states en route. Originally, the idea was to begin the train trip in Pittsburgh and wind our way through Ohio and Indiana, ending up in Chicago. Virtually every swing state Clinton needed to carry the election was located within five hundred miles of the convention hall, so we wanted to make a big production of the president's arrival by campaigning in as many of those key states as possible.

While we were preparing the trip, though, we learned that the Secret Service would want to shut down rail travel in the cities through which the president was to pass. This caused a specific problem in Pittsburgh, which turned out to be the hub of commercial rail travel in much of the United States, so we had to cancel the plans to begin the trip there. In the process, I learned a great deal about Hillary's attitude toward the Secret Service.

In her memoir, the former first lady strikes the gracious and generous pose toward the Secret Service that one would expect from the HILLARY brand. "The Secret Service adapted to our needs, and we to theirs," she writes. Hillary describes the "tone of cooperation and flexibility that came to characterize our relationships with the agents sworn to protect us."

As we planned the train trip, though, the friction between the Service and the first lady was palpable. During a meeting in the White House Map Room, Hillary warned that the Secret Service "will shut down the entire Eastern Seaboard just to embarrass us if we give them the excuse [by going to Pittsburgh]. How will it look if all trains are shut down? They do this to us all the time. They're mainly Republicans. They hate us. They always take the most extreme option just to cause us embarrassment. We enter a city and they close down all traffic. We can't go to Pittsburgh."

A second example of Hillary's growing paranoia came a few weeks before the Democratic Convention. Bill had recently celebrated his fiftieth birthday at Radio City Music Hall to raise funds for the party. Hecklers from the radical gay group Act Up interrupted the president's speech with catcalls, demanding more action on gay issues. As they were hauled out by the police, Clinton interrupted his speech to urge the cops to be careful and remember that the demonstrators had rights, too.

In a meeting to plan the convention, Hillary alluded to the Radio City experience and pointed out that they had been sitting in the most expensive seats nearest the podium. "How could they afford five-hundred dollar tickets?" she demanded. She said she was sure that the Republicans had paid for the seats for the demonstrators and said she expected them to use similar tactics at our convention.

Her solution? "I want tight control on who gets tickets and screening to keep out protesters," she proposed. "I want us to know who goes into that hall and where they come from." I had visions of the news stories likely to result from such a public show of both paranoia and vulnerability. When I raised my concerns with the president later, he told me he'd heard nothing about Hillary's idea and assured me he wouldn't do anything like she suggested. There were no hecklers at the convention, and no screening either.

Time and again, Bill Clinton would leaven Hillary's paranoia and allow us to overlook her more brazen attempts to exert control and stifle criticism. Hillary's outbursts were never the final word. A cooler head with a more detached, professional outlook, Bill would make the final decisions. In a Hillary presidency, however, the roles would be reversed. With Hillary making the decisions, Bill Clinton might be reduced to sending impotent alarms whenever disaster was near.

If the 1996 Chicago convention was a theatrical production, Hillary was starring in the role of hometown girl. She arrived at the convention several days before Bill so she could accompany reporters to all of the sites with which she was familiar as a child.

Some of us in the campaign worried about holding the convention in Chicago in the first place. The comparisons with the 1968 convention—with its tear gas, night sticks, and blood—could hurt our attempt to moderate the Democrats' image. On the other hand, Hillary loved having it in Chicago, a city where she could play a featured role.

But HILLARY is a New York brand, so in *Living History* she gives the city of her childhood short shrift. "I arrived in Chicago on Sunday, August 25, three days ahead of Bill," she writes. "Betsy Ebeling had organized a gathering of my family and friends at Riva's Restaurant, which sits on Navy Pier overlooking Lake Michigan. I quickly caught Chicago's excitement about hosting the convention."

And that's it. As she reinvents herself as a New Yorker, Chicago seems to have become a distant memory. At the time, though, her trip back to her childhood haunts loomed large to her, and became central to our plans to carry the swing state of Illinois.

Hillary focused intently on her speech to the convention. Her first appearance on the national stage since the 1994 elections, it was a vital opportunity to reinvent herself as an education and child care expert and distance herself from the health care debacle.

Like most people, I was always very impressed with how Hillary protected Chelsea from the media. She realized that if she and Bill put Chelsea out there, the reporters would take shots. But if they avoided trying to exploit her too overtly, she would remain more or less off limits.

Of course, Hillary took her daughter with her whenever she could on her trips, but the press seemed to feel that her mere presence at Mom's side was all right.

Before the convention, I called Hillary to suggest that Chelsea second Bill's nomination. "That isn't going to happen," she said flatly. "And I don't want to hear anything more about it from you or anyone else."

Okay. Got it.

And yet, when it came time to give her speech, Hillary invoked Chelsea's name no less than six times—and often unnecessarily. Indeed, throughout the speech Hillary sought to illustrate each of the points in her husband's program with examples from Chelsea's life, giving the address a distinctly *Ozzie and Harriet* feel:

- "Our daughter, Chelsea, will graduate from college in 2001, at the dawn of the next century."
- "It is hard for any of us to know what the world will look like then, much less when Chelsea is my age, in the year 2028. But one thing we know for sure is that change is certain—progress is not."
- "And Bill was with me when Chelsea was born, in the delivery room, in my hospital room, and when we brought our baby daughter home."
- "You know, Bill and I are fortunate that our jobs have allowed us to take breaks from work not only when Chelsea was born, but to attend her school events and take her to the doctor. But millions of other parents can't get time off."
- "Chelsea has spent only one night in the hospital after she had her tonsils out, but Bill and I couldn't sleep at all that night."
- "Sometimes, late at night, when I see Chelsea doing her home-work, or watching TV, or talking to a friend on the phone, I

think to myself, her life and the lives of millions of boys and girls will be better because of what all of us are doing together."

Was Hillary protecting Chelsea or just keeping her for her own political use?

With Chelsea's help, Dr. Hillary yielded to Professor Hillary, as she succeeded in burying health care in her past. Her speech was a great success. It moved her husband up two points in that night's postspeech tracking poll—the yardstick for virtue in those days.

It was a great kickoff to the campaign. And yet, once again, *Living History* makes no mention at all of her role in the general election of 1996. The text goes directly from her convention speech to election night in less than a page. What happened to the intervening two months? Why no discussion of the dozens, if not hundreds, of speeches she made on her husband's behalf?

In particular, Hillary never mentions her role in campaign fundraising. Yet it was almost as extensive as Bill's. In early 1996, President Clinton angrily told me: "You want me to issue executive orders and make speeches, but all I have time to do is to raise the money for your television ads. I can't think. I can't act. All I do is raise money. And it's all Hillary does, all Al [Gore] does, all Tipper does."

Few politicians like fund-raising; it's time-consuming and often demeaning. It's understandable that HILLARY might want to forget how much effort Hillary put into it. Understandable, but not exactly candid.

Election night was a bittersweet experience for the Clintons. Upbeat as always in her memoir, she writes: "I felt it was more than a victory for the President; it was a vindication of the American people."

Nice spin. But the fact that the Republicans retained their control of Congress (thanks to Trent Lott's late session pragmatism), even as Dole was getting trounced, bespoke a lack of real trust in the Clintons and an ardent desire to maintain healthy checks and balances in

Washington. While the president was re-elected by "a solid eight percentage points" (Hillary's phrase), a Republican Congress meant that Hillary and Bill could look forward to more committee hearings, investigations, and problems.

Bill was upset that he did not win a majority of the vote, falling short by a few tenths of a percent. The key reason was that the Clinton campaign ended the 1996 election in a nose dive, driven down by the growing scandal about their fund-raising tactics and the possible involvement of money from sources connected to the Chinese government.

As Hillary sets the stage for the second term in her memoir, she focuses on her shift "from a highly visible role as Bill's chief health care advisor . . . to a more private—but equally active—role during the two years following the mid-term elections in 1994."

But Hillary realized there was a hole in her CV. As she looked toward her own future, she knew that a record of public advocacy alone would not be enough to lay the basis for a Hillary candidacy—a lesson she'd learned back in 1990, when our polls revealed that Arkansas voters still saw her as a subset of her husband.

And so, in *Living History,* Hillary takes pains to let us know that she really had power on the inside all along. The HILLARY brand requires a resume of public achievements to put forward—and since she can't quite muster that on her own, she uses Bill's. She may have hidden it at the time, but the HILLARY of *Living History* was at the center of the action all along.

"I had begun working inside the White House," she writes, "and with other Administration officials to save vital services and programs targeted by Gingrich and the Republicans. I also spent two years helping the President's top advisors refine welfare reform and stave off cuts in legal services, the arts, education, Medicare, and Medicaid. As part of our continuing effort on health care reform, I lobbied Democrats and Republicans on Capitol Hill to initiate a comprehensive program to make vaccines available at low or no cost for children."

Fact check: Hillary did, indeed, play the key role in the vaccination program and was important to welfare reform. But the rest of this account reads like a how-to manual on padding a resume.

Her role in the budget fight with the Republicans was minimal, although she was strongly committed to the president's position. By this time Hillary recognized that she was like a red cape to the Republican bull, so she stayed largely out of sight, anxious not to inflame an already tense situation. She was involved in neither the negotiations with Congress, nor the design or content of Clinton's speeches during the period. She had little input even in the 1995 and 1996 State of the Union speeches, which I helped the president prepare. (I still have my typed copies, with his neat handwritten inserts.)

Within the administration, Hillary *was* a voice against compromise on vital programs, and for her private advocacy of the White House balanced budget plan she deserves special credit. Instead, though, the HILLARY brand is eager to take credit for advances she had little to do with.

The most important result of this series of ideological shifts, of adaptations in service of opportunity, and, yes, of newly mastered skills, is that Hillary Rodham Clinton became a political professional. The sudden need to manage her husband's career after his 1980 defeat; the experience of formulating and passing education reform in Arkansas; her shock at discovering that the state's voters nevertheless saw her as Bill's surrogate, not yet as her own person; her disastrous handling of health care reform once her husband reached the White House; the strategy of shifting her energies from backroom activism to public advocacy; the need to focus on incremental improvements rather than unreachable solutions; her use of foreign travel; and her balancing of the traditional with the novel in the first lady's role: All have come to define the politician that she is today.

But there was another side to Hillary's experiences during her husband's first term. Constantly, continuously, she was under fire for scandals that were laid at her doorstep. Weary of rehashing the controversy of that period, one is tempted to pass it by, simply to forget about it.

HILLARY hasn't forgotten the controversy. But neither has she remembered it . . . not accurately, anyway. Instead she stoutly defends her innocence, assails her critics, and continues to misrepresent the facts. Perhaps she is just trying to salvage what she can from a series of unfortunate episodes. But it seems equally likely that she has really not learned from them. To understand the significance of her lapses of memory, to help us judge whether Hillary's ethical boundaries remain as porous today as they have proved in the past, we must examine the record of how HILLARY has hidden Hillary's more worldly—not to say acquisitive—face.

6

HIDING HILLARY:
THE MATERIAL GIRL

Future generations, when asked to free-associate the words "Clinton" and "scandal," will probably summon up only the name "Lewinsky," since that particular outrage led to the historic impeachment of a president. But the string of Hillary-generated scandals during the two Clinton administrations is stunningly impressive on its own.

The Whitewater investment; the firing of the White House Travel Office employees; the legal work for the Madison Bank; the hide-and-seek game with billing records; Vince Foster's suicide; the misuse of FBI files; the source of payments to Webb Hubbell: Every one of these was a Hillary Clinton scandal. Even the wanton award of presidential pardons during the last days of the second term, which can be laid at Bill Clinton's feet, weren't his work alone: Among the recipients were her brothers' clients, and some of her most ardent supporters.

Echoing through all of Hillary's scandals—and distinguishing her troubles from the ones that nearly brought down her husband—is the sound of money. Bill had his scandals; Hillary had hers. George Stephanopoulos puts it this way in his memoir, *All Too Human:* "On [Whitewater], Clinton wasn't commander in chief, just a husband beholden to his wife. Hillary was always the first to defend him on

145

bimbo eruptions; now [on Hillary's financial scandals] he had to do the same for her."

At first, one is inclined to forgive Hillary's financial misdeeds. After all, the amounts involved were not large and Bill and Hillary were not wealthy. Sandwiched in between the millionaire presidencies of Carter, Reagan, Bush, and Bush, the Clintons' willingness to cut corners to salt away some savings is not necessarily grounds for outright condemnation.

But as the Clintons have amassed great wealth through their $18 million in book deals and Bill's $10 million annual income, Hillary's avarice has not abated. Her recent conduct suggests that her insensitivity to conflicts of interest and ethics rules, so much in evidence during her Arkansas days, has not changed. If anything, getting away with her past conduct seems to have emboldened her and desensitized her further to ethical lines.

And then there is Hillary's book. If *Living History* is a window on the current evolution of Hillary's ethical sensibilities, we are in for a very tough time if she ever becomes president. Hillary's memoir is one continuous cover-up. Coming so gratuitously, almost four years after she left the White House, the cover-up is more disturbing than the scandals themselves. If Hillary truly believes what she writes about Whitewater, her commodities trading, the gifts, and such, she hasn't learned a thing from her scandals—except to feel free to do it all again.

But what *can* she say? you may ask. She can't very well reverse her statements over the decades and admit fault, can she?

Perhaps not. At the very least, though, she could indicate in general terms that she has learned from her experiences. But she doesn't do that. Instead, to preserve HILLARY's reputation, she reasserts her innocence at the top of her lungs, twisting and spinning the evidence to her advantage, determinedly absolving herself of any blame for anything.

Has she learned? Her account of each of the Hillary scandals in *Living History* suggests not.

It's not terribly difficult to find the source of Hillary's early financial scandals. From the start of the Clintons' political career, Hillary claims that she was in a chronic state of financial insecurity, citing Bill's $35,000 salary as governor. With everything in her husband's life subordinated to the search for political power, according to her, it was her job—and her burden—to care for the Clinton family's material needs.

In *Living History,* she repeats the family mantra: "Money means almost nothing to Bill Clinton. He is not opposed to making money or owning property; it has simply never been a priority. He's happy when he has enough to buy books, watch movies, go out to dinner, and travel. . . . But I worried that because politics is an inherently unstable profession, we needed to build up a nest egg."

Certainly $35,000 a year is no huge amount of money for a family of three, but it is misleading to compare Clinton's salary as governor with a normal family paycheck. In the Arkansas Governor's Mansion, the Clintons got free luxurious housing, furniture, meals, entertainment, transportation, babysitting, housekeeping, servants, state automobiles including fuel and insurance, chauffeurs, telephones, utilities, home repairs, health insurance, and homeowners' insurance. In addition to a substantial entertainment budget, the governor also received a food allowance of more than $50,000 per year. A state credit card paid for travel. And none of these perks was taxable. Indeed, about the only things the Clintons actually had to pay for were books, clothing, and restaurant meals. And, of course, Hillary was making substantially more than $35,000 per year.

Add it up: Combining Bill's salary with her own and throwing in the food budget, the governor's entertainment allowance, and the various free services that came with the Mansion, the Clintons were quite well off—and carried very few financial obligations.

Yet Hillary felt broke—so much so that, early in her husband's political career, the Clintons actually donated his used underwear to charity two separate years to garner the tax deduction.

It was this mind-set—this combination of perceived deprivation with a sense of entitlement—that led Hillary to take extraordinary risks at the start of Bill's governorship to make money. Whitewater, the commodities trading, and her representation of the Madison Bank were all indications of Hillary's increasingly insatiable desire for money, always masquerading as a need for security.

And there was nothing the Clintons wanted that they couldn't get somebody to give them. When Chelsea was young, Hillary wanted to build a swimming pool for her on the grounds of the Mansion. Determined not to pay for it herself, and savvy enough not to use tax money, she arranged for private donors—the same type of fat cat friends who would dominate their White House years—to chip in for Chelsea's pool.

When she told me of her plans, I was astounded. I felt that voters of that very poor state would see the pool as a symbol of pretentious wealth, and hold it against the Clintons at the next election. And what special favors would the donors have gotten for their money, other than the satisfaction of knowing that Hillary could do her laps? "How could you even think of that?" I asked. "You'll get killed."

"Well, it's not really for us," Hillary replied evenly. "The mansion is for all future governors of the state; they'll be able to use it."

"You'll never be able to sell that argument," I shot back. "The next time you fly over Little Rock, look down and count the number of swimming pools." I asked her a pointed question: "The next time I do a poll, do you want me to ask whether people have swimming pools?"

That got her mad. "Why can't we lead the lives of normal people? They can give their daughters swimming pools; why can't we?"

"You can—you just have to pay for it," I muttered as she stalked off.

After the election, when nobody was looking, the Clintons passed the hat and built the pool.

After years of making a lawyer's six-figure salary, augmented by Bill's income and the substantial perks of his office, Hillary still saw herself as a victim who had sacrificed a life of financial security.

The fact that she lived in a mansion, surrounded by servants, chauffeurs, and other staff, seems not to have mattered.

At the other end of Bill's political career, Hillary again took extraordinary risks to make money. The prospect of losing their government-subsidized luxurious lifestyle at last apparently drove Hillary into panic.

No surprise: It would take a truly extraordinary annual income to afford all the perks that came for free with the governorship of Arkansas, much less the presidency. Not only is the White House one of the most luxurious residences in the world, it offers a panoply of cooks, florists, beauty experts, drivers, cars, jets, helicopters, pilots, a vacation home at Camp David, a movie theater, pool, Jacuzzi, tennis court, hot tub, bowling alley, workout gym, the presidential box at the Kennedy Center, any painting at the National Gallery, elegant parties, the ability to invite any entertainer to perform anything at any time or any thinker to lecture: The Clintons had the world at their fingertips, a combination of privileges that's not for sale at any price.

Faced with such a prodigious loss, at the end of her husband's presidency Hillary reached out for money in every way she could. As with her Arkansas swimming pool, her solution was to solicit donations and gifts, taking huge political risks in the process.

Like bookends on Bill's career, Hillary's early greed in Whitewater and the commodities scandals, and her later greed in her huge book deal, call for gifts, and massive expropriation of furniture and other presents intended for the White House, triggered financial scandals that almost eradicated the good work her husband was trying to do in between.

In part, her latter-day avarice was disguised as a need to pay the massive legal bills she racked up defending her investments and Bill's affairs. But one wonders if these legal bills are, in fact, ever going to be paid, or if they live on only as an excuse for Hillary's acquisitiveness. The Clintons' financial statements show continued debt for legal work, and few payments, despite their massive increases in income. They certainly are in no hurry to pay their lawyers, even as they rake in money hand over fist.

But mere acquisitiveness does not explain Hillary's grasping. After all, the Clintons have shown an amazing ability to make money after their White House years. Bill's book deal exceeds $10 million; hers was worth $8 million. Added to that, of course, is the former president's almost unlimited ability to make money giving speeches. So why the grasping materialism and financial insecurity? Why take the kinds of risks she has?

Her sense of entitlement seems to have lingered long after any perceived financial need has been satisfied. By the end of her husband's governorship, Hillary had come to embrace the idea that she was the one who gave up the beckoning blue chip legal career in downtown New York or Chicago, forsaking a cushy future for a life on the hustings in Arkansas. Repeated constantly, this account of history—revisionist though it may be—lay at the core of Hillary's self-image.

And even at the Rose Law Firm in Little Rock, Hillary would point out, she could never make the kind of money she might have earned, because of the demands on her schedule—campaigning for her husband, heading the education task force, not to mention doing the job of Arkansas first lady. The leaves of absence and days away from the office made it impossible, even here, to realize her financial potential.

Her sense of deprivation and feeling of entitlement were interdependent. Was she not sacrificing everything to promote the public good through her husband's election to public office? Had she not ventured into the heartland of deprivation—the 49th state—to bring progress and enlightenment? When she received material compensation, minimal as it was, was that not truly her just reward for such sacrifice?

It is likely that this sense of entitlement—not simple greed—was what led Hillary to take the risks she has to make money. For all of her vaunted discipline, this is the one area where her self-control goes on frequent, extended holiday. Her need to extract what she feels is just compensation for all her good work is one of the controlling forces in her life.

Such avarice is very dangerous in politics. Politicians and presidents are always being offered opportunities for personal enrichment. Some are ethical. Others are not. Anyone in public life needs sensitive antennae to tell which is which. Of our recent presidents, Truman, Eisenhower, Kennedy, Ford, Carter, Reagan, and Bush Sr. clearly had an internal sense that made them back off when there was an ethical question. Johnson, Nixon, and Clinton did not.

Where is Hillary likely to fall on that list? Some might argue that Hillary's newfound wealth will eliminate the temptation to cross the line. But Hillary's refusal, in *Living History,* to admit that there even *is* a line—or that she has ever crossed it—gives one pause.

CONFLICTS OF INTEREST

All elected officials, and the members of their immediate families, must make a special effort to resist propositions that entail conflicts of interest. If they wish to avoid reproach (and prison), they must be able to distinguish between an honest offer and an obvious bribe.

Thus far, Hillary has had three narrow escapes during her political career. Her dealings in commodities, the Whitewater real estate deal, and her legal representation of the Madison Bank at the Rose Law Firm all might easily have ruined her, and dragged Bill down as well. But her lengthy defense of her conduct in *Living History* reminds one of the Bourbon kings of France, of whom Talleyrand reportedly observed, "they learn nothing and they forget nothing."

Scandal one, the commodities deal, raises serious questions. The only reason there was not a public inquiry about this issue was that the statute of limitations had lapsed by the time it was disclosed. And the timing was no accident: The Clintons had concealed Hillary's trading profits by refusing to release their tax returns for the relevant years. By the time the media had unearthed the scandal, and pressure for a prosecution started to build, she was out of the woods.

In *Living History,* Hillary writes that her trading gains were "examined *ad infinitum* after Bill became President," and that "the conclusion was that, like many investors at the time, I'd been fortunate." But the only truly fortunate thing about the affair for the Clintons was the fact that Hillary managed to avoid any investigation. And just to be clear about the record: There was never any *official* investigation of her trades—only the work of enterprising investigative reporters. And thus there was no consensus "conclusion" that Hillary had just been lucky. That self-serving judgment was hers alone.

At around the time when her husband was being elected governor in 1978, Hillary began investing in commodities futures, under the guidance of her friend Jim Blair. There she parlayed a $1,000 investment into $100,000, making more than $6,000 on the first day.

Hillary's advisors, attorney Jim Blair and broker Robert L. "Red" Bone, were especially knowledgeable about the flow of cattle onto the market: Blair was actively working as outside counsel for Tyson Foods, and Bone had also been associated with the company. By gauging and anticipating the ups and downs of the industry, they were able to give Hillary key guidance about her investments. And, as numerous reporters have since established in great detail, Hillary's advisors were rewarded handsomely, in any number of ways, for the insights they shared with the first lady of Arkansas.

The Clintons knew that their commodities trades would sound alarm bells if they ever came to light. I know, because I watched them try to cover them up.

In 1982, as they were campaigning to win back the governorship, it became obvious to me that the Clintons were determined to hide something on their tax returns from public view. During the campaign, I urged them to release their income tax returns. It would be a good issue against Frank White, the Republican incumbent we had to beat. After all, I figured, Republicans often resist releasing their tax returns because of their business dealings. And I had totally bought into the myth that the Clintons were frugal, parsimonious people who cared little about money; what could they ever have done that might look embarrassing on a tax return?

So I asked Bill if he and Hillary would make their returns public, so that we could challenge White to reveal his.

"Of course," Bill answered. "No problem." But when the time came to release them, he turned finicky. "I'll give them out for the last two years only," he said.

"But what about the time you served in office as governor?" I asked.

"No," he replied firmly. "I'm only releasing two years."

"But if we are going to use the issue against Frank White, we need to release returns for the years you were governor. Otherwise, why should he have to?"

Bill glared at me; the discussion was clearly over. The Clintons released their tax returns, but not for 1978 or 1979. *Why not?* I wondered. When the scandal about Hillary's winnings in cattle futures emerged, I had my answer: They were apparently anxious to hide her profits, lest there be questions about insider trading—or for a *quid pro quo* with Blair of state action in return for private benefit. After all, how *did* Hillary acquire the acumen to turn $1,000 into almost $100,000 in such a specialized market?

When the question was first raised in public, Hillary claimed that she had studied the *Wall Street Journal* to educate herself on the market. But then the *Journal* pulled the rug out from under her. Having examined its archives, James Stewart reported in *Blood Sport* that "It was obvious that they would have been of scant value to any trader. Ultimately . . . the first lady backed off the claim, acknowledging that it was Blair who had guided her trading."

Was Hillary's trading based on insider information and hence illegal? The difference between legal and illegal inputs in commodities trading, it turns out, is quite a hair to split. But, as judges are fond of saying, we do not have to "reach" that issue. The real question is, why did he share it with Hillary Clinton? Hillary acts as if friendship were the sole reason. But here's what Blair and Tyson Foods, his client, got from the Clintons over the years:

- The *New York Times* reported that "Tyson benefited from a variety of state actions, including $9 million in government loans, the placement of company executives on important state boards and favorable decisions on environmental issues."
- Blair was appointed chairman of the board of the University of Arkansas by Governor Clinton.
- President Clinton named Blair's wife, Diane, to the board of the Corporation for Public Broadcasting.
- As Arkansas attorney general, Clinton intervened in a lawsuit that helped Tyson Foods.
- Governor Clinton reappointed a Tyson veterinarian to the Livestock and Poultry Commission, which regulated Tyson Foods.
- When a Tyson plant leaked waste into a creek that eventually polluted the water supply of the town of Dry Creek, Arkansas, the state never enforced an order making the company treat its wastes. After nearby families began to get sick, Clinton had to declare the town a disaster area.
- According to the *Times,* Ron Brown, Clinton's secretary of commerce, "reversed course and instituted rules that would allow Arctic Alaska (a Tyson subsidiary) and other big trawlers to dominate the nation's $100 million whiting catch."

Although James Blair was never charged with any wrongdoing, he was not helping Hillary and Bill Clinton solely out of the goodness of his heart. Only their deft concealment of the transactions, until the statute of limitations had put them out of reach, helped the Clintons avoid scrutiny for their behavior. And this is no mere archeological artifact to be dug up by those seeking to skewer a future Hillary candidacy: Senator Clinton's misleading account of the affair in *Living History* clearly puts the issue back into play—lies, ob-fuscations, and all.

For example, Hillary writes that "Our tax returns from 1979 . . . had been audited by the IRS and our records were all in order."

Not true. In fact, Hillary *did not* report her commodities profits on her 1980 tax returns; indeed, she reported a loss of $1,000.00. In April 1994, Clinton attorney David Kendall had to announce that the Clintons were paying $14,615.00 in additional taxes, interest, and penalty on their underreported income for these years.

And Hillary keeps up the charade that she figured out which investments to make on her own. In *Living History,* she writes: "I started looking for opportunities I could afford [to invest money]. My friend Diane Blair was married to someone who knew the intricacies of the commodities market, and he was willing to share his expertise."

The world is *filled* with people who are willing to be very, very nice to those in power. Newly elected officials are suddenly inundated with new best friends, and many of them come bearing gifts. Hillary's failure to wonder why Blair's husband was so willing to share his expertise can, perhaps, be chalked up to naiveté. She was, after all, only thirty-two at the time. But it's a little more difficult to forgive her continuing, blithe refusal to see through his generosity, even at the mature age of fifty-six.

And Hillary also knows that after she cashed out, the brokers who assisted her were prosecuted by market regulators for the same kind of practices that allowed Hillary to amass such huge profits. She does admit, in *Living History,* that they did not make out as well as she did. What she neglects to mention is that they were investigated and punished.

The *Washington Post*'s account suggests what probably happened. Hillary's brokers would "allocate losing investments to some of [their] clients in order to benefit preferred customers." John Troelstrup, then regional counsel for the Commodity Futures Trading Commission, said "one aspect of the investigation by the exchange focused on 'block trading,' in which . . . [they] entered large numbers of contract orders without identifying the appropriate client accounts." According to Troelstrup, their conduct "could give someone the opportunity, to divvy up trading profits and losses however they saw fit"—that is, to credit clients like Hillary with the winning calls, and other, less prized clients with the losing ones.

For such conduct—intended to help Hillary and other favored customers—the brokerage firm's president was eventually suspended from trading for six months, the firm itself was fined $250,000, and Hillary's broker got a three-year suspension.

Did Hillary's narrow brush with the law teach her a lesson? Her self-righteous defense of her commodities profits suggest otherwise.

Even now, it is hard to fathom Hillary's decision to take such appalling political risks right at the beginning of her husband's governorship. When the profits came rolling in, Hillary must have known she was getting preferential treatment from someone who expected state favors in return. Otherwise, why would she have gone to such lengths to avoid releasing her tax returns for those years?

Scandal two, the Whitewater real estate deal, was another clear conflict of interest. Behind all the complexity, it looks like another straight quid pro quo.

Here's what Bill and Hillary got:

- Jim and Susan McDougal paid 91 percent of the costs associated with the deal, but let Bill and Hillary Clinton retain 50 percent of the equity.
- When the property began to lose money, the McDougals paid off the loan the Clintons had taken out to finance their down payment.
- McDougal hired Hillary, at a retainer of $2,000 per month, to represent the Madison Guaranty Savings and Loan Association as its attorney.
- Jim McDougal held a fund-raiser that netted $35,000 for Bill's gubernatorial campaign.

And here's what McDougal got:

- Clinton appointed McDougal's close friend, Beverly Lambert, as Arkansas Banking Commissioner. McDougal also got "control" of the Savings and Loan Board through several appointments he says he "arranged." Clinton, McDougal explains, was "amenable" to his suggestions to fill these positions.
- Lambert approved McDougal's purchase of a bank in Kingston, Arkansas. "It was good to have the right connections in state government," McDougal said.
- Clinton named Beverly Bassett, McDougal's candidate, as securities commissioner.
- Bassett allowed Madison to issue preferred stock to raise capital. Hillary was McDougal's attorney on the deal.
- Clinton sat in on a meeting McDougal had with the state's Health Department after a state inspector refused to grant septic permits to a subcontractor on one of his developments. McDougal got the permits. As the banker put it: "if I kept up my connection with Clinton, I would never encounter any bureaucratic roadblocks."

The Whitewater investment turned out to be ill-timed. Interest rates soared in the next few years, which cut into the demand for vacation homes. The cash flow that was to have paid the mortgage never materialized, and the deal lost money. But McDougal decided to bail out the Clintons: "I felt a responsibility," he claimed, "for bringing the Clintons into an unprofitable deal and I decided to make the payments myself rather than ask Bill and Hillary for more money."

The Clintons keep saying that they never made money on the deal, but that misses the point. McDougal stopped them from losing their shirts. There was nothing complicated about this classic quid pro quo—a largely questionable relationship between a governor and his wife and a banker/developer. The fact that McDougal was insulating the Clintons from losses, rather than paying them profits, matters little. A favor is a favor.

Hillary cut some big corners during the Whitewater deal—and *Living History* indicates that she's still cutting them. Instead of coming clean on Whitewater, or even avoiding the subject, Hillary perpetuates the cover-up, using the occasion to revisit the Clintons' shopworn roster of hollow Whitewater defenses. To review them one by one:

In *Living History,* HILLARY writes: "Jim [McDougal] asked us [the Clintons] to write checks to help make interest payments or other contributions, and we never questioned his judgment."

The fact is: They paid only about one tenth of what McDougal paid for Whitewater.

HILLARY writes: "Bill and I never deposited money in Madison Guaranty and never borrowed from it."

The fact is: According to McDougal, the Clintons got at least two payoffs, one for $27,600 and another for $5,081.82.

HILLARY writes: "Bill . . . knew he hadn't done anything as Governor to favor McDougal . . ."

The fact is: As noted above, Bill did plenty to help Jim McDougal.

HILLARY writes: McDougal never hired her for legal work; it was really "Rick Massey, a young lawyer at the Rose Law Firm," who arranged for the retainer. She was listed as "the billing partner," she claims, "because Massey was merely an associate."

The fact is: Massey denied her story under oath—and McDougal says he hired Hillary because Bill asked him to.

HILLARY writes: When McDougal offered to buy the Clintons out of their half of Whitewater, "I thought it was a great idea."

The fact is: According to Stewart's Blood Sport, *when Susan McDougal wanted to buy the Clintons out, Hillary said: "No! Jim [McDougal] told me that this was going to pay for college for Chelsea. I still expect it to do that!"*

HILLARY denies that she "knew of any money that could have gone from Madison [Bank] . . . to any of [her] husband's political campaigns."

The fact is: Certainly she knew that Madison had aided his fund-raising efforts: On page 327 of Living History, *Hillary herself mentions a fund-raiser at the Madison Bank.*

HILLARY claims that the final report of the Office of Independent Counsel on Whitewater exonerated her—that the report found no wrongdoing.

The fact is: All the Independent Counsel said was that "the evidence was insufficient" to prove that the Clintons did anything wrong. Why were they unable to find the evidence? Well, Jim McDougal was dead and Susan was jailed for contempt rather than cooperate with the investigation. She was probably waiting it out expecting a presidential pardon as payback for her silence. She ended up getting one. So who was there to testify? The IC's final report was a far cry from exoneration.

Hillary writes warmly of Susan McDougal for choosing years in jail rather than answer Starr's questions. "Susan was suffering in jail for refusing to testify before the Whitewater Grand Jury."

But Hillary hasn't always been so nice about Susan McDougal. When it looked as though she might turn on the Clintons, Hillary told me: "She is such a liar. She worked for [the famous conductor] Zubin Mehta and stole his silver. She's crazy, unstable, and totally dishonest. You can't trust a thing she says." (Susan was eventually acquitted of stealing from Mehta.)

Probably the best indication of the Clintons' actual culpability in Whitewater is that they didn't get their legal fees reimbursed by the federal government. According to the statute under which the Independent Counsel operates, anyone who is the object of a special prosecutor's scrutiny is entitled to reimbursement for legal fees if charges are not filed and if the targets of the inquiry "show that a career prosecutor would not have pursued a similar investigation or delved as deeply."

But the panel that reviewed the Clintons' petition for $3.5 million in reimbursement ruled that their request was without merit, and awarded them only 3 percent of the amount requested (the amount due their lawyers for reviewing the final report). By contrast, President Ronald Reagan was reimbursed for 75 percent of his legal costs in the Iran-Contra scandal; George H. W. Bush got 59 percent. The clear message: Regardless of the final, inconclusive verdict, any competent prosecutor would have smelled something rotten in Whitewater.

STONEWALLING

The real reason the Whitewater scandal remained in the headlines year after year, however, had less to do with the initial deal than with the Clintons' ongoing efforts to cover up the scandal. Rather than provide the press with the information it craved, Hillary "locked down"— in the words of former Clinton aide Lanny Davis—and stonewalled Ken Starr's investigation. At several critical junctures in the twisted trail through Whitewater, all Hillary had to do was to face the media honestly and let them have all the documents. After all, the amount involved in the scandal was petty, it was a long time ago, and it all happened long before Clinton became president. But instead she refused. Over and over again, she cited privacy while her husband claimed executive privilege. It was a disastrous policy—and one for which she nevertheless shows no regret.

In *Living History,* Hillary blandly insists that she cooperated fully with federal investigators, saying that she instructed her lawyer, David Kendall, "to advise the government investigators that we would voluntarily provide them with all documents and cooperate with a grand jury investigation."

Others remember differently. No sooner did Jeff Gerth's initial story about their investment with the McDougals appear in the *New*

York Times than Hillary's damage control team went into overdrive. Gail Sheehy reports that their tactics became known among Clinton campaign staffers as the "fuck you, Jeff Gerth" strategy.

Sheehy relates how "a whole subgroup [in the Clinton campaign] was tasked with defusing this [Whitewater] bombshell. Hillary put Susan Thomases in charge of it. . . . Webb Hubbell and Vince Foster, were assigned to examine all of the Whitewater records and those relating to the Madison Bank . . . they decided what to 'give up' to The New York Times . . . [Finally Thomases] provided fewer than twenty documents."

No doubt this is because, as the *New York Post* reported on January 20, 1996, Hillary told federal banking officials that in 1988 she had sent many of the key documents about her work for Madison Guaranty to be shredded by the Rose Law Firm.

In her answers to written interrogatories, Hillary said that "While I have no personal recollection . . . I am informed that the Rose Law Firm . . . asked its members to review their old files to determine whether the firm could save money by reducing the number of closed, stored files. I cooperated with this effort and indicated that many of my closed client files, apparently including certain files relating to the firm's representation of Madison Guaranty, did not need to be retained."

The *Post* noted that "Mrs. Clinton's decision to have her Madison records destroyed came at a time when Madison was collapsing amid fraud allegations. The S&L failed the following year costing taxpayers an estimated $65 million." Sheehy describes the document destruction in more dramatic terms: "After hours, in the dimly lit Rose Law Firm offices, Vince Foster and Webb Hubbell scoured [Hillary's] records. . . . Withheld were Hillary's billing records, which over the years were to take on the dark nimbus of a smoking gun. The firm's computer hard drives were later 'vacuumed.'"

In *Living History*, Hillary claims that when the *Washington Post* first asked for information about Whitewater, she wondered, "Should we answer questions? Show them documents? If so, which ones?"

Hillary decided to stiff the media and release the documents to the Justice Department alone, which Clinton controlled. The press, of course, smelled something fishy, and stepped up the drumbeat for the appointment of a special prosecutor. Even Democrats demanded that Clinton ask his Justice Department to name one. Hillary resisted every inch of the way, but her refusal to turn over documents had started a forest fire she could not control.

Reflecting on this unfortunate series of decisions, Hillary sees a situation that called not for more candor, but less. "We will never know whether releasing an inevitably incomplete set of personal documents to the *Washington Post* would have averted a special prosecutor. With the wisdom of hindsight, I wish I had fought harder and not let myself be persuaded to take the path of least resistance." (Reminder: The documents were "inevitably incomplete," of course, because she had shredded them!)

While I was working for the Clintons, I had a firsthand experience with the tactics they used to distract, delay, and derail the work of Special Prosecutor Kenneth Starr. The episode concerned the Clintons and U.S. District Court Judge Harry Woods.

In *Living History,* Hillary blasts Starr for getting Woods disqualified from presiding over the Whitewater prosecutions of Jim and Susan McDougal and Arkansas Governor Jim Guy Tucker. "In more than fifteen years on the bench, Judge Woods had earned a reputation for fair, nearly airtight decisions that were rarely overturned— until he got in Starr's way."

Yet in point of fact, Judge Woods had just been overturned—on a Whitewater-related case. And one more fact goes unmentioned in *Living History*: Woods was an old Arkansas buddy of the Clintons, one who had been invited to the White House and even slept in the infamous Lincoln Bedroom.

In July 1995, Janet Reno had intervened in Whitewater by advising Judge Woods that, in her opinion, Starr had jurisdiction to prosecute a potential player in the Whitewater scandal. Shortly thereafter, an emissary called me on behalf of one figure, who was alarmed at the possible ramifications of Reno's move. The emissary reached me late one Friday night, and said he had a message for President Clinton from this old Arkansas acquaintance. "Furious" at the president, the acquaintance had "screamed": "If Clinton is going to play the game that way, you tell that son of a bitch that I know all about the IDC."

IDC was another name for a shady real estate deal more commonly known as Castle Grande—a phony setup where McDougal used Webb Hubbell's father-in-law as a front man to buy property because federal regulators wouldn't let him do it himself.

The attorney for the IDC/Castle Grande deal? Hillary Clinton.

Mrs. Clinton had a dilemma. If she admitted she did the legal work on IDC/Castle Grande, she would be acknowledging that she helped a deal go through that was later found to be fraudulent. But she had billed Madison for her legal work on the deal as part of her effort to justify the $2,000 monthly retainer the bank was paying to the Rose Law Firm. On the other hand, if she claimed she *hadn't* done the legal work on IDC, it would raise questions about overbilling her client—possibly landing her in the same soup as Webb Hubbell, whose overbilling had resulted in a criminal conviction and time in federal prison. She was between a rock and a hard place.

To complicate matters, Hillary had already testified, under oath, that she had never worked on Castle Grande, but in her testimony had never mentioned her work on IDC, the other name for Castle Grande. To be sure, she had left herself an out: Hillary later told Barbara Walters that she "did work for . . . IDC"—but claimed that it "was not related to Castle Grande." As Joyce Milton writes: "when she was asked [about Castle Grande] she decided not to take the risk of telling the whole truth. Like her husband . . . she seemed to see testimony under oath as a kind of word game, in which she gave answers that might be technically compliant, but that appeared to be lies to people who did not have the benefit of Ivy League law degrees."

All of this raised even more suspicion when the relevant billing records disappeared. When they finally turned up a year later, they showed that Hillary had actually billed for sixty hours of legal work for Madison. In *Living History,* Hillary describes this work as "minimal." Some might argue that sixty hours isn't exactly minimal; either way, though, it's easy to see why the implied threat to reveal the story of IDC would have alarmed the Clintons. After receiving the call from Arkansas, I called Bill Clinton at the White House residence at 12:30 A.M., waking him up. "I have some information you need to hear about," I said as Clinton answered the phone blearily.

"Can it wait until Monday?" he asked, instantly awake.

"No," I replied, obviously implying that we shouldn't discuss the matter over the phone.

"Come to see me right after the radio address tomorrow," Clinton said and hung up.

I asked Eileen to accompany me on the trip from Connecticut to Washington. I knew the elves on the White House staff would be surprised to see me in the building on a Saturday, but my wife's presence would make them more likely to chalk the visit up as a social call. But that didn't stop George Stephanopoulos from nosing around, trying to figure out what I was up to. (Years later, in his book, George recalled my alerting him to Clinton's problems with Reno.)

Eileen and I joined the president in the Oval Office right after his speech. I let Eileen, the lawyer, tell him the story of the call. As he listened, the president turned white—whiter than I had ever seen him. He sat heavily in his desk chair and let out a sigh, running his hand over his face.

"What do you think he meant?" Clinton asked.

"I don't know, but I think he thinks you know," she answered.

Clinton was silent for a few minutes, and then fell all over himself thanking us for coming to give him the information. Before I left, though, he pointed his long forefinger in my face angrily and hissed: "Janet Reno is the single worst mistake I ever made. The worst appointment I have ever made."

After Eileen and I returned home to Connecticut, Clinton called me late that night. "I just wanted to thank you for coming to see me today," Clinton said. Then he added, "I took care of that problem." We hung up.

Imagine my surprise a few weeks later, when Judge Woods ruled that Starr had no jurisdiction—just as the person threatening Clinton had wanted. The decision stank to high heaven; it was quickly reversed on appeal—and the appellate court took the unusual step of removing Woods from the case, so strongly did they object to his decision and suspect his motive for making it.

What had Clinton done? I wondered. *Had he called the judge? Intervened in the proceedings? And possibly even committed an impeachable offense in the process?* I had no idea. But my mind reeled at the lengths it seemed he would go to protect Hillary.

A year later I got another call, this time seeking a favor. This caller asked me to pass along a message from Jim Guy Tucker, who had been convicted and removed from office as Arkansas governor. "You tell that son of a bitch that he owes me a pardon. He owes me a pardon. He owes me a pardon."

I declined to pass the message on to Clinton. Let them both stew, I thought. I decided I didn't want to be involved in any more message-passing, and that was the end of it.

Whitewater and the Madison Guaranty–Castle Grande scandals had each started with the corrupting pursuit of relatively small amounts of money. The corruption led to a lie, and the first lie, as it often does, led to another and another.

Will Hillary stop doing this kind of thing if she moves back into the White House? Her consuming need for money, and the frustrated sense of entitlement that it kindled, may have diminished since her Arkansas days, though the lesson of other presidents with similar money fixations is not encouraging. But what about the self-righteous perfectionism that led to the cover-up? Or Hillary's inability, indeed refusal, to admit the slightest degree of error?

This brittle defensiveness resonates through the pages of *Living History*. Hillary—or, rather, HILLARY—never does anything wrong. She is always perfect, always the victim. Others are always getting her wrong. As long as she refuses reflexively to admit to wrongdoing, though, she may be susceptible to such temptations in the future. A second Clinton presidency will always be at risk of falling into one of these endless scandals that delight Washington and drive the rest of us crazy.

Publisher and columnist Tina Brown has an interesting take on why many high-profile women tend to be perfectionists. Commenting on the Martha Stewart case, she said, "There is no doubt that women like Hillary, women like Martha, carry the freight of knowing exactly the kind of flack that's going to ensue if they put one misstep. Men are not fretted with that as much. Men could think, 'you know what? I'll go down. I'll say it was a mistake. You know, it will be fine. I'll get away with it.' . . . [But women think] 'Oh my God, I have made a mistake. I'm going to get torn from limb to limb.' . . . That's what made her [Martha Stewart] lie in the first place."

Hillary's own perspective on the Stewart verdict was more predictable. "It is often . . . that women in positions of visibility are held to another standard. I hope that wasn't in play here." Another high-profile woman caught under the harsh light of public scrutiny—and another class action defense!

That same instinct to cover up wrongdoing seems to have been behind the Clintons' efforts to funnel money to Webb Hubbell, Hillary's former Rose Law Firm partner and Bill's associate attorney general, even as he went to prison for overbilling, in a case brought by Starr for the main purpose of pressuring Webb to talk.

Hubbell had swindled the Rose Law Firm, including his partner, Hillary. Within a few months of his resignation from the Justice Department, though, the Clintons and their friends had helped him get more than $500,000 in consulting contracts.

In *Living History*, Hillary says that she didn't know about Hubbell's overbilling when she encouraged Clintonistas to arrange for this largesse, saying that "I assumed that Webb was also being falsely accused."

But the *New York Times* reported that "President Clinton's closest confidants, attorneys James B. Blair and David E. Kendall, were aware of the seriousness of legal problems facing former Associate Attorney General Webster L. Hubbell, even before he resigned in March 1994." According to the *Times*, "Blair was told [that the Rose] law firm . . . had strong proof of wrongdoing by Hubbell, and warned [the] Clintons that Hubbell needed to resign from the department as quickly as possible." So Hillary likely knew about the overbilling, three months before Webb quit. But she had to pretend she didn't know. Otherwise, how could she defend all the consulting deals she threw his way?

But Hillary would have been concerned about ensuring Hubbell's silence. As Jim McDougal said, "Webb Hubbell is a person who had all the documents in his personal possession when they cleaned out the Rose Law Firm to come to Washington. He knows all the twists and turns . . . he knows where the bodies are buried. Webb Hubbell is the guy they [the special prosecutor] have to get to talk."

In her attack on Richard Nixon in *Living History*, Hillary condemns him for "paying off witnesses to silence them or influence their testimony." How else would she describe the White House efforts to help get money to Webb Hubbell?

One other bit of housekeeping.

In *Living History*, Hillary writes that "In late 1995, Dick Morris came to see me to deliver a bizarre message: I was going to be indicted for something as yet undefined and 'people close to Starr' suggested I accept the indictment and ask Bill to pardon me before trial. I assumed Morris was carrying water for his Republican clients or contacts, so I chose my words very carefully. 'Tell your sources to report to Starr's people that even though I have done nothing wrong, I'm well aware that, in the immortal words of Edward Bennett Williams, 'a prosecutor can indict a ham sandwich if he chooses.' And if Starr does, I would never ask for a pardon. I will go to trial and show Starr up for the fraud he is."

She quotes me as saying: "Are you sure you want me to say that?"

And she says she answered: "Word for word."

The conversation she's referring to actually took place much later—in early 1997—and over the phone.

President Clinton had asked me what I thought of the idea of pardoning Harold Ickes, who was the object of attack in the campaign fund-raising scandal, along with an array of Whitewater figures including Susan and Jim McDougal, Jim Guy Tucker, and others. He said he thought he could start the second term off completely clean, putting the problems of the first term behind him and moving on. He cited President George Bush's 1992 pardon of former Defense Secretary Caspar Weinberger and others implicated in the Iran-Contra affair.

"But Bush was leaving the White House," I said. "You still have another term. You'll be badly hurt if you issue pardons. It won't kill the issue. It will merely fan the flames."

Clinton persisted: "But these people have done nothing wrong. They've racked up huge legal bills, and Starr will keep going after them unless I shut the whole thing down now with pardons."

"Would you pardon Hillary, too?" I asked.

"I might," he answered.

"You'll get killed for that. It would be like Ford's pardon of Nixon. You'd never live it down."

Worried that Clinton might be seriously considering such a disastrous course, I called Hillary and asked her how she would feel about a pardon. I did not say I was an emissary from Starr, and I wasn't. I had not discussed the matter with Starr—I didn't even know him, and had never spoken to him. I had merely talked to her husband about it. I didn't say she would be indicted, I only mentioned the possibility of a pardon that would prevent her from being indicted—a pardon I thought would be a mistake.

Her memory of her own reaction, though, is accurate: She rejected the idea of a pardon out of hand. "If he [Starr] wants to stoop that low, I'll fight to clear my name," she said. "I won't accept a pardon! I wouldn't let Bill pardon me! I'd just go into court and show Starr up for the fraud he is." I was relieved by her attitude, and inwardly impressed by her courage. But I had no knowledge of anything going on within Starr's camp, and she is wrong to suggest I did.

I hadn't spoken to Starr, but as it happened I had heard from his people—in a manner of speaking. Several days after I returned home from the Democratic National Convention at the end of August 1996, the private security guards we had hired to keep the swarming media at bay outside our Redding, Connecticut, home informed us that two FBI agents were coming up our driveway—with papers in hand. It was a subpoena to Starr's grand jury in Washington. And it asked that I bring all papers and documents related to my work for the Clinton campaign.

I was very suspicious about why Starr would want campaign documents, particularly the weekly agendas I used as the outlines for my strategy meetings with the president. The agendas had nothing to do with Whitewater, Filegate, Travelgate, or any of the scandals. But they did contain our private, in-house campaign plans and polling data.

I was determined not to give him those documents until the day after the election. I was not about to hand over our campaign playbook to a Republican prosecutor eight weeks before the balloting.

At Eileen's suggestion, I retained Jerry McDevitt from the Pittsburgh office of the law firm of Kirkpatrick and Lockhart as my attorney. She had met McDevitt during her brief foray into the world of professional wrestling, when she represented an odd but huge client, former wrestler David "Dr. Death" Schultz, who was locked in litigation with his former boss Vince McMahon of the World Wrestling Federation. McDevitt, who represented McMahon, was no member of the Washington establishment, which Eileen distrusted, but he had proven himself one hell of a lawyer. Eileen told me she'd never met a more brutal, tenacious, obnoxious, talented, and effective lawyer. He was perfect for the job of taking on the special prosecutor.

Jerry immediately contacted the Starr prosecutors and arranged for a delay of several weeks while he moved to quash the subpoena. I told him I would never give Starr the agendas before the election, no matter what. Once the voting was over, they could have them.

But the prosecutors were pushing for me to immediately appear before the grand jury, agendas in hand. Jerry delayed it for several weeks, but at length I received another subpoena ordering me to appear on the Thursday before election day. Obviously, they wanted to make a show of having me testify on the weekend before the election. I was deeply determined not to hand over the agendas, and I was relieved when Jerry finally called to say that my testimony was postponed.

I did not hear from Starr's office again for eighteen months—until, in July 1998, I was interviewed by the FBI at my New York City apartment with my old friend attorney David Lenefsky in attendance. (An accomplished New York litigator, David had worked with Jerry on the earlier subpoena issues.)

The FBI wanted to know about a phone call I had with President Clinton in April 1996. I did not immediately remember the call; but when I checked my records, I realized that it had taken place on Easter Sunday. I had been in Paris with some family members. I remembered that I had talked to the president about advertising scripts. *What could they want to know that for?* I wondered. Only later did I learn the reason: This call was one of those that interrupted a Clinton/Monica moment; the FBI was trying to corroborate Lewinsky's testimony.

Several weeks later, I was finally required to testify at the Grand Jury in Washington about my conversations with the president after the Lewinsky story broke.

FAMILY AND FRIENDS

The two most corrupt administrations in American history—those of Warren G. Harding and Ulysses S. Grant—were headed by presidents who probably never stole a dime for themselves.

Both Harding and Grant saw their administrations destroyed by the greed, poor judgment, and arrogance of their family and friends. Grant's brother-in-law, and the businessmen who hung around the president, got him into big trouble. Virtually every member of Harding's weekly poker game stole money from the nation—probably excepting poor old Harding himself. Both presidents crashed and burned because they trusted their friends and family, and because they couldn't say no.

As president, Hillary Clinton could have the same problem with her family, and with her friends.

Family

Hillary has two younger brothers, Hugh and Tony Rodham.

These two are a piece of work.

Hugh Rodham persuaded President Clinton to pardon Carlos Anabel Vignali. All he was convicted of, after all, was shipping *half a ton* of cocaine to Minnesota. He got fifteen years. Former U.S. Attorney Todd Jones called Vignali "a major source in keeping a drug organization fed with dope." Charming.

But he had redeeming features. Vignali's father donated $150,000 to Los Angeles Democrats, and $10,000 to the national committee. More important, he paid Hugh Rodham $200,000 to get his son cleared. And it worked: Clinton commuted the drug dealer's sentence to time served.

Hugh also got more than $200,000 for securing a pardon for Almon Glenn Braswell, who was sentenced to three years in jail for touting a phony cure for baldness, and peddling a remedy for prostate problems, using photos of athletes like racer Richard Perry, football player Len Dawson, and Stan "the Man" Musial, all of whom sued him. Braswell received a full pardon from Clinton.

Tony Rodham, meanwhile, acted as a "consultant" for carnival owners Edward and Vonna Jo Gregory, who had been convicted of bank fraud in 1982. Tony arranged for the Gregorys to stage two carnivals on White House grounds, and to visit the Clintons at Camp David. The couple contributed $102,000 to Hillary and other Democratic causes. And they got pardoned.

Hillary's brothers aren't going away. If she runs for national office, they'll still be there licking their chops. If she can't handle their greed any better than she has in the past, she is in for a rocky ride if she ever becomes president.

Hillary says she simply didn't know about her brothers and the pardons. Barbara Olson catalogued her multiple denials in *The Final Days:*

- "I did not have any involvement in the pardons that were granted."
- "I didn't know about it and I'm very regretful that it occurred, that I didn't know about it."
- "I don't know anything other than what has now come out and I did not learn about that until very recently."
- "I did not know my brother was involved in any way in any of this."
- "I did not know any specific information until late Monday night."
- "I love my brother. I'm just extremely disappointed in this terrible misjudgment that he made."
- "I was very disturbed when I heard about it."
- "If I'd had any knowledge or notice of it, I believe I might have been able to prevent it. . . . I did not."
- "I don't personally have any information."

Doth the lady protest too much?

How likely is it that Hugh and Tony Rodham managed to persuade Bill Clinton to pardon their clients, without ever letting on to their sister what they were after?

Well, it's *possible,* theoretically at least. They knew she was running for Senate; they could have guessed that the pardons might prove embarrassing to her. So they might have taken some measures to ensure plausible deniability for their sister.

But both Hugh and Tony were basically living at the White House at the time. And of course Bill himself knew they were lobbying for the pardons. Is it at all conceivable that Bill Clinton said nothing to his wife about the pardons her brothers were promoting? Is it possible he didn't know that the Rodhams were behind the pardons?

No and no. Each of these pardons left a long paper trail of investigations and argument. The Justice Department opposed them vigorously, as did the prosecuting attorneys who were involved. It is inconceivable that Bill Clinton did not know that Hillary's brothers were involved. To conclude that he was ignorant, one would have to believe that every single member of his staff, who handled these applications systematically, hid Hillary's brothers' involvement from him—and that neither brother ever buttonholed Bill personally to press their case.

And is it credible that Bill didn't tell Hillary? After his wife had been elected to the Senate, is it conceivable that Bill took an action that might directly have implicated her brothers in a blatant conflict-of-interest and influence-peddling scheme—and did so without consulting her?

Knowing the Clintons, it seems highly unlikely. And yet: If we assume that Bill did tell Hillary, why did she let it happen, and risk the political fallout? It's conceivable that Hillary failed to anticipate the furor that followed. And yet: Given the outcry she endured after her husband pardoned several Puerto Rican terrorists the year before—a move widely decried as an attempt to curry favor with the New York Hispanic voting bloc Hillary was courting at the time—she must have known how this new round of presidential forgiveness would look.

So is it possible that Hillary's brothers had a hold over her that made her agree to the granting of the pardons? Or made Bill understand that she had no choice?

Any way you look at it, the granting of pardons to three felons who were paying money to your brothers-in-law marked a low point in the American presidency.

Not surprisingly, Hillary's memoirs contain not one single word about the pardons. The HILLARY brand can't afford brothers who get paid hundreds of thousands of dollars to secure pardons for convicted felons.

Friends

You can't pick your family. But you can choose your friends. And Hillary had a special friend: Harry Thomason, the Hollywood producer of *Designing Women* and *Evening Shade,* who produced many of the ads and videos for Bill Clinton's campaigns, choreographed the 1992 Democratic convention, and handled the pomp and ceremony of the Clintons' inaugural.

No doubt Harry thought all his hard work deserved recognition. And Thomason happened to be part owner of an air charter consulting firm.

Ann Coulter and others have documented how vigorously Thomason pushed Hillary, and Hillary pushed David Watkins, to fire the White House Travel Office staff. Her tactics included getting former Rose Law Firm partner David Kennedy to investigate Billy Dale, the head of the Travel Office; as a result, Dale was charged with financial misconduct, though he was later acquitted.

What the sad Travel Office affair shows us is just how far Hillary will go to accommodate her friends—specifically, in this case, to reward Harry Thomason with some business. Unless Hillary Clinton wants her prospective presidential administration to be a replay of the Ulysses S. Grant story—where favors to friends ruined his years in office—Hillary had better rethink her relationships and rein in her desire to punish enemies and reward friends with official favors.

The Travel Office affair also demonstrates how Hillary's obsessive revisionism leads her into deeper and deeper trouble. It wasn't illegal for Hillary to fire the Travel Office staff. But rather than frankly admit that she wanted Bush's people replaced with her own, the HILLARY brand had to find some justification for firing them. HILLARY could not be tainted by a scent of political patronage. She had to cloak her ambition, and her perfectly human desire to reward her friends, in a garb of pseudo-morality—by pretending that the real reason was a finding of financial dishonesty.

But eventually things got serious. In 1995, Hillary testified under oath that she had not initiated the Travel Office firings. This was the turning point in the Travelgate story—not the initial action, but Hillary Clinton's clumsy attempt to cover it up.

In *Living History,* Hillary claims that she and Bill were "cleared" in the Travelgate investigation that followed. But that's exceedingly wishful thinking. In his final report, Special Prosecutor Robert Ray, who succeeded Kenneth Starr, reported that the evidence was overwhelming that Hillary Clinton's statements about the Travel Office were "factually inaccurate." As ABC's Peter Jennings reported, "The Independent Counsel said . . . that Mrs. Clinton gave false testimony about her role in the firing of White House travel workers seven years ago."

Fox News described Ray's report as "the strongest criticism of Mrs. Clinton from any independent counsel investigation so far. The issue for prosecutors was whether anybody in the White House tried to cover up alleged mismanagement of the firings. Under oath, Mrs. Clinton flatly denied any role and denied that she had any input . . . [But] Independent Counsel Robert Ray cited eight separate conversations between the first lady and senior staff and concluded: 'Mrs. Clinton's input into the process was significant, if not the significant factor influencing the pace of events in the Travel Office firings and the ultimate decision to fire the employees.'"

Why wasn't Hillary indicted? As the Fox News story reported, "Prosecutors decided not to seek perjury charges because they said a key element, intent, would have been difficult to prove. The report said that when Mrs. Clinton testified she did not have a role, she might not have understood the impact of her conversations on White House staff."

And in *Living History* Hillary seizes on exactly that difficulty, claiming that it was her "offhand comment" that led—inadvertently, of course—to the firings.

Hillary makes a poor-little-me case in her own defense: "I was still learning the ropes and still discovering what it meant to be America's first lady. . . . Suddenly the people around you spend a lot of time anticipating what will make you happy. . . . Everything you say is amplified."

Most people make offhand comments. Hillary does not. She is never casual. Either she says nothing, or she says it emphatically. The idea of Hillary Clinton making an "offhand" comment about firing the Travel Office staff calls to mind Henry II's famous line, "Will no one rid me of this troublesome priest?"—which resulted in the assassination of Thomas Becket.

But the HILLARY brand can only wonder, in bemusement, at how easily a little miscommunication can lead to trouble—rather than learning any kind of lesson from yet another cover-up attempt that blew up in her face.

Gifts

Nothing in politics is more dangerous than a gift. It sits innocently on a table in an anteroom, a thoughtful display of friendship from a true comrade. Or is it? Is that china set, or expensive lamp, or luxury golf bag, a token of friendship—or a bid for influence?

There is no duplicity to match that of the Washington power structure. When you're on top, they shower you with attention. When you fall, they run screaming in the other direction.

Bob Crandall, the former CEO of American Airlines, once told me the difference between New York and Washington: "New York," he said, "is tough but it's not mean. They will battle over every dime in the contract, and then afterward you'll go out to dinner together and become friends. Washington is not tough, but it is mean. To your face, they'll give you anything you want. And as you walk away, they'll shoot you in the back just because it's fun to watch you die."

There is a good reason for the legislation that bars senators and congressmen from receiving gifts valued at more than fifty dollars. Those wise to the ways of our nation's capital understand that gifts are the currency of bribery in Washington. Give a politician a paper bag full of twenty-dollar bills, and you insult his integrity. Hand him an oriental vase worth as much, and he'll consider you a friend. Most elected officials are very careful about receiving gifts. The implication of favoritism and influence peddling may adhere long after the gift itself is consigned to a closet shelf.

But Hillary Clinton showed no such care about accepting, and likely soliciting, almost $200,000 worth of gifts . . . and helping herself to many more presents that were intended not for her, but for the White House.

Most of this massive deluge of gifts came in the few short weeks between her election to the Senate in November 2000, and her swearing-in during the first week of January 2001. Already elected, she felt politically free to take gifts, and before she took office she was legally able to do so. Soliciting presents in a way that defied tact and defiled taste, Hillary displayed an eagerness that verged on frenzy. Time was of the essence: Anxious to obey the letter of the law as she openly flouted its spirit, Hillary scrambled to collect every gift she could before the Senate ethics prohibition kicked in.

In *Living History,* of course, Hillary makes no mention of any such gifts. HILLARY doesn't take gifts.

In her final book, *The Final Days,* Barbara Olson included a list of some of the presents the Clintons accumulated. It's one thing to lump the gifts together and chalk it up to the eccentricity of the outgoing first lady. But to read each item—to absorb the amount of the "gift"—is to realize how massive Hillary's circumvention of the Senate ethics rules really was:

- Barbara Allen, Belfast, Northern Ireland, $650 watercolor of Clinton ancestral homestead
- Georgetown Alumni, class of 1968, $38,000 Dale Chihuly basket set
- Arthur Athis, Los Angeles, California, $2,400 dining chairs
- Dendez Badarch, Ulan Bator, Mongolia, $1,300 drawings of Mongolian landscapes
- Robert Berks, Orient, New York, $2,500 bust of Harry Truman
- Bruce Bernson, Santa Barbara, California, $300 golf putter
- Mr. and Mrs. Bill Brandt, Winnetka, Illinois, $5,000 china
- Ken Burns, Walpole, New Hampshire, $800 photograph of Duke Ellington
- Ely Callaway, Carlsbad, California, $499 golf driver
- Iris Cantor, New York, New York, $4,992 china
- Robin Carnahan and Nina Ganci, St. Louis, Missouri, $340 two sweaters
- Glen Eden Carpets, Calhoun, Georgia, $6,282 two carpets
- Dale Chihuly, Seattle, Washington, $22,000 glass sculpture
- Ted Danson and Mary Steenburgen, $4,800 china
- Colette D'Etremont, New Brunswick, Canada, $300 flatware
- Dennis Doucette, Coral Gables, Florida, $310 golf bag, clothing, book
- Ronald and Beth Dozoretz, $7,000, dining room table, server, and golf clubs (Beth Dozoretz is a friend of Denise Rich, who spoke to the president about the Marc Rich pardon)
- Martin Patrick Evans, Chicago, Illinois, $5,000 rug
- Lee Ficks, Cincinnati, Ohio, $3,650 kitchen table and four chairs
- Lynn Forester, New York, New York, $1,353 cashmere sweater
- Paul Goldenberg, La Habra, California, $2,993 TV and DVD player

- Myra Greenspun, Green Valley, Nevada, $1,588 flatware
- Vinod Gupta, Omaha, Nebraska, $450 leather jacket
- Richard C. Helmstetter, Carlsbad, California, $525 golf driver and balls
- Hal Hunnicutt, Conway, Arkansas, $360 golf irons
- Ghada Irani, Los Angeles, California, $4,944 flatware
- Jill and Ken Iscol, Pound Ridge, New York, $2,110 china and jacket
- Mr. and Mrs. Walter Kaye, New York, New York, $9,683 cigar travel humidor, china cabinet, and copy of President Lincoln's Cooper Union speech
- David Kilgarriff, North Yorkshire, United Kingdom, $300 golf driver
- Steve Leutkehans, Morton Grove, Illinois, $650 golf driver
- David Martinous, Little Rock, Arkansas, $1,000 needlepoint rug
- Steve Mittman, New York, New York, $19,900 two sofas, easy chair, and ottoman
- Katsuhiro Miura, Japan, $500 golf driver
- Jan Munro, Sarasota, Florida, $650 painting of New York City
- Brad Noe, High Point, North Carolina, $2,843 sofa
- Margaret O'Leary, San Francisco, California, $595 pantsuit and sweater
- Mr. and Mrs. Joe Panko, Concord, North Carolina, $300 three putters
- Mr. and Mrs. Paolo Papini, Florence, Italy, $425 Italian leather box
- Mr. and Mrs. Morris Pynoos, Beverly Hills, California, $5,767 cashmere shawl and flatware
- Brian Ready, Chappaqua, New York, $300 painting of Buddy, the Clintons' dog
- Denise Rich, ex-wife of fugitive Marc Rich, $7,300 coffee table and chairs (Ms. Rich also donated $450,000 to the Clinton Presidential Library, $72,000 to the Hillary Clinton campaign and committees supporting her candidacy, $1 million to the Democratic Party and its candidates, and $10,000 to the Clintons' legal defense fund)

- David Rowland, Springfield, Illinois, $500 check signed by President Harry Truman in 1934
- Stuart Shiller, Haileah, Florida, $1,170 lamps
- Steven Spielberg, $4,920 china
- Sylvester Stallone, $300 boxing gloves
- Mr. and Mrs. Vo Viet Thanh, Ho Chi Minh City, Vietnam, $350 framed tapestry
- Joan Tumpson, Miami, Florida, $3,000 painting
- Edith Wasserman, Beverly Hills, California, $4,967 flatware
- Mr. and Mrs. Allen Whiting, West Tisbury, Massachusetts, $300 painting
- James Lee Witt, Alexandria, Virginia, $450 cowboy boots
- Mr. and Mrs. Bud Yorkin, Los Angeles, California, $500 antique book on President Washington

One might ask, how did all of these different people know to buy the same expensive china patterns? As ABC News reported on January 25, 2001, "Clinton supporters even took the extraordinary step of setting up an account akin to a gift registry with Borsheim's, a high-end jewelry and china dealership owned by billionaire financier Warren Buffett. . . . Clinton's friend Rita Pynoos of Beverly Hills, asked other supporters to give generously to help the first family launch their new life. A source close to one of those solicited confirmed Pynoos had suggested a $5,000 contribution. . . . Rather than send a check to the White House, the Clinton backer was asked to send a check to Borsheim's. The donor also was asked to rush the payment in before January 3, when Senate ethics rules would bar Sen. Clinton from receiving such gifts. Other supporters confirm they too were asked to contact Borsheim's."

In all, the Clintons received $190,000 in gifts. As Olson reports, "Mrs. Clinton pulled in over $50,000 of china and flatware." Mr. Clinton didn't fare as well, getting only about $4,000 worth of golf equipment.

(Those golf clubs wouldn't have been overlooked by the president, though. When Eileen and I were preparing to go for a vacation in Morocco over Christmas 1995, the president told me to tell the King—if we bumped into him—how much he loved the driver His Majesty had given him. "It takes ten strokes off my score, and nobody knows that it's the driver, not me," he said. The next year, the day after Elizabeth Dole delivered her riveting Oprah-like speech at the Republican convention, I spoke with Clinton and he was mad as hell—not at the speech, but at the fact that his favorite golf driver had just broken. The man takes his golf seriously.)

Asked by Tim Russert on *Meet the Press* whether the gifts were the result of an active solicitation, former White House Chief of Staff John Podesta confirmed that an appeal of some sort did, indeed, take place:

RUSSERT: "In the final weeks, did friends of Mrs. Clinton not solicit others and say 'Would you please buy this silverware, these gifts for Mrs. Clinton for her new house?'"
PODESTA: "Yes, that happened."

So extensive was the negative publicity about the avalanche of gifts that the Clintons agreed to pay back $86,000, about half their value. As Olson notes, "no one explained exactly how that compromise was arrived at."

But these last-minute gifts, given voluntarily to the Clintons, account for only part of the spoils the Clintons plundered during their time at the White House. As Hillary prepared to leave Washington for Chappaqua, she and the former president took with them an additional $360,000 worth of gifts given to the White House itself, including $173,000 in art objects and books, $69,000 in furniture, $26,000 in golf items, and $24,000 in clothing. The *Washington Post* reports that the gifts even included 137 five-piece china settings, representing five patterns and costing $38,000.

Moreover, a House Committee charged that many of the gifts were undervalued—including "An Yves Saint Laurent suit valued at $249, slightly below the threshold for triggering public reporting. A Ferragamo coat worth $1,350 was valued at $800, a set of men's Spalding golf clubs and canvas bag accepted at a $200 value were worth $500 to $600, and a Tiffany silver necklace listed at $150 was worth $450 to $1,000."

When many of the original donors of these gifts learned that the Clintons had expropriated their donations to furnish their new house, they were outraged. Businessman Brad Noe, surprised that his $3,000 couch had made it to Chappaqua, was furious and said that he "would never give a gift to the Clintons." Eventually the Clintons were forced to return $28,000 of sofas, chairs, and other pieces of furniture to the White House.

Olson explains how the Clintons got away with their legal burglary: "While still in office, Bill and Hillary shipped seventy museum pieces, donated to the White House by prominent American artists, to the Clinton Presidential Library in Little Rock. The items were part of a White House Americans Craft Collection and featured a Dale Chihuly glass piece. . . . White House curator Betty Monkman said the decision to move them was made by 'Mrs. Clinton herself.' " Once these items were in the possession of the library, the compliant board of directors, appointed by Clinton, could do with them as they wished.

The looting continued. "In January, 2000, the Clintons began shipping furniture to their . . . Chappaqua home, despite [the fact that] they were government property, donated as part of a $396,000 White House redecoration project in 1993."

Former White House Counsel Vince Foster "sent a March 24, 1993, memo requiring that the gifts be accepted with formal acknowledgments, thereby making them government property."

Olson notes that "The Clintons reportedly returned 'a truckload of couches, lamps, and other furnishings taken from the White House.

Unfortunately, no one knows for sure how much the Clintons got away with. That information has been withheld despite numerous attempts for disclosure. All everyone knows is that they tried." Approximately $28,000 worth of gifts made to the White House were removed by the Clintons, even after the chief usher objected. These gifts, which had never been disclosed, included a hand-painted television armoire, a custom wood gaming table, and a wicker center table with a wood top.

This gifting orgy points up the raging materialism Hillary must have been holding in check throughout most of her husband's governorship and presidency. Once the Clintons were facing the loss of the opulent lifestyle they'd led since their days in the Arkansas Governor's Mansion, Hillary seems to have gone into a panic, anxious to hold on to as many of the luxurious trappings as she could.

And yet, once again, HILLARY has found a way to rewrite this bit of unflattering history. What caused the gift scandal? A "clerical error," according to *Living History*. While she doesn't mention the gifts she got before entering the Senate, she does defend herself against the charge that she appropriated White House gifts with one short sentence: "The culture of investigation followed us out the door of the White House when clerical errors in the recording of gifts mushroomed into a full-blown flap, generating hundreds of news stories over several months."

But those news stories weren't generated by any "clerical error." They were the direct result of the Clintons' decision to back a moving truck up to the White House and take tens of thousands of dollars' worth of furniture and other objects that belonged not to them, but to the American people. It was greed, not a bookkeeping mistake, that gave rise to the scandal—and it was only the massive negative publicity that forced them to return as many of the gifts as they did.

Of all the Hillary scandals, this final one may come closest to suggesting the kinds of difficulties she, and the nation, might face if she should ever be elected president.

Why? For one thing, it is the most recent, so fresh that it can't be dismissed as an old story or the behavior of an immature young political wife. Many of Hillary's other scandals began far back into her husband's governorship; the cattle futures trades and Whitewater affairs date back to the late 1970s (though her efforts to cover them up penetrated deep into her husband's presidency). Other scandals, such as Travelgate and the FBI file episode, occurred in Bill's first term.

Perhaps more to the point, it is the scandal for which Hillary is most directly responsible. It was Jim Blair's pursuit of influence that likely led him to entice Hillary into trading cattle futures. Jim McDougal was clearly guilty of a wide array of criminal activity, of which Hillary might have known nothing when she first got to know him. Others may have pushed Hillary to fire the Travel Office employees. Her brothers were at the heart of the pardon scandal. But the gifts were Hillary's own project. No one can imagine Bill caring about what kind of china he had. (To him, the only important China was a country.) This was pure Hillary.

Hillary's brazen solicitation of lavish gifts demonstrates that she is absolutely fearless in doing things that are unseemly at best and corrupt at worst. She obviously knew the gifts would be a problem politically. That's why she delayed taking them until after she was elected to the Senate. But her success at escaping the consequences of her previous scandals seems only to have kindled an arrogance within her that verges on delusions of invulnerability.

Finally, it reminds us that Hillary lies at the center of a network of friends, who are willing to shower her with presents for one of two motives: either deep admiration or consummate opportunism. Some of these gifts may have been tokens of genuine admiration, even affection. But how many were down payments in a campaign to win her favor and gain influence? Can anyone fully insulate him- or herself from the feelings of obligation that must accompany the receipt of each gift? Only a true ingrate could accept such gifts without feeling warm—and indebted—toward the giver.

THE BOOK DEAL: HAVING HER CAKE AND EATING IT TOO

How ironic that *Living History* itself should offer one final window onto Hillary's latter-day priorities—not only in its content, but also in the terms under which she arranged to publish it.

As with the gifts Hillary received, the book deal Hillary struck with Simon & Schuster had to be consummated in the narrow but busy window between the election and her inauguration as senator. And for the same reason: Such a deal was unseemly for a Senate candidate, legal for a first lady, but probably illegal for a senator.

During her Senate campaign, Hillary said nothing to let on that she was planning to sign an enormous book deal as soon as she was elected. Indeed, she practiced a particularly Clintonian sleight of hand over the matter, telling Lucinda Franks of *Talk* magazine in September 1999 that she had "turned down a $5 million book offer" earlier that year.

The implication, of course, was that she would not indulge in writing a get-rich-quick book; instead, HILLARY would focus her full attention on her senatorial duties. Who would have imagined that the real reason she turned down the $5 million was that it wasn't enough?

Ultimately, Simon & Schuster won the auction for Hillary's book, giving the former first lady and future senator an $8 million advance against royalties. While members of the House of Representatives may not accept advances for books—only royalties based on actual sales—senators allow themselves to collect advances on their works as long as they are "usual and customary."

As Gary Ruskin, director of the Congressional Accountability Project put it "an $8 million advance is not a usual or customary contractual term. It's very, very gargantuan."

And who gave Hillary the $8 million up front? Simon & Schuster—part of the Viacom media empire, which includes Paramount Pictures, CBS Television, MTV, UPN, and Blockbuster video stores. As Olson noted, "the entertainment giant has substantial interest in what happens in Washington ranging from television station licensing to potential federal regulation of broadcast violence."

Senator John McCain wrote Mrs. Clinton to express his concern that her book might "violate Senate rules regarding conflicts of interest." McCain added "the sheer size of your $8 million book advance raises questions about whether you and Senate processes may be affected by large cash payments from a major media conglomerate. This book contract, with its uniquely lavish advance for an elected official, may be, in fact, a way for that corporation to place money into your pockets, perhaps to curry favor with you."

The Clintons had been quite critical of House Speaker Newt Gingrich for receiving a $4.5 million advance on his book from HarperCollins. Under fire for the contract, Gingrich eventually caved in to the pressure and agreed to forgo the advance, receiving only royalties for the book. Safely ensconced in the more forgiving Senate, Hillary Clinton happily accepted the far bigger advance she was offered—and went on to see *Living History* become one of the biggest nonfiction bestsellers of its year.

How did this idealistic young commencement speaker at Wellesley College grow to be such an intensely material girl, grasping for money as she exploited technicalities in her quest to square her greed with the ethics regulations of her profession?

As we ponder Hillary's early willingness to cut corners and bend the rules in her own financial interest—and her later use of loopholes to make very big money by soliciting gifts and an enormous book advance—it is the intensity of her desire to get rich that lingers in the mind. Public servants are generally forced to avoid opportunities for personal enrichment, in return for preserving their idealism (or, at the very least, preventing any impropriety, real or imagined). Hillary has succeeded in having it both ways.

As president, would the fact that she and her husband have made close to $20 million writing books diminish her appetite for money? Will his $10 million annual income quench her thirst for security? Or will her sense of entitlement, and the temptation to use her position to help her friends, still burn so brightly that it might consume a second Clinton presidency as it did the first?

The answer is unknowable, of course—and of course, as the prospectuses remind us, past history is no guarantee of future performance. But Hillary's past performance is also the best information we have.

7

HIDING HILLARY: THE INQUISITOR

Hard-nosed politician. Ideologue. Materialist. Each of these personae has been carefully hidden beneath the mask of the HILLARY brand. But none of them is uglier than Hillary in vindictive mode. Of all the disturbing entries on Hillary's White House record, probably the most serious is the way she chose to defend Bill against charges of perjury during the Monica Lewinsky scandal.

Writing today, all these years after the country was consumed with what more than one political columnist called "Hurricane Monica," one is almost inclined to ask: Who cares? So what? Did any of it really matter? Yes, in effect Hillary actually defended her husband's adultery. And, yes, she knew what she was doing. But is any of this relevant to a possible Clinton II presidency? After all, what else could she do? Even if she knew it was true, she had very few options. She certainly could never tell what she knew. Nor could she publicly chastise him, without endangering his position and hers. Defending him was clearly the best alternative of a bad lot. And if her motives for doing so were self-serving, so were those of Clinton's critics—the people behind the Paula Jones litigation.

But it is not the fact that Hillary defended her husband that should give us pause. It is, rather, *the way* she did so that calls into question her suitability for the presidency.

When a married couple is in the middle of a personal and political scandal, it's quite natural for them to take a "you and me against the world" attitude, temporarily suspending personal pain in order to get past the assaults of outsiders. That can hardly be easy when the couple in question is the president and first lady, and a Grand Jury investigation is parading their personal pain on the front page of every newspaper. Under those circumstances, any such couple would find it tempting to blame those who report their mistakes instead of blaming themselves. A personal scandal, of course, never really ends until you accept responsibility for your own flaws. Even so, Hillary's insistence on her husband's innocence was really the only position she could take. She had a right to defend his presidency against the forces trying to oust him, and she was determined to do so.

But defending your husband in public is one thing. Declaring war on the prosecutors, witnesses, and reporters investigating him is something very different. The tactics she used to defend Bill drew out the absolute worst of Hillary Clinton. Hiring private detectives, releasing opponents' confidential personnel files, stonewalling the investigation, and outright lying to save their joint political career, this woman who had helped impeach Richard Nixon came more and more to resemble her former target.

The stakes for Hillary were high. She had re-learned in Washington the hard lesson of Little Rock, that her political power was doubly derivative: dependent on both Bill's tenure in office and the survival of their marriage. If either should capsize, her power would disappear.

And, in a strange way, even though she must have known the reports of Clinton's personal transgressions were true, her revulsion at the equally low tactics of her husband's enemies permitted her to get past the betrayal and become the leader of Team Clinton. Her memoirs make it clear that she has a supreme ability to compartmentalize difficult matters, and in this case she clearly did so. With the Clinton presidency on the line, she kept his infidelity inside an emotional box—one she could open and examine when the fire had receded.

But is there, perhaps, a deeper and more self-serving reason that led her to stand by her man so often, and in the face of such difficult and repetitive behavior? In the dynamics of the relationship, did Hillary recognize that doing so could bring her great rewards?

Throughout their history, whenever Hillary publicly came to Bill's defense and pulled him through a crisis, she became more powerful in both their personal relationship and their joint professional one. In the 1992 campaign, when she defended Clinton against Gennifer Flowers (whose charges he later admitted to be true), he showed his gratitude by giving her the health care reform task force to run. After Hillary saved him from impeachment in the Lewinsky affair, he did everything he could to get her elected to the Senate.

But Hillary's star was not always in ascendancy. There were many periods in their marriage when Hillary had far less access to power. One such time was immediately before Bill's race for president.

Gail Sheehy quotes Betsey Wright describing Bill's increasing irritation with Hillary in Arkansas: "I think that there have been many times when [Bill] would have liked to go home and turn on the TV and escape or just read a book. And she would be in with a list of things people had called her about that day or had to be done. And he was like 'Ah, couldn't you just be a sweet little wife instead of being this person helping me be what I'm supposed to be?"

By 1989, the Clintons were considering divorce. David Maraniss describes how "Clinton was broaching the subject of divorce in conversations with some of his colleagues, governors from other states who had survived the collapse of their marriages." He reports that "there were great screaming matches at the mansion. Once a counselor was called out to mediate."

A year before all that, Bill asked me what kind of political impact I thought he could expect if his marriage to Hillary should break up. I told him I thought he could survive it, and offered my home in Key West as a place for him to hang out and think it over.

By whatever narrow margin, the marriage survived. But Hillary was still way out of the loop, so far out that in 1990 she didn't even know if Bill would seek re-election. As Maraniss reports, on the day before he announced his decision to the public, Hillary called Gloria Cabe, her husband's campaign manager, "and asked whether she had any inside information on what Clinton had decided."

Then came the 1992 campaign, and Gennifer Flowers. So valuable was Hillary's contribution to saving his candidacy that Clinton showered power and favor on her. She inherited health care reform, once more taking command of the signature initiative of her husband's administration as she had with education during his governorship.

But after the Republicans won the 1994 elections—in part by excoriating Hillary's health care proposals—the first lady gradually lost her influence, just as she had in the mid-1980s. Having reached dizzying peaks in the two years after her husband's election, her failure on health care reform and her poor political advice eroded the president's formerly high opinion of her abilities. As I was coming into the administration in November 1994, she was clearly on her way out of it, avoiding the appearance—and to a significant extent the reality—of hidden power, and embracing instead foreign travel and her writing to keep her head above the political water.

Through his rearrangement of the White House after the 1994 election, Clinton made it quite clear that he felt that Hillary had lured him too far to the left, letting her liberal ideology get in the way of pragmatic good judgment. But while he was vociferous in his criticism of "the children who got me elected" (Stephanopoulos in particular), he never spoke ill of Hillary. The only tip-off to his true feelings was that he stopped saying good things about her, too. He simply stopped bringing her up at all. Neither she nor her staff came to strategy meetings. Her advice was no longer registering on his radar screen.

The closest Bill ever came to criticizing Hillary to me was in March 1994, after the *New York Times* published Jeff Gerth's revelations about Hillary's commodities trading. On the night the story appeared, Bill took me aside at a White House social function and asked: "What are we going to *do* about Hillary?" I was stunned. This was the very first—and would prove the only—time he ever came near criticizing her in front of me.

Later that evening, all the guests were invited to view the latest Coen Brothers movie, *The Hudsucker Proxy,* in the White House theater. Eileen and I sat directly behind the Clintons. Not once did they even look at each other, let alone speak. The frost between them chilled the room.

I really came to appreciate how far out of the loop Hillary was when she called to ask my help in getting her longtime friend Ann Lewis—a Democratic activist and sister of Congressman Barney Frank—named as White House director of communications.

I wanted to see the job go to Don Baer, a brilliant and articulate political moderate, who wanted the president to move to the center. But Hillary was pushing Ann. *Why does she need my help?* I wondered. When she called me about it for the third time, I asked why she was hounding me. "You sleep next to the president every night. What do you need my support for?"

"It would be helpful," was all she said in a chilly reply. When the first lady doesn't have enough clout with the president to get a friend a job, she is in the doghouse. (Eventually, I helped arrange for Ann to become director of communications not for the White House but at the Democratic National Committee, where she could do little damage. Baer, who got the White House job, was essential to Clinton's repositioning.)

Just as she had been in the late 1980s, Hillary was out in the cold again. He didn't need her. Indeed, he felt the need to shake her ideologically driven posturing so that he could pursue compromise with the Republicans. And it's no coincidence that it was during Hillary's period of relative disempowerment, from 1995–1997, that Clinton accomplished virtually all of his major achievements as president: welfare reform, balancing the budget, raising the minimum wage, and passing portability of health benefits. Hillary, meanwhile, seemed to accept the hand she was dealt: a life of symbolic foreign trips and periodic intervention on issues that mattered to her. No longer the de facto chief of staff, Hillary wasn't even Bill's top advisor.

All that changed, however, when Bill's indiscretions stopped being a private embarrassment and became a public scandal. Just as in 1992, he pulled Hillary back to his side, and gave her all the power, influence—and, one suspects, affection—she ever needed or craved.

In January 1998, when the president was accused of having an affair with an unnamed intern (only later would we learn the name Monica Lewinsky), Hillary's power came back in a rush. The coup was silent and bloodless, but Hillary was back in charge at 1600 Pennsylvania Avenue, orchestrating the scandal defense, rallying Democrats in the Senate, battling on television and plotting strategy in private, all the time feigning ignorance of her husband's increasingly obvious guilt.

This time, her reward was even more substantial: A year after admitting to a relationship with Monica, Clinton turned the White House over to Hillary to help her gain the Senate seat in New York. No effort was too great; every element of Bill's presidential power was fixed on a solitary objective: electing Hillary.

This pattern of betrayal and reward, too obvious to ignore, likely explains a great deal about Hillary's decision to stay in her marriage despite its obvious drawbacks.

But Hillary also understood that she could not let it appear that power was her true priority. At all costs, she needed to play the role of first lady first and her husband's defender second. To reverse the order would be to cast suspicion on their marriage, and to invite charges that she was just using Bill to get power—charges that could cost Hillary the moral standing she needed to pull her drowning husband to safety.

Hiding her pain at his infidelities was an essential part of this strategy. Later, when denial finally became untenable, there would be time to showcase her pain—and her ability to forgive. But

Hillary's emotions could never trump the need to keep up presidential appearances.

Obviously, it's hard for any outsider to judge the state of a marriage or the emotions of either husband or wife. But my conversations with Hillary over the years lead me to believe that theirs is a genuine love affair, at least on her side. She appears to suffer real pain and grief when Bill strays—or at least when it is so clear that he is doing so that she can't pretend otherwise.

During one phone call, Hillary ended up sobbing: "Why can't anybody understand that I truly love this man? Why don't people get it?" There's no doubt in my mind that she was telling the truth. Just as I have no doubt that the affection isn't always requited in quite the way she would prefer. Hillary may appear far cooler than her husband, but in my observation she actually possesses a normal range of human emotions, from rage to love. Bill, on the other hand, is emotionally stunted. Supremely capable of empathy with every stranger he meets, he finds emotional attachment of any sort difficult.

In public, Bill Clinton always seems very emotional. In fact, that energy merely demonstrates his talent for reflecting the feelings of those around him. Absorbing their joy or pain through his ultra-sensitive antennae, he projects the same in return. Like a reflector on a highway that seems to give off light, he only gives back what you send his way. When the car passes, the reflector goes dark.

Indeed, if there is one crucial trait that Bill Clinton manifests to all who know him, it is elusiveness. Sometimes he is there—very much there. On top of you, around you, before you, and behind you all at once. When his needs pass, though, he is nowhere to be found. To be a woman in love with Bill Clinton must be a very frustrating experience. It was hard enough just being his consultant—he never called unless he needed something. The rest of the time, working with Bill reminded me of the Jimmy Buffet song: "If the phone doesn't ring, it's me."

David Maraniss believes that Bill and Hillary had different attitudes toward one another from the very beginning of their relationship: "When he had thought about marrying her, it was not so much the sight of the young woman that overwhelmed him as an image of an older version: Hillary, he told friends, was the one woman with whom he could imagine growing old and not getting bored. Her feelings about him seemed more immediate and passionate; she adored him, one friend said, with 'a romantic, fifteen-year-old, poetic, teenage love.'" Maraniss also notes that "by the mid-1980s, those early dynamics were still apparent." It's often occurred to me that what held Hillary and Bill together was their shared love . . . for Bill Clinton. But Hillary had to do a lot—and give up a great deal—to win Bill's inconstant affection, and to gain political power by saving him. The price she paid was huge. But her willingness to pay it gives us a great clue to what sort of president she might be.

At first, Hillary may not have understood how deadly Bill's affairs would be for his political career. In the early 1980s, they were sufficiently discreet—and the press tame enough—that they went unnoticed. Gail Sheehy describes how Hillary "told herself that [adultery] was a very small, unimportant part of her husband's life— a pastime, like when he'd get up in the middle of the night and go down to the basement and hang over the pinball machine for hours. In no way did she see a connection between his sexual escapades and their relationship."

Back then, nobody had any idea of the extent of Governor Clinton's infidelities, except perhaps Betsey Wright, his chief of staff. In his statewide races in Arkansas in 1976, 1978, 1980, 1982, 1984, and 1986, his transgressions never surfaced as an issue, though each new primary and election was bitterly contested.

The first time Bill's extracurricular activities really affected his career—or Hillary's—came when he had to forgo a race for president because of his extensive and serial infidelities. The American political world was rocked in 1987 when Senator Gary Hart of Colorado withdrew from the Democratic primary race after the discovery of his affair with Donna Rice. With Hart out of the running, the way seemed open for a young moderate like Bill Clinton.

In describing her husband's decision not to run for president in 1988, Hillary writes: "Much has been written about the reasons for his decision not to run, but it finally came down to one word: Chelsea."

Hillary is right that the decision not to run "finally came down to one word." But the word wasn't "Chelsea." It was "women."

In our meetings to discuss his possible candidacy, Clinton focused obsessively on the possibility that scandal could drive him from the race as surely as it had Gary Hart. He never admitted to having affairs, but he kept philosophizing about whether the American media was ready to accept a candidate who had made personal mistakes. He was clearly trying to convince himself that he could get away with running.

But Betsey Wright soon put a stop to that. David Maraniss describes the scene: "The time had come, [Betsey] felt, for Clinton to get past what she considered his self-denial tendencies and face the issue squarely. . . . She started listing the names of women he had allegedly had affairs with and the places where they were said to have occurred. 'Now,' she concluded, 'I want you to tell me the truth about every one.'" After hearing the sorry tale, Betsey "suggested that he should not get into the [presidential] race."

With Gary Hart's political corpse lying in the street, it's hard to see how Clinton could have managed to run for president. 1988 was clearly not the year the media was going to forgive womanizing by a presidential candidate.

We can only wonder how Hillary must have felt. After all her investment in this man, his personal behavior had prevented him from seeking the presidency. Photos of the announcement of his withdrawal show her wiping away a tear.

But Hillary seemed to emerge from that experience with a coldly calculating new perspective: Instead of making sure that Bill changed his ways, she realized that she must keep his recklessness out of the public eye if either of them wanted to make it to Washington.

Years before, Eileen and I had a preview of what was to come. In December 1981, during Clinton's visit to New York to film television commercials for his campaign to retake the Governor's Mansion, Eileen and I invited Bill and Hillary out to dinner at New York's Four Seasons restaurant. At the last minute, Bill told me that Hillary was stuck in Washington and couldn't make it, but Bill asked if he could bring a reporter to dinner. I asked if we could talk in front of the journalist. "Oh, it's okay," he said dismissively. "Don't worry."

When Eileen and I arrived at the restaurant, the "reporter" turned out to be a young and attractive woman with hair long enough to sit on.

Of course, she wasn't *really* a reporter. He had met her during the 1980 campaign, when she was an intern for a media outlet.

The couple held hands and rubbed knees under the table, not much caring if we noticed. Eileen and I were amazed that this man who was desperately seeking re-election would be so reckless in a public place.

As we left dinner, Bill turned to his friend and asked if she had ever seen the Christmas Tree at Rockefeller Center, just five blocks away. On cue, she batted her eyelashes and said "why, no." Bill gallantly offered to take her, turning to say, "I'll drop her off at her hotel later; you don't need to wait for us."

That wasn't the only time. In 1984, Bill came to our Manhattan apartment at 5 P.M. for a poll briefing. Nervously glancing at his watch, he said he had to make the last shuttle flight back to Washington at nine. "It won't be a problem," I assured him.

"But I have a business meeting, first, at 116th and Broadway." *Nobody has a business meeting at Barnard College at night,* I remember thinking.

I assured him it still should work out all right.

When we finished, I showed him upstairs to our bathroom. The phone rang: It was Betsey, trying to locate her charge. I went up to tell Bill, only to find him brushing his teeth and washing his chest

in the sink to prepare for his "business meeting." He came downstairs to the phone without a shirt, smoking his toothbrush like it
was a pipe.

SEND IN THE DETECTIVES

It was around the time Eileen and I encountered Bill cutting a swath
through Manhattan that Hillary first started to run interference for
him. As soon as she recognized the need to protect her husband from
himself, she formulated her response strategy: She would form an alliance with a sleazy group of men and women who worked as private
detectives. These gumshoes—I came to call them the "secret police"—gave the Clintons a set of allies as dangerous to the political
system as they were humiliating to their clients.

Nothing is more dangerous in Hillary's political style than her reliance on private eyes. America has a long history of scandals involving inappropriate or illegal government intrusion into the private
lives of our citizens—from J. Edgar Hoover's wiretapping tactics, to
Nixon's plumbers unit, to the off-the-shelf alternative foreign policy
unit in the Reagan National Security Council that led to the Iran-
Contra scandal.

When detectives get into the act, they can be hard to stop and
harder to control. They push civil liberties boundaries to the limit,
and often exceed them. But when their ruthless talents are used to
invade the privacy of private citizens, as happened frequently during
Hillary's orchestration of her husband's scandal defense, they can be
quite terrifying—even more so when they have the power of the
presidency behind them.

Hillary reportedly first used detectives in 1981, hiring Ivan
Duda, a Little Rock investigator, to compile a list of her husband's infidelities. According to Duda, Hillary hired him not to acquire evidence for a divorce, or even to rein Bill in, but because "she wanted
to be prepared for any charges that might come up in the course of
the campaign."

In 1990, Hillary hired private detectives once again—this time to dig up negative material on millionaire utility executive Sheffield Nelson, Bill's Republican opponent in the gubernatorial race and a man whose wealth made him a serious threat.

The campaign hired the Investigative Group International (IGI), run by Terry Lenzner, to investigate Nelson's role in a natural gas deal involving the Arkla Company, which he headed. The deal had enriched Jimmy Jones, who later bought the Dallas Cowboys, and there were serious questions about Nelson's role. Since I was creating the negative ads about the scandal to throw at Nelson, I was delighted at the sudden appearance of a constant flow of material to use in attacking the Republican. Until I read about it years later, I had no idea that it was coming from a private investigator rather than from public sources.

Hillary had known Lenzner for years, since he was director of the Office of Legal Services, a federal agency charged with representing poor people in civil suits, and Hillary was chairman of its board. Hillary's relationship with Lenzner became even closer once she was first lady. Brooke Shearer, her close friend and the wife of Strobe Talbott, joined Hillary's staff after leaving a position in Lenzner's firm, where her talents included "dumpster diving"—that is, sifting through other people's garbage.

Lest anyone assume that such tactics are normal in American politics, they are not. The use of detectives to scour the backgrounds of one's adversaries was not—and *is* not—common in American politics. Hillary and Bill were pioneers in this seamy pastime.

Then, as scandals threatened Bill's 1992 presidential bid, the campaign hired detectives, at a cost of more than $100,000, to find information to discredit the women who posed potential problems, and to use that information to "convince" them to remain silent.

And Hillary was in it up to her ears. She enlisted Vince Foster to work with Bill's confidant Bruce Lindsay in setting up a damage control operation. Joyce Milton writes: "Foster farmed out the job of investigating Clinton's affairs to a Little Rock private detective named

Jerry Luther Parks." Parks, who had been named by Clinton to the Arkansas Board of Private Investigators, also got a contract in 1992 to handle security for the Clinton campaign headquarters. "Quite soon, Lindsay and Foster had a list" of Clinton girlfriends to work with.

Eventually, the damage control operation grew into an extensive, professional organization. To run it, Hillary called back her good friend Betsey Wright from her teaching post at the Kennedy School of Government in Boston; she would head up the thankless task of protecting Clinton from his own past.

Ever since 1987, when she had talked Bill out of running for president by confronting him with his alleged affairs with other women, Betsey Wright had been the repository of information about Bill's extramarital relationships. Curious about the potential damage rumors of this sort might inflict on Clinton, I asked Betsey about them.

"He's usually quite careful," she told me. "He usually gets involved with people who have as much to lose as he does, married women and such." How extensive were his activities? Betsey told me about a friend who had just come from a meeting with Clinton and told her how he had fulminated about the stories of his personal life. "I don't know most of the women they're talking about," he screamed. "I don't do what they say I do." Bewildered, she told Betsey: "you know, I began to wonder if he had actually forgotten that we had slept together!"

Betsey was soon overwhelmed. She later told *Washington Post* and *Newsweek* reporter Michael Isikoff that "there have been nineteen allegations from women purporting to have had intimate relations with Bill Clinton." She noted that this "follows seven earlier allegations."

But Betsey was no pro at sleuthing. So she hired someone who, she said mildly, "has the skills as an attorney to interview witnesses that I don't have": Jack Palladino.

As the *Washington Post* reported, Jack Palladino was "a San Francisco attorney who heads a major private investigative firm, Palladino and Sutherland." The paper quoted a 1990 article in the *San Jose Mercury News*, which called Palladino and Sutherland "one of

America's most successful investigative agencies." The *Post* added, "It operates out of a San Francisco mansion, employs about 10 detectives and charges clients $200 an hour or up to $2,000 a day for the services of its principal partners."

Palladino boasted to Gail Sheehy: "I am somebody you call in when the house is on fire, not when there's smoke in the kitchen. You ask me to deal with that fire, to save you, to do whatever has to be done."

Sheehy reports that "Hillary knew Palladino from the summer she had worked in San Francisco on the Black Panthers case. Palladino had done investigations for Panthers lawyer Charles Garry in defense of Bobby Seale, Huey Newton, and Eldridge Cleaver. He had also helped Hell's Angels beat drug charges."

Initially the Clinton campaign paid Palladino $28,000, routing the money through Jim Lyons, a Denver attorney President Clinton later named to the federal judiciary. Subsequent payments to Palladino—including federal matching funds—were even larger.

Palladino's job? "Bimbo eruptions," as Betsey told Michael Isikoff for the *Washington Post*. Palladino was to "figure out where and why some of these charges [against Clinton] are being leveled."

One by one, Palladino and Hillary's other detectives interviewed the women, seeking affidavits denying any intimate relations. As Sheehy writes, "When Palladino ran into resistance, he would visit relatives and former boyfriends and develop compromising material to convince the women to remain silent. He would eventually gather affidavits from six of the Jane Does later subpoenaed by Ken Starr." The fact that these affidavits were coerced lies, which the women mostly later repudiated, didn't matter. They were enough to cover Bill Clinton until election day.

The detectives left behind a trail of sleaze, blackmail, and intimidation possibly unique in the annals of presidential campaigns:

- In 1994, former Clinton girlfriend Sally Perdue told the *London Telegraph* that she had been offered a bribe to shut up. If she didn't, a "Democratic operative" told her, he "couldn't guarantee the safety of her pretty little legs." Perdue's car window was broken, and she found a spent shotgun shell on her car seat.

- Loren Kirk, Gennifer Flowers's roommate, reported that Palladino asked her: "Is Gennifer Flowers the sort of person who would commit suicide?"
- Kathleen Willey, who described to a grand jury how she was groped by President Clinton in the Oval Office, said that "her tires were punctured with nails and her cat was stolen—then a strange jogger approached her in her neighborhood near Richmond, Virginia, and asked her about her cat, her tires, and her children by name. 'Did you get the message?' the stranger reportedly asked Willey before disappearing."
- Former Miss America Elizabeth Ward Gracen says she was offered acting jobs through the Hollywood-connected Clinton operative Mickey Kantor in return for denying a sexual encounter with Clinton. She also reports that her hotel room was ransacked—and $2,000 left untouched—in what she suspects was an effort to find incriminating tapes.
- Arkansas state trooper and Clinton accuser L. D. Brown says he was approached in London by Clinton operatives who offered him $100,000 to recant his stories of Clinton womanizing.
- Dolly Kyle Browning, who claims to have had a longtime affair with Clinton, reports that campaign operatives threatened to "destroy you" if she came forward.

But the most serious challenge to Clinton's campaign came when Gennifer Flowers exposed her twelve-year affair with the governor. To substantiate her charges, she released audiotapes of an intimate conversation with Bill. The Clintons had to destroy the credibility of the Flowers tapes. So *someone*—David Kendall, Clinton's lawyer, denies that it was the campaign—hired detective Anthony Pellicano, who examined the recordings and pronounced them doctored and unreliable, thus blunting their impact in the media. (Flowers submitted the tapes to another service, Truth Verification Labs, which found them to be completely authentic.)

Pellicano is a hot potato these days, having been accused of using thuggish tactics on *Los Angeles Times* reporter Anita Busch to stop her from working on a story critical of one of Pellicano's clients. Investigating the charge, the FBI arrested him for illegal weapon possession. They found he had a drawer full of hand grenades and, in the words of one agent, enough plastique to "take out a 747." The police also came across evidence that Pellicano may have used illegal wiretaps.

Did Hillary ever stop to think about the kind of people she was employing? On a campaign for president of the United States? How had this lifelong advocate for the rights of women stooped to employing sleazy gumshoes to intimidate them?

In *Living History,* Hillary regrets the way the investigations of Clinton scandals "unfairly invaded the lives of innocent people." But she clearly isn't thinking of the ultimate innocents—the women who said yes to Bill, or who—like Kathleen Willey—said no.

The "Bimbo Patrol" worked. Bill Clinton was elected.

When the Monica Lewinsky scandal broke, once again the detectives were called out:

- The *Washington Post* reported that Terry Lenzner was hired to probe Monica's past, to discredit her in the event that she turned on the president.
- Lenzner investigated Monica's friend Linda Tripp, who leaked the affair to Ken Starr.
- Pellicano was reported to have turned up Monica Lewinsky's former boyfriend Andy Bleiler four days after the Lewinsky story broke in January 1998. Through his lawyer, Terry Giles, Bleiler said that Monica had stalked him, and that when she got her job in Washington she had quipped that she was going to have to get "presidential knee pads." When *New York Post* reporter Andrea

Peyser asked Pellicano if he was the one who found Bleiler, he
told her, "you're a smart girl. No comment."

- White House staffer Sidney Blumenthal is reported to have tried
to place a story that a member of Special Prosecutor Kenneth
Starr's staff was gay.

- Blumenthal also reportedly encouraged journalists to investigate
the past life of House Judiciary Committee Chairman Henry
Hyde, uncovering evidence of a thirty-year-old affair.

- A lobbyist for Planned Parenthood accused House Government
Oversight Committee Chairman Dan Burton, a persistent thorn
in the Clintons' side, of groping her. How coincidental that her
boss when the incident allegedly took place was Ann Lewis,
Hillary's confidante and partisan.

- During the impeachment proceedings, House Speaker Bob Liv-
ingston resigned after reports of infidelity were leaked to the
press. ABC News reporter Cokie Roberts said she had gotten advance word of the scandal by a source close to the White House.
Other reports had White House operatives "peddling" the story
to ABC's Linda Douglas.

Shortly after America learned that Monica Lewinsky had confessed her affair with Clinton to Linda Tripp, who had taped her
calls, Jane Mayer of the *New Yorker* reported that Tripp had lied on
her Pentagon personnel questionnaire. Asked if she had ever been arrested, she answered no, ignoring her teenage detention by police in
Greenwood Lake, New York, over a missing wallet and watch.

My wife, Eileen, immediately surmised that the leak to Mayer
must have been illegal, since personnel files are confidential. In February 1998, I published a column accusing the Pentagon press office
of violating Tripp's rights under the Privacy Law.

Apparently, Kenneth Bacon, chief Pentagon spokesman and a
former colleague of Mayer at the *Wall Street Journal,* had permitted
the improper release of the information. On November 4, 2003, the
Pentagon agreed to pay Tripp $595,000 to settle a lawsuit brought

by Judicial Watch. The Defense Department admitted that it had released data from her personnel file, and had violated the Privacy Act.

My own feelings about the Clintons changed as I saw their tactics in defending against impeachment. I did not think Bill Clinton should be impeached. But I could not countenance the Clintons' use of secret police digging up dirt on innocent people, a tactic that turned my stomach. I had never used such tools in political campaigns, no matter how bare-knuckled they got. I was stunned that the Clintons were doing so.

How far Hillary had fallen! How different her life had become from what she must have imagined it would be. Describing her work for the Senate Watergate Committee in *Living History*, Hillary recalls that "The charges against President Nixon included . . . directing the FBI and the Secret Service to spy on Americans and maintaining a secret investigative unit within the Office of the President."

But how was any of that different from what Hillary herself did? Hillary's legal team kept a phalanx of detectives on the payroll throughout the impeachment imbroglio to find incriminating information about their enemies. The fact that they were paid for by private funds, and were not government officials, is a detail. They worked for the president and the first lady, and their job was to spy on American citizens.

The history of underhanded investigative tactics in American politics is long and ignoble. Former FBI head J. Edgar Hoover is reported to have snooped on presidential opponents for decades, and was famous for his voluminous files detailing the private lives of members of Congress and other high government officials.

But Hoover's techniques have been so roundly repudiated that it's unlikely the FBI can ever be so misused again. Richard Nixon's "Plumbers Unit," established to plug leaks in the administration by running down the source using wiretaps and the like, was exposed when they broke into the offices of Daniel Ellsberg's psychiatrist to discredit him for releasing the Pentagon Papers. When the plumbers broke into the Democratic National Committee headquarters at the

Watergate to plant eavesdropping bugs, they had committed one burglary too many; the resulting scandal, as everyone knows, led to Nixon's resignation.

Hillary Clinton's efforts to protect her husband and silence his opponents picked up where Hoover and Nixon left off. She has resurrected a style of politics and campaigning that had died a much-needed death.

SAY IT NEVER HAPPENED

In *Living History,* Hillary repeats all the charges against her husband, and all the predictable Clinton denials, again and again. Granted, the lies of a woman standing by her husband in a time of great trial deserve some consideration. But the misrepresentations of an author trying to make good on an $8 million book deal deserve much less. It was one thing to attack Gennifer Flowers's credibility while Bill was running for president. It is quite another to keep up the pretense now, even after the man himself has admitted under oath to having had an affair with her. But in *Living History,* even now, Hillary, arrogantly—and falsely—dismisses Flowers's accusations as "a whale of a tale."

Barbara Walters didn't let Hillary get away with denying the Flowers affair in her interview promoting the publication of *Living History.* Walters asked: "When Governor Clinton decided to run for president, a woman named Gennifer Flowers claimed that she had a twelve-year affair with your husband. Your husband told you it wasn't true. Did you believe him?"

Hillary dutifully answered "I did."

Then Walters closed in. "Years later, under oath in a deposition in the [Jones] lawsuit, your husband did admit that he did have a sexual encounter with Gennifer Flowers. How did you reconcile that with what he told you all the years earlier?"

Hillary double talked her way through her answer: "Well, you know, Barbara, we've been through a lot together now, over many years. And as I also write in the book, we have spent some time having marriage counseling, which I highly recommend to people, especially people who led such busy lives as we did over so many years together. And I think I'll leave it at that."

For a trial lawyer, the refusal ever to admit guilt is key in litigation strategy. The defendant's right not to incriminate himself is so fundamental that it's in the Bill of Rights. We do not expect those who have committed crimes to tell the truth. They can refuse to testify one way or the other. We make prosecutors prove that they committed the crimes using forensic and other evidence. A confessional style of justice would inevitably bring back the rack and the thumbscrew.

But as a lawyer, Hillary mistakenly applies the right of refusal to politics, where trust is the key factor. From the very beginning of their political career, Bill and Hillary have understood that any allegation of personal misconduct becomes a "he said, she said" situation, in which denial is the first and best weapon to defeat scandal. Until DNA testing transformed a stain on a blue dress into a trigger for impeachment, the denial defense carried them through all their scandals.

But at what price to Bill Clinton's credibility? He will never escape his finger-wagging denial of a relationship with Monica Lewinsky. This brazen lie is engraved in our minds forever, sullying his place in our memories and in history.

As with so much else involving the Clintons, I had a preview of the "say-it-never-happened defense." It occurred in 1990, during Bill Clinton's final race for re-election as governor. Though it showed me a side of Bill's personality—his capacity for rage—for the first time, and I found it scary indeed, it was Hillary who made the deeper impression on me—with the coolness with which she asked me to lie and pretend the incident had never happened.

Clinton was locked in an unexpectedly tough Democratic primary against a virtually unknown challenger, Hal McRae. The race looked like it might go either way, and Clinton was rattled by its closeness. Defeat seemed a real possibility.

I had dental surgery earlier that day as I prepared to fly to Little Rock to present the latest polling data—which was not good news. The pain in my dry socket did nothing to improve my mood, especially since I resisted taking painkillers because I needed to be clear-headed when I met with the Clintons.

Bill was late. He had cancelled our earlier evening meeting to do a TV show, and returned around midnight to the Governor's Mansion for our strategy session. Campaign manager Gloria Cabe, Hillary, and I joined him in the breakfast room adjoining the kitchen in the Mansion. On seeing the poll data, Bill ripped into me like he never had before. "You got me into this race," he screamed, "so you could make some extra money off me. That was the only reason. And now you give me no attention, no attention at all. I'm about to lose this election, lose this primary, against a nobody, and you're too busy with the little legislative races that Betsey [Wright] got you to give me any attention at all. I pay your expenses, and you come down here and you work on Betsey's races, not on mine. You've forgotten me. You've dismissed me. You don't care about me. You've turned your back on me." Growing red in the face, he kept it up: "I don't get *shit* from you anymore. You're screwing me! You're screwing me!"

In pain, angry, tired, fed up, I stormed out of the Mansion, yelling back at him: "Thank you. Thank you. Thank you very much. You've just solved my problem. I'm getting shit from [Lee] Atwater and shit from [Trent] Lott for working for you, and now I can solve my problem. I'm quitting your campaign—I'll be a free agent. I can be a fifty-state Republican, and I won't have to take your shit." As I marched through the kitchen to leave the Mansion, I heard hoofbeats. Bill came up at a run, threw me to the ground, and drew his fist back to punch me. Hillary was on him in a flash, grabbing his arm and screaming at him: "Bill! Stop! Think! Get control! What are you doing? Bill!"

Red faced, breathing hard, Clinton jumped to his feet spewing apologies. Realizing he'd gone too far, he switched instantly to damage control, trying desperately to keep me on his reservation.

Hillary leapt forward and followed me out of the Mansion as I stalked off to the parking lot. "Dick, Dick, I'm sorry—I'm so sorry. Don't go. Bill didn't mean it. Please don't go. Calm down. *Dick.*" Then she said something I have pondered ever since. I offer no explanation of its meaning; I leave it to readers to make of it what they will. She said: "He only does this to people he loves."

Eileen wanted me to swear out a warrant for his arrest on assault charges. I didn't, but our relationship was never the same. There was a new formality to it, with an undercurrent of warning: Don't go too far again. I continued to work for him in the 1990 election out of a sense of duty, but after 1990 we parted ways, probably figuring we would never meet again.

Perhaps I was engaging in denial myself. Because after their defeat in the congressional races of 1994, Hillary called to ask me to come back and work for Bill. In *Living History,* she describes me as reluctant. She says I told her: "I don't like the way I was treated, Hillary . . . people were so mean to me."

"I know, I know, Dick, but people find you difficult," she says she replied.

Baloney. I never felt "people were mean to me," and never said anything of the sort. Hillary knows why I was reluctant—our fight at the Mansion. I had resolved never to work with Clinton again. Why did I? The allure of power, prestige, money, and everything else was too great. Like so many people in Bill Clinton's life, I gave in.

During the 1992 campaign, reporters got wind of what had happened and pressed me for an account. A reporter for the *Los Angeles Times* called me after the Rodney King riots in L.A., claiming he wanted a comment on their impact on the election. His call turned out to be a ruse to get into my home very early one morning to ask about the Mansion episode. I rushed down in my bathrobe and threw him out. I wondered if there had been a photographer in his car; I could just imagine a photo of me, with wild, slept-on hair, hollering at the reporter in my slippers and bathrobe, finding its way onto the *Times*'s front page.

I called Betsey Wright to ask how to handle the questions. She checked with Hillary and called back: "Hillary said to say it never happened," Betsey reported.

"Say it never happened." It was my first direct, inside taste of how the Clinton rapid response team worked. Operatives who first heard about negative attacks that might be building against the Clinton campaign reported to central command: Hillary. She would orchestrate the response. And the central insight was this: If it happened in private, say it never happened and it will go away. From my altercation with the governor in the Mansion, to Bill's affairs, to his confrontation with Paula Jones, the instructions were always the same: "Say it never happened." This line of defense worked well until a blue dress ripped it apart.

To this day, spokesmen for the Clintons—although not Bill or Hillary themselves—deny that he attacked me. But Gloria Cabe, Clinton's 1990 campaign manager and still a loyalist, confirmed the incident to David Maraniss: "Clinton . . . slugged Morris, sending him reeling." From where she was standing, my fall must have looked like it was in response to a punch.

Bill Clinton didn't punch me. But he did tackle me. Years later, when I was asked about Cabe's account, I called the president. "Deny it," he said. "I didn't punch you."

"But you tackled me," I answered.

"Right, but I didn't punch you," he replied.

"If you had, I would have undoubtedly decked you," I joked. Even six years later, though, it wasn't that funny.

(In *Behind the Oval Office*, my 1997 memoir of the Clinton years, I tried to protect the president with a sanitized account: "Clinton charged up behind me as I stalked toward the door, grabbed me from behind, and wrapped his arms around me to stop me from leaving. I slipped to the floor. Hillary helped me to my feet." When I read this account to Clinton over the phone before the book was published, he chuckled and said "that's right—I was trying to stop you from leaving.")

~~~

The "say-it-never-happened" tactic was, of course, a daily feature of the president's defense while the Monica Lewinsky scandal was convulsing the country. But for Hillary still to be relying on it six years later is a bit much. Yet in *Living History*, she hews to the party line that Bill lied to her.

But did he really lie to Hillary?

He didn't lie to me that same morning when we spoke by phone. "Ever since I became president I've had to shut myself down, sexually I mean," he told me. "But I screwed up with this girl. I didn't do what they said I did, but I may have done enough that I cannot prove my innocence."

I had no earthly idea what the president meant, and I wasn't about to ask him. It was months before I realized, like the rest of the country, what he actually was saying that morning. I did not reveal my conversation with the president until I was summoned to a Grand Jury.

In June 2003, on the Fox News Channel's *Hannity & Colmes*, former Dukakis campaign manager Susan Estrich, a friend of the president's and a top lawyer, indicated that Clinton also told her the truth about Monica Lewinsky.

I leave it to the reader to decide whether, if the president told Susan Estrich and me, he lied to Hillary. But even if he didn't tell her the truth, was she born yesterday?

If your husband has a history of kleptomania and he's accused of shoplifting, you don't take his denials at face value. After Gennifer Flowers, Paula Jones, Elizabeth Ward Gracen, Dolly Kyle Browning, Kathleen Willey, Sally Perdue, the testimony of state troopers L. D.

Brown and Danny Ferguson, Betsey Wright's warning about the women problems that would arise if Bill ran for president in 1988, and dozens of others, *is Hillary seriously asking us to believe that she gave Bill the benefit of the doubt?*

And when it came out that Bill had spoken to Monica more than one hundred times in person or on the phone—including late night calls—didn't Hillary think twice about Bill's limited admission that he had "talked to her a few times?"

We have to assume she knew that Bill was guilty.

But, if so, why did she pretend she thought he was innocent, and why does she perpetuate that pretense in *Living History*?

At the time the Lewinsky scandal broke, it made complete political sense for Hillary to say that she believed in Bill's innocence. His presidency—and her own first ladyship—was hanging by a thread. Demands for his resignation were rife. Hillary acknowledges as much in *Living History*. Had Hillary not publicly defended him, they both would likely have been forced out of the White House. Had Hillary failed to defend him, her own loyalists—and even at her lowest ebb, she still retained the affection of millions of Americans, most of them hardcore liberal Democrats—would have turned against the president, tipping the balance and likely forcing both Clintons out of the White House.

Hillary could not publicly defend her husband without asserting his innocence. To have done so would have been to make everyone realize that she would put up with the most unbelievable public humiliation just to hang on to power. It would have made a sham of her claims that she had a real marriage based on love, trust, and affection. It was only by pretending not to believe the charges that she could stand up and defend his—and her—status and power.

But why lie now? Why even address the issue of Monica in *Living History*? Hillary's pious statement in her book that "in a better world, this sort of conversation between a husband and wife would be no one's business but our own" is nothing more than verbal sleight-of-hand. No one made her write this book; nor did anyone hound her for an explanation of January 21, 1998. Hillary could have written her memoir and glossed over this aspect of her personal life. She might not have made $8 million, but she could have settled for a smaller sum and avoided repeating her lie. But she wanted the money. Her initial fabrication in January 1998 was an attempt to save her husband's presidency, and her own proximity to power. Her transparent lying in *Living History* was designed solely to make money.

Just as in the gift scandals that followed Hillary out of the White House, she was willing to incur political harm for financial gain—a tendency that augers ill for a president.

As for Bill Clinton, he had faced the question of whether to commit perjury or admit his adulteries before. In June 1996, as he prepared to testify in the trial of Jim and Susan McDougal and Jim Guy Tucker, Clinton asked me what he should say "if they ask about my relationship with Susan McDougal."

I didn't press him but wondered if he meant that he had an affair with her and wanted to know how to handle it. "Tell the truth," I said. "If you had an affair with her, admit it. You'll drop ten points [in the poll] and you'll only be seven points ahead, but we'll get those points back. Just don't commit perjury. Then nobody can help you." He was never asked, and Susan McDougal repeatedly denied any such relationship.

President Clinton was deeply aware of the mess he had gotten himself into by lying about Lewinsky in his Jones deposition. When we spoke on January 21, the day the story broke in the *Washington Post,* I told him he should consider telling the truth to the American people about the affair, since they were generous and inclined to forgive. "But what about the legal situation?" he asked.

"If the public forgives you, no prosecutor will be able to move against you," I assured him.

Then I conducted a survey for him that indicated while the voters would, indeed, forgive the adultery, they would not overlook perjury. Misunderstanding my advice, he decided to keep on lying. And he did it in the most emphatic way possible, wagging his finger on national television. Here is how Hillary describes the event: "The President issued a forceful denial that he'd had sexual relations with Lewinsky. I thought his show of anger was justified under the circumstances, as I understood them."

Hillary stood by, bobbing her head in agreement.

Absent from her description is any sense of outrage, anger, or even concern at the aggressiveness with which the president lied to the people. It remains the single most blatant lie ever told on national television by a president of the United States, and represents an assault from which American politics has yet to recover.

Hillary, though, was applying her standard tactic in "he said, she said" situations: Say it never happened. Hillary reflected her confidence on the *Today* show in January 1998, just seven days after the allegations had come out. "If all that [Bill's affair and perjury] were proven true, I think that would be a very serious offense. This is not going to be proven true."

And it never would have been, were it not for DNA.

Hillary is at her most disingenuous when she describes the denouement of the Monica story. She writes, in *Living History,* that she "knew the prosecution had requested a blood sample from the President without specifying its significance." What did she think they wanted the blood sample for? To test his cholesterol?

Then she writes with anguish of how she finally learned the truth: "I could hardly breathe. Gulping for air, I started crying and yelling at him, 'What do you mean? What are you saying? Why did you lie to me?'"

Is her story credible? By August 1998:

- Hillary knew that Linda Tripp had taped Monica describing her affair explicitly.
- Hillary knew that Lewinsky had visited the White House more than three dozen times since leaving her job there.
- Hillary knew that her friend Evelyn Lieberman, Clinton's deputy chief of staff, had transferred Monica from the White House to the Pentagon because she was around Bill too much.

- Hillary knew that Clinton had lied to her about his relationship with Gennifer Flowers.
- Hillary knew that Betty Currie, Clinton's loyal secretary, was often listed as the cover for Monica's meetings with him.
- Hillary knew that Monica Lewinsky had told Vernon Jordan that "she had had sex with Clinton and that she planned to lie to the court."
- Hillary knew that Bill had given Monica a copy of Walt Whitman's *Leaves of Grass,* the same book he'd given Hillary "after our second date."
- Hillary knew that Starr had asked for a blood sample from the president, and press leaks linked it to Monica's blue dress.

In short, Hillary's account of the August confrontation with her husband is very likely her most egregious and elaborate lie. She couldn't admit to knowing that Bill and Monica were an item until August 15 because that would make it impossible for her to stand by her man in public. And impossible to hold at bay the forces that wanted him—and therefore her—out of the White House.

If she were to take up residence there again, would President Hillary Clinton use the same stonewalling tactics as the ones she adopted when first lady? Presidents can draw on a deep wellspring of forgiveness in sustaining their administrations. It is only when they get stuck—hunker down in a position and lose their flexibility—that they get badly hurt.

Johnson on Vietnam, Nixon on Watergate, Clinton on Monica, and, perhaps, Bush on weapons of mass destruction in Iraq are all examples of getting stuck. Losing her ability to maneuver, a chief executive who stonewalls takes a serious political risk. Hillary's record indicates that she may fall again into the same trap.

BLAME THE RIGHT WING

The most consistent theme running through Hillary's scorched-earth defense of her husband's administration is an obsession with the

Clintons' ideological enemies. As Gail Sheehy writes of the 1992 campaign: "Hillary turned a different face to the world. The stories of her husband's infidelities appeared to register, consciously at least, as having nothing to do with their marriage, but rather as evidence of the depths to which the hit men behind George Bush would stoop."

Sheehy quotes Hillary's friend, former newspaper publisher Dorothy Stuck, saying, "it doesn't make any difference [to Hillary] what people say about her. Whatever criticism or belittling, she doesn't take it personally, because the cause is always more important. It may very well be the way she insulates herself from hurt. And I think in the past ten or twelve years with Bill she may have done that to protect her sanity."

Most famously, Hillary sought to blame the entire Lewinsky scandal not on Bill, but on enemies of the progressive cause. It was on the *Today* show, shortly after the Monica scandal broke, that Hillary famously said of Ken Starr's investigation: "I do believe that this is a battle. I mean, look at the very people who are involved in this. They have popped up in other settings. This is—the great story here for anybody willing to find it and write about it and explain it is this vast right-wing conspiracy that has been conspiring against my husband since the day he announced for president. . . .'"

In *Living History,* she writes: "Looking back, I see that I might have phrased my point more artfully, but I stand by the characterization of Starr's investigation. . . . I do believe there was, and still is, an interlocking network of groups and individuals who want to turn the clock back on many of the advances our country has made, from civil rights and woman's rights to consumer and environmental regulation, and they use all the tools at their disposal—money, power, influence, media, and politics—to achieve their ends."

On the *Today* show that morning, the HILLARY mask slipped and we glimpsed the real Hillary underneath—the one all of us who know her well are used to: partisan, combative, and angry. And, always, anxious to deflect an attack on her husband's character into an assault on civil rights, woman's rights, consumer's rights, and environmentalism—anything but what the criticism actually concerned.

But Hillary's rhetoric is not just an effort to channel the scandal into defensible pathways; it also reflects her actual inner thinking. To Hillary, objective guilt or innocence is not nearly as important as the motivations and ideology of those who are bringing the charges. Good people—like herself—cannot really be guilty; bad people—like her conservative critics—are never really innocent. Nothing is objective. All is seen through the prism of ideology.

THE LOCKDOWN

Hillary's defense tactics—private investigators, character assassination, denial, and even turning scandal into ideological warfare—have backfired over and over again. But *Living History* would indicate that she has learned nothing.

In fact, the entire catastrophe, beginning with Clinton's perjury in the Paula Jones deposition, and ending with the subsequent impeachment and his trial in the Senate, could have been averted had she been willing to listen to reason and be a bit flexible.

Lanny Davis, a key Clinton defender, ruminated to Gail Sheehy on what might have been if Hillary had not stonewalled the media requests for information. "One can speculate that the whole chain of events that led up to the Whitewater investigation, then led to Ken Starr, which then led to the investigation of Monica and finally to impeachment can be traced back to . . . [Hillary's] first instinct—to lock down."

Davis is absolutely right. Both Ken Starr's original Whitewater investigation, and the Paula Jones lawsuit in which Clinton lied under oath, could have been stopped early on had Hillary been less reflexively insistent on stonewalling. In fact, no special prosecutor would have been appointed had she been more forthcoming in answering the media's requests for information on Whitewater. And had she accepted Paula Jones's offers to settle her lawsuit, Bill would never have been summoned to a deposition in the first place.

The settlement offer was actually quite generous. Jones, a former Arkansas state employee, sued Clinton saying that she had been led to his hotel room by a state trooper on some pretext. Once there, she said, the governor behaved lewdly and propositioned her. To settle her lawsuit, Jones just wanted Clinton to affirm her good moral character and rebut the accusations of the president's defenders that she had asked the trooper to take her to Clinton's room in hopes of having an affair with the governor. All Jones wanted Clinton to say was: "I do not deny meeting Paula Jones on May 8, 1991, in a room at the Excelsior Hotel. She did not engage in any improper or sexual conduct. I believe her to be a truthful and moral person." That was it. No money. No admission of inappropriate behavior.

But Hillary's strategy was to lock down.

In *Living History*, she writes that she wouldn't settle because it would create "a terrible precedent . . . the lawsuits would never end."

But that wasn't the real reason she rejected Jones's offer.

To have accepted it would have been to admit that a state trooper brought Paula Jones to "a room at the Excelsior Hotel" in Little Rock. To admit that this was how Clinton used troopers would have lent credibility to the charges of retired Arkansas cops that they had procured women for Clinton while he was governor.

By then, the tapestry of lies Hillary had created in defense of Bill was so densely interwoven that she could not admit the truth in one sector without imperiling her defense of her husband in another. Pull one thread, and the whole design unraveled. So for the sake of covering up the trooper scandal (for which Clinton could not have been impeached, for it concerned his conduct as governor and was not criminal), she let the Jones suit continue, until it mushroomed into perjury by the president—an impeachable offense. And, to her credit, in *Living History* Hillary admits to the mistake: "With the wisdom of hindsight, of course, not settling the Jones suit early on was the second biggest tactical mistake made in handling the barrage of investigations and lawsuits." She can't resist adding, "The first was requesting an independent counsel at all."

But then, she goes on to remind the reader that "Judge Susan Webber Wright had decided to throw out the Paula Jones lawsuit, finding that it lacked factual or legal merit."

So why did Bill settle the case and pay Jones $850,000?

Hillary explains: "Although he hated to settle a case he'd already won . . . Bill decided that there was no other sure way to put this episode to rest."

But that's a far, far cry from what actually happened.

The truth is that Judge Wright threw out the Jones lawsuit, finding that her case did not rise to the level required to take a sexual harassment case to a federal jury, since Jones had neither been punished for withholding sexual favors, nor was the single incident sufficient to create a hostile workplace environment. Nonetheless, she found the president of the United States to be in civil contempt of court and referred the matter to the Arkansas Supreme Court for disciplinary action. The result: Clinton's law license was suspended for five years. Incredibly, none of this makes it into *Living History*.

The idea that paying Jones almost $1 million was not an admission of guilt is absurd. Why would anyone pay almost a million dollars to settle a lawsuit that had been dismissed? The sum amounted to a good part of the Clintons' life savings at the time (and the settlement specified that they could not pay it out of their legal defense fund, but had to write a personal check, although an insurance policy paid for part of it).

COUNTER-ATTACK

For connoisseurs of seamy political activity, Hillary's defense of her husband was a banquet with many courses. One of the most distasteful was her attempt, in 1992, to plant a story in the press about George H. W. Bush's alleged infidelities.

Far from decrying what she called "tabloid journalism," she now found herself defending Bill by peddling smut.

Author Gail Sheehy reports Hillary's attempts to plant the story firsthand: "Then Hillary went a little too far. It was not by chance that during a formal interview with me . . . [she] purposefully planted a toxic tidbit in my tape recorder: 'Why does the press shy away from investigating rumors about George Bush's extramarital life?' she complained. She told me a little story. 'I had tea with Anne Cox Chambers . . . and she's sittin' here in her sunroom saying 'You know, I just don't understand why they think they can get away with this—everybody knows about George Bush.' And then she launches into this long description of, you know, Bush and his carrying on, all of which is apparently well known in Washington. I'm convinced part of it is that the establishment—regardless of party—sticks together. They're going to circle the wagons on Jennifer and all these other people.' "

"Jennifer" refers, Sheehy explains, to a "decade long Bush staffer who by then enjoyed a senior State Department position."

Once again, the stench of private detectives lurks around the edges of Hillary's story. *Vanity Fair* reported the contention of a former member of Lenzner's staff that Cody Shearer, brother of Hillary's staffer Brooke Shearer, "was working on the Bush love thing with IGI [Lenzner's firm]. He did it in writing. I know it didn't stop, because Cody kept coming around." Lenzner and Cody Shearer both "adamantly deny" the story. But then Hillary tries to plant the story with Sheehy? Strange.

When Sheehy later told Hillary that "I had independently confirmed the story she had told me about Jennifer and Bush . . . [Hillary] gave me a glittery lizard eye blink." Her voice went cold as a courtroom witness: "I have no independent recollection of such a conversation."

Regardless of whether any affair took place, though, Sheehy had something remarkable on tape: the future first lady, dishing dirt to hurt her husband's opponent and his wife.

THE BOTTOM LINE

Hillary's defense of Bill against accusations of scandal shows her at the worst. Her use of detectives, stonewalling, lying, deception, and counter-attack presents her in the most unflattering light imaginable.

Of course, we could hardly expect Hillary to be at her best when goaded beyond endurance by attacks and accusations on the one hand, and by the irresponsible behavior of her husband on the other. It's important to realize that she did not descend into this netherworld of spies and detectives on her own. Nor did she do it to defend her own personal conduct. She was, at least partly, lured into the use of such squalid tactics by the circumstances of her husband's career and conduct.

But not entirely. Bill's weaknesses certainly are what prompted Hillary to defend him with every weapon at her disposal. The choice of those weapons, and the use to which she put them, is Hillary's responsibility alone. She has demonstrated that we cannot rely on her conscience to keep her from using the most sordid and virulent methods when she feels that her grasp on power is threatened. Since such threats are an occupational hazard for whoever occupies the White House, we are right to wonder how many of these black arts she might bring should she continue on the path she has determined will return her there.

The first step on that path was her 2000 campaign for the United States Senate.

8

SENATOR HILLARY

The deal between the Clintons had always been this: first Bill and then Hillary. In 1990, when Bill asked me to explore the possibility of Hillary running for governor of Arkansas, he explained the bargain explicitly: "She feels we've done everything for me. My career and my needs have taken a front-row seat—now it's her turn."

It wasn't the right time for Hillary to run in 1990, but from the moment that Daniel Patrick Moynihan announced his retirement from the U.S. Senate on November 6, 1998, Hillary began to focus on running to fill his seat.

Speculation that she would run heated up after New Jersey Senator Robert Torricelli, likely on cue from the White House, aired the idea on *Meet the Press* on January 3, 1999.

A reasonable person might wonder why Hillary Clinton, of Illinois, Arkansas, and the District of Columbia, was being mentioned as a possible senator from New York. In *Living History*, even Hillary raises the issue, with remarkable understatement: "I was not a New York native." Not a native? She had never lived there, never worked there, rarely visited the city, and had no intention of moving there—unless it was to run for office.

I am very much a New York native. I grew up on the ninth floor of an apartment building on Manhattan's West Side and attended the city's public schools and Columbia University, thirty blocks north of my home. I talk about New York all the time. During the years I worked with them in Arkansas, I would often tell the Clintons about concerts, ballet, or plays I'd seen. I even made a practice of bringing a huge corned beef sandwich from the Carnegie Deli— New York's best—to Little Rock and presenting it with great ceremony to media creator David Watkins, usually in front of Hillary. I called it my "New York Care Package." And, as I've mentioned, on plenty of occasions I celebrated (or bemoaned) the performance of the New York Yankees in front of the Clintons.

I saw Hillary frequently from 1980 until 1990. But never, not once, did she evince the slightest, remotest interest in New York, city or state. She never asked what it was like to live there, or to grow up in Manhattan. She showed no curiosity about the city's schools, crime, taxes, drug problems, politics or anything else. She seemed as interested in New York as she was in Detroit or anyplace else. In fact, during one Clinton visit to New York, shortly after Chelsea's birth, I gave Hillary a copy of the local weekly newspaper for my community at the time, called the *Chelsea Clinton News*. ("Chelsea" referred to the area between 14th and 34th streets on the West Side; "Clinton" was the name of the neighborhood between 34th and 59th.) Hillary did a double take and asked if we had gotten the paper printed up especially for her.

So when Hillary registered her interest in running for Senate in my native state, I reacted with disbelief. As a lifelong New Yorker, I bristled at the idea of an interloper *pretending* to be one of us, for the sole purpose of *leaving* us to go to Washington to *represent* us. Whenever I heard her say "we New Yorkers . . ." it struck my ears like nails on a chalkboard.

I also felt keenly disappointed that Hillary would launch her political career with so obvious a deception. In my weekly column in the *New York Post*, I suggested that she should wait until 2004, when a Senate seat in Illinois came up for grabs. I felt she might become a good senator, but not from a state she had never met.

Hillary, of course, sees nothing problematic about her choice. In *Living History*, she writes that her reason for running was that "I had spoken out about the importance of women participating in politics and government, seeking elective office and using the power of their own voices to shape public policy and chart their nations' future. How could I pass up an opportunity to do the same?" As in so many other cases, Hillary chose to treat the prospect of making a Senate run herself as a referendum on group identity rather than her own qualifications. She redefined the decision, in *Living History* and likely in her own mind, from "Should *this* woman run for *this* Senate seat from *this* state?" to "Should *a* woman run for *a* seat?"

But Hillary pulled it off: She won the seat.

The audacity—and success—of the move left me amazed. I'd never really believed she would have the chutzpah to run in a state where she'd never even lived. And even once it became clear she was serious about running, I never thought she had a chance of getting elected, for Rudy Giuliani would easily defeat her. Wrong and wrong. She ran and Rudy dropped out, leaving her pitted against an unknown young congressman named Rick Lazio who had little time to establish himself.

More important, I did not know what Hillary knew: that demographic changes reflected in the federal census of 2000 (which were not yet public during the campaign), had dramatically shifted New York from a swing state to a solidly Democratic one. She would likely have known that the population shifts were in her favor, and that would certainly have influenced her decision.

Hillary's Senate campaign is both her most splendid achievement and her most original effort. And a close examination of its ups and downs—and its treatment in *Living History*—offers a fascinating window on the real world of Hillary Clinton.

THE CLINTON MARRIAGE
GEARS FOR BATTLE

Hillary's Senate run finally gave her the chance to pull away, by some measure at least, from Bill's gravitational pull. In *Living*

History, Hillary deals frankly with the opportunity: "My dilemma was unique. Some worried that Bill was still so popular in New York and such a towering political figure in America that I would never be able to establish an independent political voice. Others thought the controversy attached to him would overwhelm my message. . . ."

As she ran, Hillary said she relished her independence. She told Lucinda Franks of *Talk* magazine: "I want independence. I want to be judged on my own merits. Now for the first time I am making my own decisions. I can feel the difference. It's a great relief."

But even though Hillary was calling the shots, she needed Bill more than ever. It seemed like a role reversal. He had needed her to become—and remain—president; now she needed him to help her win the Senate race. Hillary notes that "he was anxious to be helpful and I welcomed his expertise. . . . The tables were now turned, as he played for me the role I had always performed for him." And of course Bill was very, very supportive. But to suggest that he played the same role that she had long played in his campaigns is ridiculous. Hillary had always campaigned for Bill and weighed in on ideas and policy. She was always supportive, and was an asset in every one of his campaigns.

But that is a far cry from having unfettered access to an advisor who is a two-term president with an encyclopedic knowledge of the federal budget and every single federal program, who is the sitting commander-in-chief, who has negotiated peace accords, developed landmark federal legislation, and worked with the Congress for eight years. Bill Clinton was no ordinary supportive husband. And, of course, as president, he had a staff of experts on every subject, an experienced political team, a stable of generous donors, and access to every Democrat in the country. On his own, he is a brilliant political strategist. In addition, he had a fleet of planes, an almost limitless entertainment budget, absolute access to the media, a boundless ability to raise money, and a personal popularity that was always way ahead of Hillary's.

With all of the power of the federal government, he could, at any time, create a focus on issues favorable to Hillary, as he did with the Middle East peace talks that he held during her campaign.

So this was no simple role reversal of supportive spouses. Bill Clinton wanted Hillary to win, and he did everything he could to make it happen. With the backing of the powerful Clinton political machine and the power of the White House, Hillary was in a different sphere from her opponent. Think of it: If she needed information about a foreign affairs issue, she could talk to the president, the secretary of state, or the chairman of the National Security Council in great depth, at her convenience. Whom could Rick Lazio talk to?

If she needed advice on her political strategy, she could talk to a man who had been through six gubernatorial and two presidential campaigns, and helped write hundreds of scripts for political ads. If she needed help in projecting her image, she could turn to the team that helped make Bill Clinton the first Democratic president since FDR to be elected twice.

If Hillary wanted to charm potential donors and supporters, she could—and did—invite them to fly with her on government planes, or invite them to a state dinner or sleepover in the White House. This power was alluring, of course, and it increased her charisma. Hillary masterfully marshaled all the perks of the presidency to advance her candidacy. Any other candidate would have paled by comparison. While Rick Lazio might hold a fund-raiser with local Republicans on Long Island, Hillary was feted at a Hollywood star-studded affair, surrounded by the celebrities and movie stars she admired, who had been generous donors to Bill Clinton and now supported her. It wasn't even a fair fight.

Bill's public and private involvement in Hillary's campaign was pivotal. As the sitting president, controlling the prestige and the vast resources of his office, he was the man who could turn on the spigot to finance her costly campaign. He was also the party chieftain, and could guarantee her a free ride—without a primary contest—to the

Democratic nomination in a state where she had never lived. He controlled the vast federal bureaucracy, and immense executive authority. Finally, he was about to wield the power of the budget to back up her candidacy.

But, to raise funds, donors needed to know that giving a dollar to Hillary was as good as giving one to Bill. Indeed, now that Clinton could not run again, it was better. Using the White House was the only way she could possibly raise the vast sums she needed to run.

So Hillary had to appear to be close to Bill once again, in much the same way—if for different reasons—as she had in the past.

But changing the image of the Clinton marriage to a semblance of normalcy in the post-Monica years was not an easy task. Hillary had *first* to show that they were estranged after he confessed to her, supposedly for the first time, in August 1998. *Then,* in due time, she needed to make it clear that the breach was healed. The estrangement was vital, for it helped substantiate the idea that they had a real marriage. And the *rapprochement* was essential, allowing her to attract the money and political support she would need to run.

So Hillary and Bill obligingly performed their very public melodrama—first her anger, then her forgiveness, and finally their renewed closeness—before an eager audience of potential campaign donors, party leaders, and all New Yorkers. Photos of their unforgettable walk to the helicopter on the way to Martha's Vineyard with Chelsea between them, of Hillary's adoring gaze at him as he addressed the crowds in Northern Ireland, and their joint appearance at her campaign events—such as the New York State Fair—chronicled the stages of their marital metamorphosis over the years.

Was there ever really a period of alienation between the two of them? It's not impossible. Hillary was never one to hide her anger at Bill, and it was always her style to withdraw completely and cut off anyone who displeased her. By the time the campaign was about to begin, though, it was imperative that Bill and Hillary be seen as a committed couple again.

So it was scarcely surprising, in September 1999, when Hillary took the opportunity of an interview in the inaugural edition of *Talk* magazine to publicize the opening act in the reconciliation drama. Her most intimate confederates, her closest friends, uncharacteristically opened up to author Lucinda Franks with highly personal details of the Bill/Hillary relationship. That was the tip-off. Anyone who knows anything about Hillary Clinton understands that the penalty for talking to the media about anything concerning her—never mind about her innermost secrets—is instant exclusion from her good graces. The shortest route to her list of least-favored people is to talk to the press. So anyone who talked—and still lived—was undoubtedly told to talk. And not just to talk, but to stick to a carefully developed script.

One of the goals of the story was to elaborate on the reconciliation, but it was also necessary to paint the picture of her journey back to Bill. So first Hillary had to show how angry and estranged she had been. Franks quotes "one of [Hillary's] closest aides" as saying "Hillary barely spoke to Bill from the time of the stain on the dress in August right up until the trip to North Africa." Kathie Berlin, a friend of Hillary's, told Franks that Clinton "suffered terribly from Hillary's exclusion. If he had trouble keeping focused, as people say he did, it was because she was no longer part of the equation." Bernie Nussbaum, former White House counsel and Hillary's personal friend, says that Hillary "acted like someone had died" after the Monica scandal.

Then Hillary had to show her forgiveness and enact a pantomime of Bill's redemption. Melanne Verveer, Hillary's chief of staff and longtime friend told Franks: "I think she fell in love with him again when she came here [to North Africa in the spring of 1999]. As the president has tried to make up for what he has done, we've slowly seen a physical passion come back into their lives. And it's not just for show. I've seen them together when no one is looking. And when they start talking it's electric. The power of ideas positively ignites them."

Had Melanne been this graphic without Hillary's okay, she'd be floating, figuratively, face down in the Hudson River. Like other very close friends, such as Diane Blair, who reported to the press from time to time about the Clintons' love for each other, they proved very useful in sugarcoating the couple's story to gullible, Clinton-favoring journalists. The party line was clear: The marriage is real. She did suffer. She gave him the cold shoulder for a long time. He repented. And now they're back together.

Once more, Hillary struggled mightily to feign domesticity. "I was cutting Bill's grapefruit this morning," she told Franks, "and we had the best idea we ever had about day care, and all of a sudden there's this flapping at the window and it's a seagull—a seagull at our window." (Neither Bill nor Hillary nor the seagull have yet shared the day care brainstorm.)

Hillary even made sure that *Talk* confirmed that they slept together—to showcase Hillary's renewed closeness to her chief fundraiser. The quintessentially private Hillary revealed: "We like to lie in bed," she told Franks, "and watch old movies—you know on those little individual video machines you can hold on your lap?" I knew Hillary Clinton for more than twenty years. And I can testify that her sense of privacy is so intense that it's impossible to imagine her offering a reporter such an intimate tidbit without a compelling motive—in this case to establish that they were an item again.

Of course, just because Hillary was publicly spinning their renewed relationship doesn't mean that it wasn't true that they were back together. Indeed, the lesson in dealing with the Clintons is that their public posturing about their marriage bears no necessary relationship—direct or inverse—to the truth. Their marriage has its ups and downs, but to attempt to chronicle them through their public statements is impossible.

Hillary even used the *Talk* piece to make excuses for Bill, blaming his conduct on the conflict between the two strong women of his youth—his mother and his grandmother—and on how he was abused emotionally as a child. To hear her tell the story, it wasn't his fault after all.

Hillary told Franks that, as they were packing up to move to New York, "she and her husband went through old boxes of papers and photo albums." Hillary said, "it reminds us of our past. That we have one, and that there is so much more than the extremely painful moments."

For his part, Bill made sure he was heard telling friends—and that they told Franks for inclusion in the *Talk* article—"doesn't she look beautiful?" Romance was breaking out all over.

Congressman Charlie Rangel, an early supporter of Hillary's candidacy, even told *Talk*, "You could see the guilt written all over [Clinton's] face" as he participated in talks about the viability of her candidacy. "Any man would do anything to get out of the doghouse he was in." And when that man is president of the United States, he can do quite a great deal.

The *Talk* magazine article was a punctuation mark, an announcement that the long days of pain and alienation were over. Now it was time to move on to the Senate race.

WHITE HOUSE DINNERS

Hillary always controlled the invitations to White House entertainment and state dinners, as do all First Ladies. Until her Senate campaign, the dinners were not especially targeted to attract and reward donors and ingratiate the press. Instead, the invitees were mainly White House Senior Staff, members of the cabinet and Congress, and prominent Americans, politicians, and others, who were associated with the country of the visiting dignitary.

(At one White House state dinner honoring President Zedillo of Mexico in 1995, I was introduced to quite a number of prominent Hispanic and Mexican Americans and Mexican public officials. After dinner, I noticed our friends Gene and Marta Eriquez and went to talk to them. At the time Gene was the mayor of Danbury, Connecticut, the town next to ours; he and Marta had been to our house many times. Gene asked if I had arranged the invitation, but I hadn't. Gene laughed. "I think they must think I'm Hispanic," he said. "That happens a lot with my name." [He's Italian.])

Once Hillary decided to run for the Senate, the purpose of the state dinners and other entertainment at the White House changed drastically. Instead of diplomatic events to showcase the country of the visiting head of state, they became a highly politicized vehicle for courting and rewarding Hillary's donors and supporters, and for reaching out to the national and New York press who would cover her campaign. Camp David and the Lincoln Bedroom also became overnight fund-raising sites for her voracious campaign treasury.

The *Washington Post* reported that "of 404 people invited to sleep overnight at the White House or Camp David since Hillary Clinton began her Senate race, 146 of the guests had contributed money in this election cycle, for a total of $5.5 million, 98 percent of it to Democratic entities. About 100 of the sleepovers have contributed to committees supporting Mrs. Clinton's race, for a total of $624,000. Overnight guests contributed a total of $2.5 million to the Democratic National Committee."

At the height of the fund-raising frenzy, guests were staying overnight at the White House at an average rate of twenty-nine times each month—nearly one per day. It was an occupancy rate any Washington hotel would envy.

In September 2000, Hillary exploited a state dinner honoring Indian Prime Minister Atai Bihari Vajpayee: Hillary seized upon it as an opportunity to reward donors, court New York political reporters, and stroke Empire State politicians. Nearly every guest had some potential connection to Hillary's campaign. According to *Newsweek*, "more than 100 of the 646 guests . . . donated money to Hillary's Senate campaign or several soft money funds set up to benefit her."

Among the most interesting guests were Sydny Weinberg Miner, vice president and senior editor at Simon & Schuster, and Carolyn

Reidy and Michael Selleck from their trade division. Was their memoir deal already in the works?

Hillary's most blatant use of the White House and the social prestige and power of the presidency to raise funds for her campaign was the Millennium Dinner at the White House. Nearly a thousand people were invited to celebrate the arrival of the twenty-first century that evening, but the list was so politically sensitive that the White House refused to release all of it.

At Hillary's table was Dennis Rivera, New York local president of the Service Employees International Union—a key player in local politics. The union donated $10,000 to her campaign, and mobilized its 300,000 members on her behalf. Bernard Schwartz, head of the Loral Corporation, also joined Hillary at her table. Loral is best remembered for being accused of selling satellite technology information to China, but it should not be forgotten that Schwartz and his wife had donated $40,000 to support Hillary's campaign.

At the president's table, of course, was Terry McAuliffe, his chief fund-raiser. Also there were Walter Shorenstein, one of the Democratic Party's top fifty soft-money patrons, and S. Daniel Abraham, founder of Slim-Fast, who contributed $76,000 to Hillary's campaign and affiliated committees.

Also attending was Beth Dozhoretz, the fund-raiser who lobbied for Marc Rich's pardon and who provided the Clintons with their dining room table and other gifts. Walter Kaye, a donor and gift-giver who got Monica Lewinsky her job at the White House, was there. Jill Abramson of the *New York Times* was on the guest list, as was E. J. Dionne of the *Washington Post*. According to the *Post,* the Millennium event "evolved into an off the record fund-raiser, with corporate sponsors shelling out millions to mingle with the Clintons and their celebrity guests."

Hillary even planned to publish a book about White House entertaining during her Senate campaign. But the publicity about her blatant use of these state dinners to court political supporters likely induced her to postpone publication until after the election was over.

The idea for the book probably stemmed from a story that appeared in the *Washington Post* shortly after White House Social Secretary Ann Stock left her position in October 1997. The small article announced that Stock and then-White House chef Walter Scheib were planning to write a book together based on their experiences planning parties at the Clinton White House. The book would include recipes from state dinners and other White House events and tips on entertaining.

Remember how much Hillary likes her staff to speak out on their own? Well, before the ink had dried on that *Post* article, somebody must have had quite a talking-to. The Stock/Scheib book disappeared, but by the end of the Clinton presidency, a very similar book hit the shelves. The author? Hillary Rodham Clinton.

An Invitation to the White House: At Home with History was published by Simon & Schuster on November 14, 2000. The book featured more than one hundred flattering photographs (including a cover shot) of a sophisticated Hillary as the hostess at various White House events. Hillary was shown with Lauren Bacall, Meryl Streep, Willie Nelson, John F. Kennedy Jr., Ricky Martin, Princess Diana, the Rev. Billy Graham, the Rev. Jesse Jackson; with the president, she was pictured with Nelson Mandela, Queen Noor and the late King Hussein of Jordan, former President and Mrs. Kim of Korea, the Emperor and Empress of Japan, the king and queen of Spain, Tony and Cherie Blair, Stevie Wonder, Czech President Vaclav Havel, Harry Belafonte, and on and on. It was the ultimate manifestation of Hillary's addiction to celebrities.

The book even shows photos of a 1998 carnival on the White House grounds. Yet it fails to mention that the company operating the fair was run by Edward and Vonna Jo Gregory—the pair who were convicted of bank fraud in 1982 and who then hired Hillary's brother, Tony Rodham, to get them a pardon. Bill came through with the coveted pardon after the Gregorys contributed to Hillary's campaign. But Hillary apparently found none of this important to mention; her accompanying text merely recalls: "In 1998 Capricia

Marshall and I decided to stage an old-fashioned carnival, complete with Ferris Wheel, daredevil rides, cotton candy, and balloon artists for the children" (and presidential pardons for the carnival's owners).

THE POWER OF THE PRESIDENCY . . . AT HILLARY'S DISPOSAL

White House dinners weren't the only way that the Clintons courted donors. President Clinton used the broad power of the presidency to raise funds for Hillary. According to *U.S. News and World Report,* on October 27, 1999, Clinton asked the president of the European Community to allow American aircraft landing in Europe to be equipped with "hush kits" to abate noise. One leading manufacturer of these kits is ABS Partnership, whose principals, Sandra Wagenfeld and Francine Goldstein, gave $160,000 to Hillary's campaign right before Clinton's intervention. The two women had also given $301,000 to the Democratic National Committee in 1999, and were guests at a White House state dinner in June of that year for the president of Hungary.

No mention of fund-raising, and certainly no allusion to the use of the White House, Camp David, or Air Force One for that purpose, appears anywhere in *Living History.* Asked about the numerous guests to White House events who contributed to her campaign, Hillary said "I don't think it is particularly newsworthy. There just really isn't any reason for anybody to raise questions about it." But Hillary used the White House in many, many other ways, as *U.S. News* reported:

- In 1999 alone, Hillary traveled to New York thirty-five times or more on military aircraft. While each of the trips had an official excuse—visiting the United Nations or inner-city schools—they also gave her the opportunity to campaign and look for a place to live.
- She used federal aircraft to fly to two fund-raisers in Los Angeles, including a $10,000 a couple dinner hosted by Steven Spielberg

and his wife. She justified the use of public planes by making a
speech in the San Fernando Valley.

- Hillary took a $25,000 contribution from Metabolife International, the maker of a weight-loss supplement, which had been
trying to stop FDA action against its product.

As the article noted, "The first lady, in a word, is finding lots of
ways to employ the advantages of incumbency without ever having
held political office."

President Clinton also used the federal budget and policy to
Hillary's advantage:

- Late in 1999, President Clinton announced a major increase in
housing aid, largely to the benefit of New York—a reversal of
seven years of cost cutting, including major increases in aid for
low income tenants.
- The president restored budget cuts in Medicaid payments to New
York's teaching hospitals, deleting a key cost reduction that had
been a centerpiece of the 1997 budget-balancing deal.
- HUD Secretary Andrew Cuomo announced that the federal government would directly fund homeless shelters in New York City,
bypassing city government, which was the usual channel for such
aid (and thereby embarrassing Hillary's then-opponent, New York
Mayor Rudy Giuliani).

Using the White House, the president, Camp David, state dinners,
government planes, government patronage, and the federal budget,
Hillary put together a massive war chest to fund her Senate campaign
in the third most populous state in the nation.

And when reporters got too close on the trail of her White House
fund-raising exploits, Hillary simply shut down access. At the Millennium party, reporters were not permitted to the larger event. When
asked about this policy, the first lady's spokesperson, Marsha Berry,
stated: "It's closed because it's closed."

Every president harnesses the machinery of the federal government to help his chances for re-election. But Hillary's unabashed use of *all* the president's resources for her Senate race is a frightening preview of how politicized her administration might be in awarding federal contracts, aid, and spending.

CHAPPAQUA

Hillary even tried to use the Clinton financial machine to buy her home in Chappaqua, a wealthy Westchester County suburb of New York City, where she moved to establish residence in her newly adopted state. At first, Hillary sought to buy the $1.7 million house with a $1.35 million mortgage guaranteed by Terry McAuliffe, the Clinton fund-raising director and future chairman of the Democratic National Committee.

On September 3, 1999, newspapers told their readers all about the new Clinton home, a "100-year-old manor house at 15 Old House Lane." The Clintons issued a neighborly statement: "We appreciate everyone who helped make our search for a new home an enjoyable experience. We particularly want to thank the homeowners, their neighbors and the real estate brokers who have been so gracious to us throughout our search."

USA Today reported that "White House aides said McAuliffe's participation was required because the type of loan the Clintons took out was a security-backed mortgage, with McAuliffe putting up the securities."

The Clintons couldn't even buy a home of their own without triggering a scandal.

The *New York Times* reported that the Clintons had originally asked former Treasury Secretary Robert Rubin and former chiefs of staff Mack McLarty and Erskine Bowles to sign the guarantee, but were turned down by all three. But "Mr. McAuliffe did not hesitate to help."

The Clintons had been genuinely concerned that they might not qualify for a mortgage because of their outstanding legal debts, now in the millions of dollars. "It weighed very heavily on Hillary," said one person close to the Clintons. "She was very worried that they were going to lose the house. She was distraught."

"Terry would do anything for them," the *Times*'s source said. "He clearly knew there were consequences to helping them and that he would put himself in harm's way, but he was ready to take the heat."

Indeed there were "consequences."

The *Times* noted that "leaders of several public watchdog groups said that the refusals by Mr. McLarty and Mr. Rubin demonstrated that the favor done by Mr. McAuliffe was even more important to the Clintons than anyone had first realized. 'This is a President who has never had any compunction about going around with a tin cup,' said Charles Lewis, the founder and executive director of the Center for Public Integrity. 'Most people would have a very, very difficult time asking someone to write a check for $1.3 million.'"

The house sale set off alarms all over Washington and New York. Was McAuliffe's guarantee a gift? The Clintons said no, because the money was to be held in escrow. Public interest advocates said yes, because McAuliffe had to put the money in a bank and was denied the use of it for the five-year term of the Clintons' mortgage. Rudy Giuliani himself questioned the deal: "A million-three is a lot of money; somebody putting it in the bank for you is quite unusual."

The problem was determining whether the guarantee was a gift, and thus subject to taxation. To handle the heat, Hillary made up a story. She said the deal had the seal of approval of the federal ethics office. "Everything that we've done has been passed on by the Office of Government Ethics and has been legally approved," she said.

Well, not quite. According to the *New York Times*, "Stephen D. Potts, the director of the independent ethics office, said that his office had ruled only on the narrower question of whether Mr. Clinton would have to report Mr. McAuliffe's involvement on his annual financial disclosure form. Mr. Potts said that the narrow question was the only one that the White House Counsel's Office had raised about the arrangement with Mr. McAuliffe."

Potts added: "If the President's and Mrs. Clinton's statements were accurately quoted by the press, they could give the impression that the Clintons accepted the loan guarantee because O.G.E. (Office of Government Ethics) said its acceptance was not a problem. We do not know who 'legally approved' acceptance of the loan guarantee or who advised that the loan guarantee 'was not a gift.' We do know that it was not O.G.E."

Potts said he had warned the White House about that interpretation after first reading Mrs. Clinton's remarks in mid-September. But Hillary still didn't get the message. Potts said he subsequently saw President Clinton quoted in the *Washington Post* saying that he took the loan "only after receiving assurances from O.G.E. that the loan guarantee did not constitute a gift under federal law.'"

When it came out that Hillary didn't have the fig leaf of the ethics approval, she had to backtrack and get a real mortgage. On October 14, the Clintons announced that they had taken out a new mortgage loan of $1.35 million for their house without McAuliffe's guarantee.

If the Clintons had gone through with the McAuliffe guarantee, would it have been a gift? Under the terms of the new loan, *sans* guarantee, the Clintons had to pay 7.5 percent interest. The old loan, with McAuliffe standing behind the Clintons, was for 6.5 percent. The extra one percent interest, on a $1.35 million mortgage, comes to $13,500 per year for the five-year term of the mortgage—a gift of $67,500.

The Clintons' conduct in arranging their Chappaqua home purchase tells us a lot. Eight years of ducking scandal in the White House—and living to tell about it—had apparently made the Clintons so confident about their ability to get away with anything that they hardly gave a second thought to an arrangement that attracted so much criticism that they had to rescind it. And they seemed to be so tone-deaf that they failed even to anticipate the criticism.

And for what? For 1 percent? In order to shave their debt service payments by $13,500 per year—when they had $18 million in book deals in the offing—they were willing to risk a public scandal just as Hillary was approaching a Senate race in a state where she'd never lived. There's a word for this sort of attitude: arrogance.

And this arrogance is matched by their growing appetites. The Clintons I knew in the 1980s and early 1990s would put up with any financial hardship in order to survive and prevail politically. No desire for wealth would ever have stood in the way of their ambition. But here they were risking her political career to buy a great, big expensive home . . . and not even to buy it, but to save a few bucks in paying for it.

A hunger for luxury; an eye for loopholes (real or imagined); a rampant materialism and disregard of ethics rules—are these the principles on which a President Hillary would pad her own nest while presuming to steer the economy and lead our country forward?

THE PARDONS

But not all the help President Clinton gave Hillary was financial. He also used the power of pardon—supposedly the most nonpolitical power of the office—to help her get elected. In a pardon, one man—the president, who was not present at the trial—overrides the verdict of a jury and the sentencing of a magistrate with the stroke of a pen. It is a power almost uniquely absolute in our democracy, usually so governed by checks and balances.

The key difference between New York politics and those of any other state in America is its balkanization into a dozen or more ethnic voting blocs. As the initial destination for many of America's legal immigrants—and a goodly share of the illegal entrants—New York's ethnic groups are not homogenized. Russians, Poles, Chinese, Koreans, Dominicans, Salvadorans, Mexicans, Haitians, and the rest remain fiercely separate, their communities vibrant and distinct.

Most of these constituencies lean to the Democratic Party anyway, but two—Puerto Ricans and Hasidic Jews—have shown considerable independence. New York's Republican governor, George Pataki, won a surprising share of the Puerto Rican vote in his 2002 bid for a third term. Hasidic Jews, at odds with New York's African American community, have increasingly turned their backs on the Democrats and embraced Republican candidates. Wild cards in the state's ongoing political poker game, these groups are key targets for anyone seeking public office.

Every politician caters to them, as one might expect, with patronage, promises, and platitudes. But only Hillary and Bill gave them pardons.

The FALN (Fuerzas Armadas de Liberacion Nacional—The Armed Forces of National Liberation)—is the Puerto Rican equivalent of the Irish Republican Army. Determined to end their island's status as a commonwealth affiliated with the United States, they want complete independence. As Barbara Olson wrote, they are "a Marxist group responsible for a reign of terror that included 130 bombing attacks in the United States from 1974 to 1983. Chicago, New York, and Washington were prime . . . targets, with attacks against the New York office of the FBI, military recruiting centers, and the Chicago campaign headquarters of Jimmy Carter. All told, the terrorists racked up six deaths and scores of wounded. The victims included the husband of Diana Berger of Cherry Hill, New Jersey, six months pregnant with her first child when her husband fell victim to an FALN bomb. Joseph and Thomas Connor, nine and eleven, lost their father in the same bomb attack. Other attacks left police officers maimed and blind."

And yet Bill Clinton pardoned them.

After 9/11, it's hard to imagine any president pardoning a terrorist. But back in 1999, it was fashionable—in some liberal circles, anyway—to look with favor on the FALN, in much the same way that those same circles had cheered for the Black Panthers during Hillary's law school days.

New York Puerto Rican Congressman José Serrano called these figures political prisoners, and signed an open letter to President Clinton calling for their release. He was joined by former President Jimmy

Carter and South African Archbishop Desmond Tutu in urging the clemency.

But for all the hype among New York's liberals, opposition to pardoning the FALN was widespread:

- Carlos Romero-Barcelo, Puerto Rico's congressional delegate (who sits in the House of Representatives but cannot vote) came out against the pardons. "These are people who acted in cold blood with the purpose of imposing their will," he said. "These are the worst crimes in a democracy. . . . How can we responsibly set them free? What if they kill somebody else?"
- FBI Director Louis Freeh opposed the pardon.
- The Justice Department sent Clinton a memo in 1996 against the pardons.
- The FBI's assistant director of national security, Neil Gallagher, denounced the FALN as "criminals, and they are terrorists and they represent a threat to the United States."

But the potential gains for Hillary among New York's Puerto Rican community were too good to pass up. It was a game the Clintons had played before: The president had already acted to appease the Puerto Rican community by banning the use of live ammunition tests at the Navy Training Base in Vieques, Puerto Rico, long a grievance of the island's residents and émigrés. Pardoning the FALN was the next step.

So, in September 1999, Bill Clinton offered pardons to sixteen FALN terrorists. (Because they had not even sought pardons—they saw themselves as political prisoners who did not need to be pardoned—the president could only "offer" the pardons rather than "grant" them. Fourteen accepted his largesse.)

When the pardons were announced, Hillary was supportive but said she had "no involvement in or prior knowledge of the decision."

As the *New Republic* noted, Hillary's statement is "hard to believe." The magazine reported that on "August 9th, two days before the president announced the clemency deal, New York City Council-man Jose Rivera personally presented Hillary with a packet on clemency, including a letter asking her to 'speak to the president and ask him to consider granting executive clemency' to the prisoners."

The magazine reported that "Hillary may also have heard some-thing about the issue from clemency advocate Dennis Rivera . . . head of the health-care workers union."

And how could President Clinton not have told his wife about the pardons? Here she was, running for Senate in the state that had the largest Puerto Rican population in the nation. The pardons di-rectly affected how she would be perceived in that community. They were, obviously, controversial. They would have a lasting impact on her candidacy. It is just not credible that he didn't tell her.

Invoking executive privilege, the president refused to release the background documents that led to his decision to grant clemency. But the outcry was enormous and instant. Police associa-tions, New York newspapers, and her then-opponent, Rudy Giu-liani, attacked the pardons and Hillary for supporting them. The *Washington Post* reported "the backlash against the offer is reported to have caught the White House by surprise." Hillary needed to run for cover. Once more, the Clintons seemed to have had no clue that releasing convicted terrorists who had not even requested it might cause a problem.

Because her husband had actually only "offered" clemency to the terrorists, they had to accept or reject his proffer. After three weeks, many of the terrorists had not yet accepted the clemency and its precondition that they pledge to abstain from violence. Hillary seized on their response to reverse her position and oppose Bill's action, saying "It's been three weeks and their silence speaks volumes." In the end, then, Hillary got to have it both ways: sup-porting clemency when it appeared beneficial, running away when it started to look costly.

Joseph Connor, whose father fell victim to the FALN, summa-rizes the pardons eloquently: "The Clinton family traded the release of terrorists for votes; votes that were promised to be delivered by New York politicians to Hillary for senate and Gore for president. That was clear."

Of course, that was not Clinton's only problematic pardon. The most controversial went to Mark Rich, a fugitive who fled the United States, renounced his American citizenship, and settled in Switzerland to avoid answering federal fraud charges. National anger over pardoning a man who wouldn't appear in court and was no longer even an American citizen—and still won't come back to the United States as of this writing—was long and loud.

Rich's estranged wife, songwriter and Clinton supporter Denise Rich, fought hard for the pardon, and distributed her financial largesse far and wide to win favorable consideration. Among her donations to Clinton-related funds was $450,000 to the Clinton Library, $10,000 to the Clintons' legal defense fund, $70,000 to the Hillary Clinton campaign or committees that supported her campaign, as well as a gift of $7,000 worth of furniture to the Clintons. Rich also gave $1 million to the Democratic Party and other Democratic candidates.

If the FALN pardons were intended to help Hillary with Hispanic voters, the pardon of the leaders of the New Square Community in Rockland County, New York, helped with Hasidic voters among New York's Orthodox Jewish Community.

The four New Square leaders had applied for and received federal scholarships for 1,500 phantom students at the religious school they ran, pocketing $40 million of taxpayer money. Sentenced to prison terms in 1999 of between two and a half and six and a half years, the community began to press for pardons.

In August 2000, while campaigning for the Senate, Hillary visited New Square and met with Rabbi David Twersky, a community leader. Her visit was most successful. In November 2000, while other Hasidic districts voted overwhelmingly for Hillary's opponent, New Square backed her by 1,400 votes to only twelve.

On December 22, 2000, with a month left in his presidency, Clinton met with the leaders of New Square at the White House about a pardon for their leaders. Hillary was present, but contends that she did not speak at the meeting. Evidently she didn't have to; all four New Square leaders received presidential pardons.

The FALN and New Square pardons go beyond the tackiness of inviting donors to sleep in the White House or at Camp David, or the questionable ethics of inviting them to taxpayer funded White House dinners. These pardons freed terrorists and swindlers from prison.

One thing that can be said with certainty about a second Clinton presidency is that the power of pardons will remain just as powerful, and as tempting, to President Hillary as it was to President Bill.

MANAGING THE MEDIA

During her Senate campaign, Hillary was still able to use her status as first lady to blunt media questions as her campaign unfolded. Members of the Secret Service kept reporters at bay, citing security concerns, and the first lady turned down interviews with reporters she considered hostile.

Fred Dicker, the *New York Post*'s Albany bureau chief, described how it worked: "She'll show up at a local event and you'll go up to her like you would any candidate and say 'Mrs. Clinton, can I ask you . . .' and she runs off and the Secret Service blocks us. She's done that time after time after time. You can't get to her. She's using the resources of the federal government to prevent us from just having the kind of access you would take for granted with any other politician."

Sometimes, the Secret Service agents even used force to keep the press away from Hillary. As Metro Network newsman Glenn Schuck recounted, at one rally "Secret Service agents literally [were] pushing press to the ground. . . . I mean they just started pushing and shoving; female camera people five feet tall were getting thrown to the ground, cameras flying. Myself, I was grabbed by the shoulder, thrown back over. I think somebody from Channel 11 landed on my back."

Most candidates could not get away with this policy of distancing the media, but Hillary used her special status as first lady to make it work.

To work for her, anyway. Politicians always prefer to control their ostensibly spontaneous appearances in front of voters, and Hillary is no exception. The most extreme example came when she appeared on *Late Show with David Letterman*. In *Living History*, Hillary says that because "late-night comics sometimes skewer their guests. . . . I was a little nervous."

She needn't have been (and she probably wasn't); after all, everything had been scripted out in advance. The highlight of the Letterman show was a quiz he gave her about New York State to test her local knowledge. She answered all the questions correctly. But the New York *Daily News* revealed that her staff, taking a page from the fixed television quiz shows of the 1950s, had been given the questions in advance. Like Mark Van Doren, the legendary cheat from the original quiz show scandals, Hillary would pretend to search her memory as Letterman asked each question, seeming to stall for time, and then blurt out the answer at the last moment—always correct. The tension mounted as Dave asked each of the ten questions in turn—but Hillary aced the test.

GIULIANI WITHDRAWS

I do not believe Hillary could have defeated her original opponent for the Senate, Rudy Giuliani. Even before his canonization after the crisis of 9/11, his popularity downstate would have made Hillary's task truly daunting. To win in New York State, a Democrat must come out of New York City with a huge margin in order to offset the enormous Republican base in the suburbs; Giuliani would have run too strongly in New York City and the suburbs for Hillary to win.

But Giuliani turned out to have two problems: prostate cancer and a bad marriage. Hillary could not have known of the former when she announced for the Senate, but the odds are that she knew about the latter. Rudy had been conducting a blatant affair with Judith Nathan, spurning his wife, Donna Hanover. It was an open secret; the entire New York press corps talked about it all the time. Hillary hardly needed her private detective to have known about Nathan.

Would the affair, by itself, have knocked Giuliani out of the Senate race? Perhaps not, but in combination with a sense of his own mortality, and the need to focus on people he truly loved, it was apparently enough to persuade him to pull out. In any event, by withdrawing from the contest Rudy virtually handed the Senate seat to Hillary.

Rick Lazio, Hillary's new opponent, was actually forty-two years old, but looked like he was twenty-five. A center-right congressman from New York's suburbs, he was a virtual unknown. Moreover, because of Giuliani's late departure from the field, Lazio had very little time to build a campaign. Before he could define himself to the voters, Hillary was all over him with negative ads painting him as a right-wing extremist, despite his pro-choice, pro-environmental voting record.

Adding to his circumstantial handicaps, Lazio soon exhibited a tactical deficiency as well. He was determined to play to the grandstands—the legion of Hillary haters—by running negative advertisements emphasizing what everyone knew already: that she was not a New Yorker. Instead of publicizing his own record, Lazio spent all of his time and money attacking her. Negative ads work when they convey new and important information. But negative ads that just restate the obvious don't work. Everyone who would ever vote against Hillary because she wasn't a New Yorker was already voting against her. The ads could do nothing to augment their ranks. Lazio learned too late that the Battle of Hillary was over and the Battle of Lazio had begun.

Many candidates, particularly Republicans, are so enamored of negative ads that they forget to run positive commercials that explain to voters what they are all about. As in baseball, where a fastball is still the best pitch, positive ads remain the most effective weapon in politics. Too bad Lazio didn't choose to run them.

What he chose, instead, was to make an issue of "soft money"—contributions above the legally allowable amount that can be donated to an individual candidate, that are given to parties for issue advertising. Soft money, in short, represented a way to circumvent the legal limit of $1,000 per person per candidate contributions to Senate elections.

Because the Republicans have historically counted on people who can afford to write checks substantially greater than $1,000, they have, in general, opposed limits on soft money. It wasn't surprising, therefore, when Hillary opened the campaign by appealing for an end to soft money donations, reflexively echoing the scripted position of the Democratic Party.

That's when reality departed from the script. Lazio found that anti-Hillary donors flooded his campaign with small contributions through the mail and e-mail, and he quickly decided to agree to ban the larger soft money donations. But Hillary, despite her stated opposition to it, needed soft money. Her donors were special interest types, who wanted to curry favor with the president.

So Hillary was on the spot. She had called for an end to soft money, but she was bluffing, and had never expected to have her bluff called. Two months before election day, Lazio had $10 million in hard money on hand; Hillary had only $7 million. So when Lazio agreed to ban soft money, she didn't know what to do. Suddenly in love with soft money, she conceded that a ban would work against her. It was typical Hillary: There was no objective issue, no fair judgment of ethics or circumstances. There were only measures that would favor the forces of goodness (her) and those that would do the opposite.

But banning soft money had been Hillary's issue. It was she who had first injected it into the Senate race, and it was highly embarrassing that she could not take Lazio's "yes" for an answer and agree not to spend soft money. That is, it would have been embarrassing for most people. In *Living History* Hillary notes, disingenuously: "I wasn't going to commit to it [the soft money ban] unilaterally."

There's only one problem with Hillary's story: Lazio had *already agreed* to cease spending soft money. There was never any question of a "unilateral" ban on these funds.

The issue erupted during their debate on September 15, 2000. Lazio, pen in hand, strode over to Hillary's lectern, hectoring her and demanding that she sign the soft money ban right then and there. "Right here, sign it right now!" Lazio said.

Young and inexperienced, Lazio had overplayed his hand. With so many anti-Hillary zealots, it was hard to focus on the sensitivities of swing voters—a lesson for anyone who runs against Hillary in the future.

The pressure on Hillary to accept the ban on soft money built up. Succumbing, she agreed to the ban on September 24, 2000. Lazio hailed the agreement as a victory, but for him it was actually a big defeat: One of his core issues went away, and Hillary had plenty of success raising enough hard money to compete with Lazio. All that remained in most voters' minds was the image of a menacing Lazio striding over to Hillary's lectern—a move that backfired just as it did for Al Gore in his third presidential debate with George W. Bush the same year.

Ultimately, it was a last-minute event and its aftermath that sealed Hillary's victory. On October 12, 2000—less than a month before the election—al Qaeda terrorists attacked the *USS Cole* in Yemen, killing seventeen American sailors. Hillary cancelled her New York events to go to the memorial service. Nothing, of course, could have been more of a campaign event—as Hillary's every move was broadcast live into the most heavily Jewish state in the nation.

And as if that wasn't bad enough for Lazio, he decided to make it a disaster.

Hillary had accepted a campaign contribution from the American Muslim Alliance, a group that some said had links to terrorists (a charge the group vehemently denied). In a "clerical error" on her disclosure forms, the organization was listed as the "American Museum Alliance." Amazing what a difference a few letters can make.

Cynics called it a deliberate misrepresentation. But Lazio was way too aggressive once more. He set up phone banks to call Jewish voters, attacking Hillary for accepting the donation. He linked it to the *Cole* attack, urging voters to tell Hillary to stop backing terrorist groups.

The charge went way too far. Many candidates think that campaign phone messages fall under the radar and won't be noticed by the establishment press. But not in New York. Lazio's phoners admitted to the calls, and the story blew up. The fact that she shouldn't have taken a donation from such a group was lost in the melee. In its place, Hillary's opponent had handed her a golden opportunity with his implication that Hillary actually "supported" terrorism.

Former New York Mayor Ed Koch, beloved of the city's Jewish voters, rebutted Lazio's charges in a television ad that undoubtedly reached many more people than had gotten the phone calls. "Rick, stop with the sleaze already," Koch said.

WHY HILLARY WON: THE DEMOGRAPHICS

However damaging Lazio's missteps were, though, the real reason for Hillary's victory lay in those demographic insights buried in the 2000 census statistics. New York State, it turned out, had undergone a dramatic population change in the decade from 1990 to 2000. The state had lost half a million people to other states—but it had absorbed an equal number of foreign immigrants. And while those who left were largely older, white Republicans, the immigrants who arrived were Democrats.

Combined, these population shifts had transformed New York from a swing state to a solidly Democratic one. Two years before

Hillary won, Democratic Congressman Chuck Schumer had defeated eighteen-year Republican incumbent Alfonse D'Amato. With Hillary's victory in 2000, New York had two Democrats in the Senate for the first time in fifty years. New York's Republican Governor George Pataki held on to office only by moving so far to the left that the GOP had a hard time recognizing him.

Hillary picked up on these demographic trends—which, remember, she would have seen and studied before the public or the Republicans had a chance—and exploited them brilliantly. I always wondered how she managed such a convincing victory. When the census came out, I understood.

. . . AND AS SENATOR?

As soon as Hillary took office, of course, she was engulfed with a thorough deluge of scandal, stemming from the orgy of White House gift-giving (and taking), her husbands' pardon-granting, and her book deal.

But then things quieted down. She settled into the job of Senator, and brought a calmness to her role that few had anticipated. Even as Washington braced for her arrival, she fooled her detractors by blending in and avoiding controversy.

But she also didn't get much done. At this writing, more than three years into her term, she still has yet to pass a single piece of legislation. She has carved out no area of expertise, and many believe she has yet to make her impact felt in any but a symbolic fashion.

Indeed, her only sustained and vigorous activity has been campaign fund-raising—at which she excels—and the promotion of her book.

The Senate has cast two key votes during her short time in office. On one, the Iraq War, she voted with Bush and the moderates to authorize the use of force against Saddam Hussein. On the other, to expand Medicare to include prescription drugs for the elderly, she voted with the doctrinaire liberals of her own party against the Bush plan. So one vote was centrist and the other leftist.

Some of her votes were motivated by neither leftist ideology nor centrist compromise, but by a desire for personal revenge. As noted, she twice voted against the confirmation of Michael Chertoff for judicial nominations to punish him for his role in the Whitewater investigation. She also opposed Ted Olson's confirmation as solicitor general, presumably to protest his late wife Barbara's role as chief of the staff of the Government Reform Committee that had haunted her and her husband over the FBI file and White House gifts scandals. (Barbara's authorship of two Hillary-bashing books couldn't have helped, either.)

Her one faux pas was to stand up in the Senate and scream that she demanded to know "what Bush knew and when he knew it" about 9/11. Her strident remarks were roundly condemned, and she was quickly chastened into silence.

Hillary visited Iraq in 2003, one step behind President Bush's surprise Thanksgiving visit to the troops. While she was there, she criticized the war, earning the condemnation of the right and the applause of the left.

But the overwhelming impression of Mrs. Clinton's Senate career has been one of mediocrity. Shying away from controversy, avoiding the spotlight, she has done precious little to justify the high hopes with which she was elected.

What she has mainly achieved in the Senate is the recovery of her public image. As each new month passes without a debilitating battle, the flaming red anger of Hillary's White House years has been replaced with a benign glow, suggesting—if not quite proving—a newfound maturity.

But the simple act of maintaining equilibrium in the Senate pales next to the real achievement of Hillary's new career—which was getting elected in the first place. With all her White House privileges and demographic advantages, with all her early gaffes and ill-judged favors, before long she righted herself, stopped making mistakes, and waged a skillful campaign. When her opponent's negative ads gave her an opening, she pounced on it wisely and well, sealing a lead she never lost.

If the first task of a president is to be a good politician, Hillary demonstrated her ability in this first outing. Drawing on her experiences as both a manager and an advocate, she managed to get her message across, and out-perform her Republican rival.

And so concluded the first act of *HILLARY: The Drama*—with its heroine riding high. Will the rest of the production be remembered as a triumph? A farce? Or a tragedy?

9

THE PERFECT STORM

At this writing, a confluence of political circumstances and trends is propelling Hillary Clinton toward the presidency—a political perfect storm where all of the forces needed to win seem to be aligning in her favor:

- The public relations triumph of her book and promotional tour.
- A safe perch in the Senate, where the wounds of Whitewater and the other Clinton scandals are healing—and our memories are fading.
- The dearth of other potential Democratic rivals: After John Kerry, who is left?
- On the Republican side, no heir apparent (always excepting yet another Bush).
- The dramatically and rapidly changing demographics of the United States, with our growing minority population.

All these are moving Hillary Clinton into the on-deck circle.

Last summer's brilliantly orchestrated marketing campaign for *Living History* improved Hillary's image, and raised her approval ratings to new heights. Through her autobiography, however distorted, Hillary defined herself, evoking sympathy and admiration. Her descriptions of her family and career, of the pain and losses she has suffered, made her appear more human, more vulnerable, and less frightening, particularly to other women. By crossing the country on her book tour, she reached out to tens of thousands of people who swarmed her signings and saw her as a star. The reviews may have been negative, but her appearance with Barbara Walters was such an example of softball journalism that it could have been a paid political advertisement. Sure that she'd receive few direct challenges to the story as she presented it in her book, Hillary was able to be positive and cheerful, smiling and happy. She was the All-New HILLARY.

At the same time, she gloried in her role as a senator. With the days of the special prosecutor behind her, the complaints about her credibility and character had dwindled. Her work as a senator was of less interest to the national press, which allowed her to restrict her public visibility and stay on message. No longer on the defensive—no longer obliged to spend her days hiding billing records or denying accusations—Hillary's popularity rose as her past scandals faded. Her handlers spent their days placing stories describing her quiet effectiveness and newfound popularity on Capitol Hill: Hillary as Miss Congeniality.

And the other Democratic contenders seemed to die on the vine. Howard Dean met with a debacle and self-destructed. Joe Lieberman faltered at takeoff. Wesley Clark started with much promise, but never fulfilled it. Dick Gephardt died a much-deserved, and hopefully final, political death. John Edwards flared briefly into prominence, but seemed to lack staying power. John Kerry won the nomination, but it was a mixed blessing indeed: Even before securing the necessary delegates, he ran into a buzz-saw of Bush negative advertising. With John Kerry as the one potential exception, Hillary was suddenly rid of all of her potential competitors for the future presidential nomination.

There was similar bad news and disarray on the Republican side. Perhaps the most ominous development for the GOP was the inexorable demographic shift that is remaking America. Every year, America becomes half a percent more black and Hispanic. Today, these two groups each account for 12 percent of the American population. The United States Census Bureau estimates that in twenty years blacks will comprise 14 percent of the population, Latinos 19 percent. So the combined black and Hispanic community, which now represents one quarter of the American population, will grow to one third by 2025. And 75 percent of Hispanic Americans live in five important states: California, New York, Illinois, Texas, and Florida. Florida—the ultimate swing state, on which the 2000 election hinged—is now 30.4 percent black and Hispanic. Texas, no longer a safe Republican stronghold, is 43.5 percent minority. California, once a swing state and now increasingly a Democratic bastion, is 39.1 percent black and Hispanic.

In 1996, while I was working for President Clinton, I calculated that in a 50–50 race for president the swing state was New Jersey. By the 2000 election, New Jersey was solidly Democratic; Florida, a state that historically leaned Republican, was the new bellwether.

Since the 2000 election, with its 543,895 popular vote margin for Gore, America has become 2 percent more black and Hispanic. This demographic transformation forces Bush to do better than he did in 2000 just to stay even, like a person running up a down escalator. If African Americans continue to vote for Democratic candidates by 8:1, and Latinos follow past habits and back them by 3:1, Republicans will find it harder than ever to defeat the Democratic nominee— particularly if she's Hillary. Add her strong showing among single white women to immense popularity among minorities, and the GOP would have to win the remaining voters by more than 2:1 in order to succeed. The Republican Party is running out of white people.

This shift in Democratic state-by-state strength is due not merely to increasing numbers of African Americans, but to their greater animosity toward the GOP. Until Ronald Reagan, African Americans didn't hate the Republican Party. Eisenhower carried black voters because they distrusted the Democratic Party, memorably represented by an aging generation of racist southern politicians. In 1959, when a crucial amendment came up to ban all-white jury trials for civil rights cases, Senator John F. Kennedy voted with the South—and

Vice President Richard Nixon broke the ensuing tie in favor of the liberals. How times have changed!

As late as 1972, Richard Nixon won a large slice of the African American vote. As the Republican Party abandoned its forward-thinking support for civil rights to embrace the cynical Southern Strategy, African American voters were increasingly turned off. When Reagan sliced discretionary federal spending and demolished many anti-poverty programs left over from Lyndon Johnson's Great Society, blacks turned solidly against the GOP. In the Reagan landslide of 1984, blacks bloc-voted for the loser even as whites were re-electing Reagan by a landslide. And no Republican has won a significant share of the African American vote in any national election since.

Likewise, the Republican Party systematically alienated Hispanics throughout the 1970s, 1980s, and 1990s by advocating English-only language laws, deriding bilingual education, castigating affirmative action, opposing social benefits for legal immigrants, and demanding that the children of illegal aliens be denied public education. In Florida and California, anti-Hispanic proposals regularly roiled state politics, driving Latinos into the waiting arms of the Democrats.

Yet the Hispanic American vote should be fertile territory for the Republican Party. Overwhelmingly Roman Catholic, Latinos are generally social conservatives. Surveys show that they are largely pro-life and deeply committed to Republican notions of the nuclear family and traditional values. (A CBS-*New York Times* survey in 2003 showed that 44 percent of Hispanics said that abortion should not be permitted; only 33 percent felt it should be legal.) It was only the aggressive rhetoric of latter-day nativists like Pat Buchanan that turned them into Democrats.

More recently, President Bush and his brother in Florida have pushed the Republican Party to adopt more Latino-friendly policies. Forcing the party to abandon anti-immigrant, English-only campaigns, the president courageously urged a program to legalize Latino workers in the United States, increase immigration, and, in effect, grant amnesty to those already in the country, even if they had arrived illegally.

It's too early to tell whether Bush's outreach will bear fruit, but the strategy is vital to his re-election. Republican victories in must-win states like Arizona, Ohio, Indiana, Texas, and Florida may well hinge on attracting the Latino vote. And if Bush fails to blunt their bloc-voting for Democrats, by 2008 America will have become so Hispanic and African American that their votes may make the Democratic nominee almost impossible to beat.

Moreover, if President Bush is re-elected in 2004, then in 2008 the Democrats will have history on their side. Six times since World War II, two-term presidents have tried to arrange their succession by a candidate from their own party—and five times they have failed. Truman couldn't get Adlai Stevenson elected. Eisenhower, despite his massive popularity, failed with Nixon. Johnson couldn't help Humphrey win. Nixon's chosen successor, Gerald Ford, lost to Carter. And Clinton failed to propel Gore into office. Only Ronald Reagan bucked the trend, propelling George H. W. Bush into office (with plenty of help, of course, from the hapless Mike Dukakis).

Why the high failure rate for two-term presidents? Often, ironically, their very success extinguishes their mandate and leaves their chosen successor with little more to do and even less to run on. Once Truman had acted to preserve the New Deal's accomplishments, who needed Stevenson? After Eisenhower secured peace and prosperity—forever, it seemed—what did voters need with Nixon? Once Johnson had passed the civil rights bills, America felt little need for Hubert Humphrey. Eight years of Clinton-era prosperity left voters feeling free to stray from the fold and vote for Bush.

Today, the very success of the Republican Party is, perversely, threatening to be its undoing. Bush has cut taxes; Clinton had already cut the welfare rolls; a combination of factors has reduced violent crime—and thus the hot button issues that animated the Republican surge of 1994 have largely dissipated. Partisan gerrymandering and the war on terror have kept voters in line behind Republican majorities in Congress, but underlying attitudes on most domestic issues have shifted sharply to the left.

Peel back the war on terror, and what are the issues that most concern Americans? According to a Fox News poll of May 20, 2003, the economy, health care, education, and social security top the list. But when the pollsters asked voters who they felt would do the better job on these domestic issues, Democrats beat Republicans on nearly every one. Voters felt that Democrats were better at handling Social Security by 46 to 32, health care by 48 to 30, and education by 40 to 35. On the economy the parties broke even, with Republicans at 40 percent to the Democrats' 39. As the war on terror winds down, the Democratic edge on these domestic issues is likely to grow.

Nor is the stable of Republican candidates lining up to succeed Bush and keep Hillary out of the White House particularly promising. The search for successors usually starts with the incumbent vice president. Eight of the last twenty candidates for president first ran for vice president. Given his age and health, though, Dick Cheney is the first vice president since Truman's Alben Barkley who does not harbor White House ambitions. This traditional springboard to the presidency is empty.

The Bush administration harbors no heir apparent. Rumsfeld is too old, Ashcroft too controversial. Ridge and Thompson have not become popular figures. The ranks of Republican governors and senators are similarly thin. Schwarzenegger is foreign-born and hence ineligible. Texas's Perry is too new, New York's Pataki too old. Majority Leader Bill Frist might run, but can he excite mass commitment? Jeb Bush? The Bushes aren't that popular. George H. W. Bush lost in 1992, attracting only 37 percent of the vote. His son lost the popular vote in 2000, and faces a tough battle in 2004. If Americans aren't tired of the Bushes by 2004, they are going to be exhausted by 2008.

The most popular potential Republican candidates are Secretary of State Colin Powell and former New York Mayor Rudy Giuliani. Powell, or for that matter Condoleezza Rice, would slice deeply into the Democratic ethnic base, breaking the stranglehold that demographics would give Hillary in 2008. Rudy Giuliani, still a hero after 9/11, would put New York's electoral votes in play for the first time since 1988.

But can either be nominated? Both are pro-choice on abortion, support gun controls, and back affirmative action. Could the GOP reverse direction on these core issues without triggering a right-wing defection? Even assuming Powell or Giuliani could prevail in conservative-dominated Republican primaries, either man would be hard-pressed to lead a united party into the election. The true believers from the NRA and the Christian Coalition might well bolt the party altogether, splitting it as disastrously as Ross Perot did in 1992.

To a gambler, then, the Democratic Party looks like the way to bet in 2008. But why bet on Hillary Clinton?

Because with or without the looming demographic perfect storm, no Democrat is likely to be able to stand up to Hurricane Hillary. Should John Kerry win, Hillary will have to bide her time for eight years instead of four. But she will emerge in 2012 as strong as ever.

Hillary's hold on a future Democratic presidential nomination stems from the control the Clinton organization has over the Democratic National Committee. Ever since 1992, the Clintons have run the Democratic Party the way a Mafia don runs his family. Their hand-picked *caporegime*, Terry McAuliffe, is its reigning leader. McAuliffe dominates the party's fund-raising efforts. Democratic fat cats give when they are told, and to whom they are instructed by the smoothly oiled national fund-raising operation. Despite Howard Dean's now-legendary Internet-driven fund-raising success, the big checks still do the talking—and the Clintons control the process.

Just as important are the "superdelegates"—the congressmen and other party and public officials who attend the Democratic National Convention by right of their position. And the former first lady is making sure she has IOUs among all these prominent Democrats throughout the land. Hillary's campaign committee says that she has participated in 127 fund-raisers for other candidates or committees since she joined the Senate—forty-five of them outside of New York or Washington.

The *Buffalo News* reports that Hillary's "fund-raising committees have given $1.66 million to Democratic candidates and causes. . . . [Mrs.] Clinton's political activities have touched at least 40 states. She has attended fund-raisers in 25 states. . . . No other senator has had a fund-raising outfit as successful as HillPAC, the senator's federal political action committee. HillPAC gave away $902,000, which is $244,000 more than the second-most-active Senate PAC, run by Senate Minority Leader Tom Daschle."

Hillary's Democratic fund-raisers have mastered the game of raking in soft money despite the ostensible prohibition against doing so in the McCain-Feingold reform law. Even though Democratic senators led the battle to ban these donations to party committees and refused to pass the legislation without this provision, Democratic fund-raisers haven't gotten the word. Instead they have simply set up "independent" committees like Move On and Americans Coming Together to take soft-money donations. As Republican Senator Mitch McConnell, an opponent of campaign finance reform, points out, "Soft money is not gone, it has just changed its address." Instead of sending checks to the Democratic National Committee, donors just mail them to these specially created front organizations. Ironically, Republicans have proven more adept at raising *hard* money under the limits of McCain-Feingold than the Democrats, generating twice as much through September 2003. Democrats use the loopholes in the finance reform law to keep the soft money flowing to offset this advantage.

And Democrats have developed guardian angels to fill their coffers. Financier George Soros and his friend Peter B. Lewis, for example, have each committed to giving $10 million in soft money to these front groups, far beyond any of the contributions Republicans have been getting. At the core of these new Democratic Party front groups is Harold Ickes, Hillary's former campaign director and chief political advisor. With one of Ickes's hands on the throttle and the other on the steering wheel, these new campaign financing vehicles are, effectively, under Hillary's control.

This combination of a dramatically improved image, proven fund-raising ability, a long trail of supporters owing her favors in virtually every state, and control of the national party apparatus gives Hillary a giant head start toward the Democratic presidential nomination in 2008.

Meanwhile, public opinion polls indicate that no other Democrat can catch Hillary. Had she decided to run in 2004, she would have won the nomination in a walk. An NBC poll in December 2003 showed that Hillary would have won 43 percent of the Democratic primary votes, with only 12 percent for the next leading candidate.

Then again, Hillary might still run for vice president in 2004. As the most popular Democrat in the nation, she would undoubtedly strengthen the Democratic ticket. The prospect of a genuinely electable female vice presidential candidate—particularly Hillary—would transform a campaign into a crusade, electrifying the Democratic base and guaranteeing a huge turnout.

Would Hillary run for VP? She might. Here's why:

- It's a free shot on goal. She doesn't have to give up her Senate seat to run. If she wins, she becomes the vice president. If she loses, she's still the United States Senator from New York, until she has to run for re-election in 2006.
- If Kerry wins in 2004—and runs for re-election in 2008—Hillary will have to keep fresh until 2012, a long time in politics. In the Senate, she would be at best an onlooker as the action moves to a Democratic White House. But as vice president, she would be the presumptive nominee when Kerry leaves.
- If Hillary doesn't run for vice president, somebody else will— and win or lose, he'll be tough competition when Hillary decides to run for president.

- Should Bush be re-elected, it won't be by much. There would be no shame for Hillary in running for vice president on a ticket that narrowly lost.
- If Hillary stays in the Senate, she may have to battle Rudy Giuliani in 2006 when she runs for re-election. Wouldn't it be the better part of valor to step aside for the hero of 9/11 and run for national office instead?

Besides, Hillary has already served as a kind of vice president and found it both enjoyable and rewarding. During the first two years of Bill's first term, she was a de facto chief of staff. Then, for the remainder of his White House tenure, she effectively became a second vice president, roaming the world, speaking out on issues she cared about, and raising money for the party. It's not a bad job.

The weather patterns—the wind, tides, waves, and clouds—all indicate, though, that 2008 may be the Perfect Storm for Hillary Clinton.

B ut what kind of storm will it be?

It's impossible not to turn once more to those devil-or-angel symbols of the 1960s, Bobby Kennedy and Richard Nixon.

As we've seen, Hillary Clinton's past carries disturbing echoes of Nixon's. Like him, she has proven susceptible to temptation, paranoia, and scandal; like him, she has allowed her fierce political instincts to darken her perspective, and contrived a deceivingly positive public face behind which to hide. If her behavior as president is much like her performance as first lady—in Arkansas or Washington, D.C.—then her supporters and critics alike have much to fear.

But the image of Bobby Kennedy reminds us that things needn't be that way—not even for Hillary Clinton.

In the years after his brother's assassination, Robert F. Kennedy grew. He saw how his tactics in hunting mobsters and communists—

and wiretapping civil rights leaders like King—undermined our constitutional rights, and he repented. He came to realize that his hawkish, primitive 1950s anti-communism had helped to lead America into the swamp of Vietnam, and to a massive neglect of our domestic problems. Civil rights and the needs of the poor, once distractions from his brother's legislative agenda, became the core of his own message, and grew into deeply rooted principles.

Robert Kennedy became a very good person.

So can Hillary. To do so, she would first have to admit her errors, if only to herself. Perfect people never change. Those who look in a mirror and see only the most insignificant of errors never grow.

Granted, a best-selling memoir by a sitting politician may not have been the place to begin a candid, introspective self-examination. It's hard to think of any such memoir that has been completely forthcoming, and for any number of reasons Hillary's *Living History* is filled with predictable ellipses, cover stories, and creative embroidery of the truth.

But as the decade unfolds, in the quiet of her Senate seat, apart from the daily duels of political dialogue, Hillary will have the chance to become the person she still can become. She will have a chance to marry her sincerely generous goals to her means. She can look back over her career and see how a minor lie—like Whitewater—can almost bring down an entire presidency. And we can hope that this time she decides the solution is not to perfect her talent for stonewalling, but not to lie in the first place.

Our current political landscape badly needs Hillary's perspective, her passionate idealism. Her willingness to fight for the underdog and her compass for issues are rare indeed in our male-dominated, profit-obsessed society. She is, as we've seen, a flawed instrument. If she continues to hide behind the HILLARY brand, a second Clinton presidency would do vastly more harm than good. But the question lingers:

Will she grow?

NOTES

Chapter 1: Deconstructing Hillary

6   "dynastic politics": Kevin Phillips, *American Dynasty* (New York: Viking, 2004).

7   "not only are . . .": Ibid., p. 4.

7   "As Phillips points . . .": Ibid., pp. 4–5.

11   "Take an apparently . . .": Todd Purdum, "Hillary Clinton Meets Man Who Gave Two L's," *New York Times,* April 3, 1995, p. A6.

11   "thought she was . . .": Ibid.

11   "So when I was . . .": Ibid.

11   "But Sir Edmund . . .": Mark Steyn, "The Mystery of Hillary Clinton," *National Review,* June 28, 1999.

12   "Chelsea had gone . . .": Hillary Clinton interview with Jane Pauley, NBC, September 18, 2001.

12   "Chelsea herself, though, flatly . . .": *Talk,* November 9, 2000.

Chapter 2: Hillary as President?

19   "opens with the . . .": Jimmy Carter, *Keeping Faith* (New York: Bantam Books, 1982), pp. 3–14.

22   "if a person . . .": John Harris, "Applying the Salve of Prayer; Clintons Use Gathering to Speak Out against Anger, Cynicism," *Washington Post,* February 7, 1997, p. A01.

22   "both George W. Bush. . .": Sean Hannity, *Deliver Us from Evil* (New York: ReganBooks, 2004).

23 "Barber grouped all . . .": David James Barber, *Presidential Character* (Englewood Cliffs, NJ: Prentice-Hall, 1972), pp. 12–13.

23 "ability to use . . .": Ibid., p. 12.

23 "seems ambitious, striving . . .": Ibid., p. 12.

23 "Adhering rigidly to . . .": Ibid., pp. 42–43.

24 "The president appears . . .": Ibid., p. 43.

24 "himself as having . . .": Ibid., p. 98.

25 "No other word . . .": Richard Hofstadter, *The Paranoid Style in American Politics* (Cambridge, MA: Harvard University Press, 1996), p. 1.

27 "delighted that his . . . made a point . . .": Jean Edward Smith, *Grant* (New York: Simon & Schuster, 2001), p. 783.

27 "Grant was not . . .": Ibid., p. 484.

28 "the fact is Grant . . .": Ibid., p. 485.

Chapter 3: The Hillary Brand

38 "I cannot and . . .": Lillian Hellman, Letter to House Committee on Un-American Activities.

40 "Hillary recalled the 'pain' . . .": Peter Baker, "First Lady Recalls Early Taste of Ethnic Tension," *Washington Post,* December 10, 1997, p. A-4.

41 "The athletic director . . .": phone interview of Jim Reese by Katie Maxwell.

43 "Jacqueline Onassis suggested . . .": Hillary Clinton, *Living History* (New York: Simon & Schuster, 2003), p. 135.

43 "showcase American culinary . . .": Ibid., p. 139.

43 "Why don't these . . .": Ibid., p. 470.

43 "to be strong . . .": Ibid., p. 480.

43 "strong advice, I . . .": Ibid., p. 394.

43 "It was Nelson Mandela . . .": Ibid., p. 470.

43 "Jacqueline Onassis said . . .": Ibid., p. 138.

43   "TV producer Linda . . .": Ibid., p. 111.

43   "encouraged me to . . .": Ibid., p. 137.

44   "newly permed short . . .": Ibid., p. 93.

45   "You know, I . . .": Ibid., p. 109.

46   "I wanted a . . .": *House Beautiful,* March 1994.

47   "Chelsea was not feeling . . .": Hillary Clinton, *Living History* (New York: Simon & Schuster, 2003), p. 136.

48   "courting couch": Ibid., p. 91.

49   "that people could . . .": Ibid., p. 140.

49   "gender stereotypes . . .": Ibid., p. 140.

50   "In my own . . .": Ibid., p. 141.

51   "granted an exclusive . . .": Ibid., p. 140.

51   "The photos were . . .": Bob Woodward, *The Agenda: Inside the Clinton White House* (New York: Simon & Schuster, 1994), p. 111.

53   "the first couple . . .": Gail Sheehy, *Hillary's Choice* (New York: Random House, 1999), pp. 10–11.

53   "Except for a . . .": Ibid., p. 11.

53   "proved to be . . .": Joyce Milton, *The First Partner: Hillary Rodham Clinton* (New York: William Morrow and Company, 1999), pp. 4–5.

53   "how difficult a . . .": Gail Sheehy, *Hillary's Choice* (New York: Random House, 1999), p. 11.

53   "Another folksy image . . .": Ibid., p. 11.

55   "speculation by some . . .": Hillary Clinton, *Living History* (New York: Simon & Schuster, 2003), p. 438.

56   "that she and . . . let it slip . . . I must say . . .": Barbara Olson, *Hell to Pay* (Washington, DC: Regnery, 1999), p. 1.

56   "it was time . . .": Hillary Clinton, *Living History* (New York: Simon & Schuster, 2003), pp. 435–436.

57   "I adopted my . . .": Ibid., p. 110.

58   "Some of the attacks . . .": Ibid., p. 110.

58   "this is the sort of thing . . .": Ibid., p. 109.

59   "about undermining the . : .": Ibid., p. 245.

59   "the purpose of the investigations . . .": Ibid., p. 194.

60   "vast right-wing . . .": Ibid., p. 445.

61   "three of his . . .": Ibid., p. 106.

61   "His generosity of . . .": Ibid., p. 235.

63   "I had taken . . .": Ibid., p. 64.

63   "but my heart . . .": Ibid., p. 64.

64   "Bill Clinton's first . . .": Ibid., p. 76.

64   "the most venerable . . .": Ibid., p. 78.

64   "Vince [Foster] and another . . .": Ibid., p. 79.

64   "already obtained an . . .": Ibid., p. 76.

65   "I was always . . .": Gail Sheehy, *Hillary's Choice* (New York: Random House, 1999), p. 162.

65   "She tried only . . .": Ibid., p. 162.

66   "I've always been a Yankees . . .": Hillary Clinton interview with Katie Couric on *Today,* June 10, 1999.

66   "I've always been a Patrick Ewing . . .": Ibid.

68   "Mahatma Ghandi—he . . .": "Indian Group Still Angry with Hillary," *Newsmax.com,* February 18, 2004.

69   "Hillary voted twice . . .": U.S. Senate Roll Call Vote, 107th Congress, 1st Session, Vote 169, May 24, 2001 (as Asst A.G).

Chapter 4: Hiding Hillary: The Politician

76   "During her early . . .": David Maraniss, *First in His Class: A Biography of Bill Clinton* (New York: Simon & Schuster, 1995), p. 426.

78   "a family endeavor": Hillary Clinton, *Living History* (New York: Simon & Schuster, 2003), p. 93.

78   "we loaded Chelsea . . .": Ibid., p. 93.

79   "avoid the appearance . . .": Ibid., pp. 91–92.

81   "In a few days . . .": Dick Morris, *Behind the Oval Office* (New York: Random House, 1997), p. 54.

89   "Within hours, the . . .": Ibid., p. 117.

90   "In the next . . .": Ibid., p. 117.

90   "Hillary, [Warren] Christopher, [Al] Gore . . .": Bob Woodward, *The Agenda: Inside the Clinton White House* (New York: Simon & Schuster, 1994), p. 59.

90   "We were also . . .": Ibid., p. 118.

90   "If another Democrat . . .": Eleanor Clift and Mark Miller, "Hillary: Behind the Scenes," *Newsweek*, December 28, 1992.

92   "Hillary does discuss . . .": Hillary Clinton, *Living History* (New York: Simon & Schuster, 2003), p. 120.

95   "Most Republican voters . . .": Ibid., p. 251.

95   "Deflated and disappointed . . .": Ibid., p. 25.

97   "I encouraged Bill . . .": Ibid., p. 289.

97   "when opposing camps . . .": Ibid., p, 290.

Chapter 5: Hiding Hillary: The Ideologue

105   "a small law . . .": Hillary Clinton, *Living History* (New York: Simon & Schuster, 2003), p. 54.

105   "Its lead partner . . .": Myrna Oliver, "Robert Truehaft, 89: Crusading Attorney," *Los Angeles Times*, November 16, 2000.

105   "And what loyal . . .": Ibid.

105   "long known as . . .": Joyce Milton, *The First Partner: Hillary Rodham Clinton* (New York: William Morrow and Company, 1999), p. 52.

106   "That world and . . .": Hillary Clinton, *Living History* (New York: Simon & Schuster, 2003), p. 45.

106   "I learned, late . . .": Ibid., pp. 44–45.

106   "clubbed, burned with . . .": John Elvin, "Hillary Hides Her Panther Fling," *Insightmag.com*, July 7, 2000.

106 "The evidence against . . .": Barbara Olson, *Hell to Pay* (Washington, DC: Regnery, 1999), p. 55.

106 "a rallying point . . .": Ibid., p. 55.

106 "The fact is . . .": "Hillary Hides Her Panther Fling," *Insightmag* .com, July 31, 2000, www.insightmag.com/news/2000/07/31 /InvestigativeReport/Hillary.Hides.Her.Panther.Fling-210660.shtml (03/14/2004).

107 "It was a . . .": Ibid.

107 "Hillary attended Black . . .": Barbara Olson, *Hell to Pay* (Washington, DC: Regnery, 1999), p. 56.

107 "For too long . . .": Ibid., p. 59.

107 "get high with . . . kill our parents": Ibid., p. 59.

107 "The combined second . . .": Ibid., p. 60.

109 "agreed that Arkansas . . .": Hillary Clinton, *Living History* (New York: Simon & Schuster, 2003), p. 94.

111 "enraged the teachers . . .": Ibid., p. 94.

113 "the explosion in . . .": Bob Woodward, *The Agenda: Inside the Clinton White House* (New York: Simon & Schuster, 1994), p. 23.

113 "In 1992, we . . .": President William J. Clinton, State of the Union Speech, 1993.

114 "we wanted a . . .": Hillary Clinton, *Living History* (New York: Simon & Schuster, 2003), p. 153.

115 "Now, you may . . .": Hillary Clinton, Speech at the Democratic National Convention, August 14, 2000.

115 "CHIP set out . . .": Jamie Court, "Toward a Seamless System of Health Care," *Consumerwatchdog.org*, September 25, 2000, http:// www.consumerwatchdog.org/ftcr/co/co000745.php3 (3/14/2004).

115 "I didn't fully . . .": Hillary Clinton, *Living History* (New York: Simon & Schuster, 2003), p. 116.

117 "a blow that . . .": Ibid., p. 153.

118   "intended to deceive . . .": Robert Pear, "Judge Rules Government Covered up Lies on Panel," *New York Times*, December 19, 1997, p. A37.

118   "The Executive Branch . . .": Ibid.

118   "The government was . . .": Ibid.

118   "they had devised . . .": Bob Woodward, *The Agenda: Inside the Clinton White House* (New York: Simon & Schuster, 1994), p. 110.

119   "a number of staffers . . .": Ibid., p. 169.

119   "I believe in . . .": Ibid., p. 169.

119   "I don't care how . . .": Ibid., p. 169.

121   "takes credit for . . .": Hillary Clinton, *Living History* (New York: Simon & Schuster, 2003), p. 248.

121   "my own missteps . . .": Ibid., p. 248.

124   "Yet Hillary thought . . .": U.S. Senate Roll Call Vote, 107th Congress, 1st Session, Vote 169, May 24, 2001 (as Asst A.G).

126   "The exercise of . . . gave me a . . .": Ibid.

127   "[Todd's] contract to . . .": "Clinton Book Raises Questions," *TheHill.com*, May 7, 2003.

128   "a captive audience": Hillary Clinton, *Living History* (New York: Simon & Schuster, 2003), p. 278.

128   "it was Mary Catherine . . .": Ibid., p. 265.

128   "I understood her . . .": Ibid., p. 265.

128   "The State Department asked me to visit . . .": Ibid., p. 268.

128   "The State Department asked me to go . . .": Ibid., p. 341.

128   "I was asked . . .": Ibid., p. 353.

129   "Some media commentators . . .": Ibid., pp. 300–301.

129   "overstated her role": Harry Wu, "Hillary's Account of My Release Untrue," *Newsmax.com*, October 12, 2003.

129   "I never believed . . .": Ibid.

130   "When I was . . . But we never . . .": Ibid.

130   "she does not . . .": Ibid.

130   "Nor were there many. . .": Maggie Farley, "China Releases Human Rights Activist Harry Wu," *Los Angeles Times,* August 25, 1998.

131   "to open my . . .": Ibid., p. x.

131   "During Hillary's second . . ." Ellen Nakashima, "White House Travel Bill: $292 million, Republican Senator Says Clinton Air Transport Expenses are 'Exorbitant'," *Washington Post,* August 18, 2000, p. A02.

133   "I remembered all . . .": Hillary Clinton, *Living History* (New York: Simon & Schuster, 2003), p. 369.

133   "Some in the . . . I told . . .": Ibid., p. 367.

134   "If he vetoed . . .": Ibid., p. 369.

136   "The Secret Service . . . tone of cooperation . . .": Ibid., p. 131.

138   "I arrived in . . .": Hillary Clinton, *Living History* (New York: Simon & Schuster, 2003), p. 374.

139   "Our daughter, Chelsea . . .": Associated Press, "THE DEMOCRATS; Excerpts From Remarks by Cuomo, Jackson, Bayh and the First Lady," *New York Times,* August 28, 1996, p. A17.

139   "It is hard . . .": Ibid.

139   "And Bill was . . .": Ibid.

139   "You know, Bill . . .": Ibid.

139   "Chelsea has spent . . .": Ibid.

139   "Sometimes, late at . . .": Ibid.

140   "I felt it . . .": Hillary Clinton, *Living History* (New York: Simon & Schuster, 2003), p. 379.

141   "a solid eight . . .": Ibid., p. 379.

141   "from a highly . . .": Ibid., p. 380.

141   "I had begun . . . and with other . . .": Ibid., p. 380.

Chapter 6: Hiding Hillary: The Material Girl

145   "On [Whitewater], Clinton . . .": George Stephanopoulos, *All Too Human* (New York: Little, Brown, 1999), pp. 227–228.

147   "Money means almost . . .": Hillary Clinton, *Living History* (New York: Simon & Schuster, 2003), pp. 85–96.

147   "the Clintons actually donated . . .": Gail Sheehy, *Hillary's Choice* (New York: Random House, 1999), p. 172.

152   "examined *ad infinitum* . . .": Hillary Clinton, *Living History* (New York: Simon & Schuster, 2003), p. 87.

153   "It was obvious . . .": James Stewart, *Blood Sport: The President and His Adversaries* (New York: Simon & Schuster, 1996), pp. 417–418.

154   "Tyson benefited from . . .": Jeff Gerth, "Top Arkansas Lawyer Helped Hillary Clinton Turn Big Profit," *New York Times,* March 18, 1994, p. A1.

154   "Blair was . . .": Ibid.

154   "President Clinton named . . .": Ibid.

154   "As Arkansas attorney general . . .": Ibid.

154   "Governor Clinton reappointed . . .": Ibid.

154   "When a Tyson . . .": Ibid.

154   "reversed course and . . .": Ibid.

155   "Our tax returns . . .": Hillary Clinton, *Living History* (New York: Simon & Schuster, 2003), p. 223.

155   "In April 1994, . . .": Joyce Milton, *The First Partner: Hillary Rodham Clinton* (New York: William Morrow and Company, 1999), p. 318.

155   "I started looking . . .": Hillary Clinton, *Living History* (New York: Simon & Schuster, 2003), p. 86.

155   "allocate losing investments . . . said one aspect . . . could give someone . . .": Howard Schneider and Charles Babcock, "First Lady Barely Avoided Future's Crash; Clinton Commodities Broker Became Target of Lawsuits, Sanctions," *Washington Post,* March 31, 1994, p. A1.

156   "For such conduct . . .": Ibid.

156   "Jim and Susan . . .": Jim McDougal and Curtis Wilkie, *Arkansas Mischief: The Birth of a National Scandal* (New York: Henry Holt, 1998), p. 212.

156   "When the property . . .": Ibid., p. 212.

156   "McDougal hired Hillary . . .": Ibid., pp. 209–210.

156   "Jim McDougal held . . .": Ibid., p. 214.

157   "Clinton appointed McDougal's . . .": Ibid., p. 171.

157   "control . . . arranged . . . amenable . . .": Ibid., p. 206.

157   "It was good . . .": Ibid., p. 171.

157   "Clinton named Beverly . . .": Ibid., p. 206.

157   "Bassett allowed Madison . . .": Ibid., pp. 214–215.

157   "Clinton sat in . . .": Ibid., p. 206.

157   "if I kept . . .": Ibid.

157   "I felt a . . .": Ibid., p. 176.

158   "Jim [McDougal] asked . . .": Hillary Clinton, *Living History* (New York: Simon & Schuster, 2003), p. 88.

158   "Bill and I . . .": Ibid., p. 193.

158   "The Clintons got . . .": Associated Press, "Statement by Independent Counsel on Conclusions in Whitewater Investigation," *New York Times,* September 21, 2000, p. A23.

158   "Bill knew he . . .": Hillary Clinton, *Living History* (New York: Simon & Schuster, 2003), p. 200.

158   "Rick Massey . . .": Ibid., p. 197.

158   "Massey denied her . . .": David Maraniss and Susan Schmidt, "Hillary Clinton and the Whitewater Controversy: A Close-up," *Washington Post,* June 2, 1996, p. A01.

158   "I thought it . . .": Hillary Clinton, *Living History* (New York: Simon & Schuster, 2003), p. 197.

158   "No! Jim [McDougal] told . . .": James Stewart, *Blood Sport: The President and His Adversaries* (New York: Simon & Schuster, 1996), p. 133.

159   "knew of any . . .": Hillary Clinton, *Living History* (New York: Simon & Schuster, 2003), p. 225.

159   "Hillary herself mentions . . .": Ibid., p. 327.

159   "the evidence was . . .": "Whitewater Affair," *World News Digest*, http://www.2facts.com/Ancillaries/Index/z00036.asp (3/14/2004).

159   "Susan was suffering . . .": Hillary Clinton, *Living History* (New York: Simon & Schuster, 2003), p. 406.

159   "show that a . . .": Carol Leonning, "Some See Politics in Court's Reimbursements to GOP," *Washington Post*, March 9, 2004, p. A1.

160   "President Ronald Reagan . . .": Ibid.

160   "to advise the . . .": Hillary Clinton, *Living History* (New York: Simon & Schuster, 2003), pp. 200–201.

161   "fuck you, Jeff . . .": Gail Sheehy, *Hillary's Choice* (New York: Random House, 1999), p. 206.

161   "a whole subgroup . . .": Ibid., pp. 206–207.

161   "While I have . . .": Marilyn Rauber, "Hillary Admits Filing Records in the Shredder," *New York Post*, January 20, 1996, p. 2.

161   "Mrs. Clinton's decision . . .": Ibid.

161   "After hours, in . . .": Gail Sheehy, *Hillary's Choice* (New York: Random House, 1999), p. 207.

161   "Should we answer . . .": Hillary Clinton, *Living History* (New York: Simon & Schuster, 2003), p. 200.

162   "We will never . . .": Ibid., p. 206.

162   "In more than . . .": Ibid., p. 348.

163   "did work for . . .": Barbara Walters interview with Hillary Clinton, *ABC*, January 19, 1996.

163 "when she was . . .": Joyce Milton, *The First Partner: Hillary Rodham Clinton* (New York: William Morrow and Company, 1999), p. 320.

164 "minimal": Hillary Clinton, *Living History* (New York: Simon & Schuster, 2003), p. 330.

166 "There is no . . .": Lloyd Grove, "Martha: Women's Verdict," *New York Daily News,* March 9, 2004, p. 21.

166 "It is often . . .": Ibid.

167 "I assumed that . . .": Hillary Clinton, *Living History* (New York: Simon & Schuster, 2003), pp. 221–222.

167 "President Clinton's closest . . .": Stephen Labaton, "Advisors Knew of Hubbell Plight," *New York Times,* May 5, 1997, p. A1.

167 "Webb Hubbell is . . .": Jim McDougal quoted in Ann Coulter, *High Crimes and Misdemeanors: The Case against Bill Clinton* (Washington, DC: Regnery, 1998), p. 197.

167 "paying off witnesses . . .": Hillary Clinton, *Living History* (New York: Simon & Schuster, 2003), p. 68.

167 "In late 1995 . . .": Ibid., p. 328.

171 "a major source . . .": Barbara Olson, *The Final Days: The Last, Desperate Abuses of Power by the Clinton White House* (Washington, DC: Regnery, 2001), p. 151.

171 "Vignali's father donated . . .": Ibid., p. 151.

172 "Hugh also got . . .": Ibid., pp. 151–153.

172 "The couple contributed $102,000 . . .": Ibid., p. 155.

172 "I did not . . .": Ibid., pp. 177–178.

174 "part owner of . . .": Ann Coulter, *High Crimes and Misdemeanors: The Case against Bill Clinton* (Washington, DC: Regnery, 1998), p. 121.

175 "cleared in the . . .": Ibid., p. 485.

175 "factually inaccurate . . . the Independent Counsel . . .": "Factually Inaccurate Hillary Skipped," *Media Research Center Cyber Alert,*

October 19, 2000 https://secure.mediaresearch.org/news/cyberalert /2000/cyb20001019.asp (3/12/2004).

175   "the strongest criticism . . .": Ibid.

176   "Prosecutors decided not . . .": Ibid.

176   "offhand comment": Hillary Clinton, *Living History* (New York: Simon & Schuster, 2003), p. 172.

176   "I was still . . .": Ibid.

177   "Barbara Olson included . . .": Barbara Olson, *The Final Days: The Last, Desperate Abuses of Power by the Clinton White House* (Washington, DC: Regnery, 2001), pp. 66–68.

180   "Clinton supporters even . . .": *ABCnews,* January 25, 2001.

180   "Mrs. Clinton pulled . . .": Barbara Olson, *The Final Days: The Last, Desperate Abuses of Power by the Clinton White House* (Washington, DC: Regnery, 2001), pp. 68–69.

181   "In the final . . .": Tim Russert quoted in Maureen Dowd, *New York Times,* February 21, 2003.

181   "So extensive was . . .": Barbara Olson, *The Final Days: The Last, Desperate Abuses of Power by the Clinton White House* (Washington, DC: Regnery, 2001), pp. 68–69.

181   "an additional $360,000 . . .": Audrey Hudson, "House Report Cites Undervalued Gifts to Clintons; GOP Member Rips 'Broken System'," *Washington Post,* February 13, 2002.

182   "An Yves Saint . . .": Ibid.

182   "would never give . . .": Martin Kettle, "Clinton Haters Still Find Rich Pickings Ex-First Couple Lose Magic as Triumph Turns to Disaster," *WashingtonSaturday,* February 10, 2001.

182   "While still in . . .": Barbara Olson, *The Final Days: The Last, Desperate Abuses of Power by the Clinton White House* (Washington, DC: Regnery, 2001), pp. 72–73.

182   "In January, 2000 . . .": Ibid., pp. 72–73.

182   "sent a March . . .": Ibid., pp. 72–73.

182   "The Clintons reportedly . . .": Ibid., pp. 72–73.

183   "clerical error": Hillary Clinton, *Living History* (New York: Simon & Schuster, 2003), p. 439.

183   "The culture of . . .": Ibid., p. 439.

185   "turned down . . .": Lucinda Franks, "The Intimate Hillary," *Talk*, September 1999.

185   "an $8 million . . .": Barbara Olson, *The Final Days: The Last, Desperate Abuses of Power by the Clinton White House* (Washington, DC: Regnery, 2001), p. 41.

185   "And who gave . . .": Ibid., p. 40.

186   "violate Senate rules . . .": Ibid., p. 41.

186   "The Clintons had . . .": Ibid., p. 42.

Chapter 7: Hiding Hillary: The Inquisitor

191   "I think that . . .": Gail Sheehy, *Hillary's Choice* (New York: Random House, 1999), p. 158.

191   "Clinton was broaching . . . there were great . . .": David Maraniss, *First in His Class: A Biography of Bill Clinton* (New York: Simon & Schuster, 1995), p. 450.

192   "Hillary called Gloria . . . and asked whether . . .": Ibid., p. 452.

196   "When he had . . .": Ibid., p. 426.

196   "by the mid-1980s . . .": Ibid., p. 426.

196   "told herself that . . .": Gail Sheehy, *Hillary's Choice* (New York: Random House, 1999), p. 157.

197   "Much has been . . .": Hillary Clinton, *Living History* (New York: Simon & Schuster, 2003), p. 9.

197   "The time had . . .": David Maraniss, *First in His Class: A Biography of Bill Clinton* (New York: Simon & Schuster, 1995), pp. 440–441.

199 "she wanted to . . .": Joyce Milton, *The First Partner: Hillary Rodham Clinton* (New York: William Morrow and Company, 1999), p. 142.

200 "The campaign hired . . .": Judy Bachrach, "The President's Private Eye," *Vanity Fair,* September 1998, p. 204.

200 "Hillary had known . . .": Ibid.

200 "Hillary's relationship with . . .": Ibid.

200 "dumpster diving": Michael Isikoff, "Clinton Team Works to Deflect Allegations on Nominee's Private Life," *Washington Post,* July 26, 1992, p. A18.

200 "at a cost . . .": Ibid.

200 "Foster farmed out . . .": Joyce Milton, *The First Partner: Hillary Rodham Clinton* (New York: William Morrow and Company, 1999), p. 212.

201 "Quite Soon, Lindsay . . .": Ibid., p. 211.

201 "Betsey was soon . . . there have been . . .": Michael Isikoff, "Clinton Team Works to Deflect Allegations on Nominee's Private Life," *Washington Post,* July 26, 1992, p. A18.

201 "has the skills . . .": Ibid.

201 "a San Francisco . . .": Ibid.

202 "I am somebody . . .": Gail Sheehy, *Hillary's Choice* (New York: Random House, 1999), p. 201.

202 "Hillary knew Palladino . . .": Ibid., p. 201.

202 "$28,000 . . .": Michael Isikoff, "Clinton Team Works to Deflect Allegations on Nominee's Private Life," *Washington Post,* July 26, 1992, p. A18.

202 "Bimbo eruptions . . . figure out . . .": Ibid.

202 "When Palladino ran . . .": Gail Sheehy, *Hillary's Choice* (New York: Random House, 1999), p. 201.

202 "Sally Perdue . . . Democratic operative . . .": Carl Limbacher, "Hillary's Private Eye Arrested in Reporter Intimidation Case," *Newsmax.com,* November 23, 2002.

203 "Loren Kirk, Gennifer . . .": Joyce Milton, *The First Partner: Hillary Rodham Clinton* (New York: William Morrow and Company, 1999), p. 232.

203 "her tires were . . .": Brian Bloomquist, "More Mystery; As Sex Files Continue; Starr Probes Weird Willey Warnings," *New York Post,* October 4, 1998, p. 12.

203 "Former Miss America . . .": Joyce Milton, *The First Partner: Hillary Rodham Clinton* (New York: William Morrow and Company, 1999), p. 226; Steve Dunleavy, "I Was Victim of Clinton Reign of Terror," *New York Post,* September 27, 1998, p. 10.

203 "Arkansas state trooper . . .": Tom Rhodes, "Trooper 'Offered Bribe in Britain' over Whitewater," *The Times,* August 23, 1997.

203 "Dolly Kyle Browning . . .": Joyce Milton, *The First Partner: Hillary Rodham Clinton* (New York: William Morrow and Company, 1999), p. 225.

203 "Pellicano, who examined . . .": "Clinton Pellicano Watch," *American Thinker,* March 14, 2004, http://www.americanthinker.com /comments.php?comments_id=95 (3/14/2004).

204 "Flowers submitted the . . .": Carl Limbacher, "Gennifer Flowers' Tapes Seen as Key to Clinton Indictment," *Newsmax.com,* December 31, 2000.

204 "take out a . . .": Carl Limbacher, "Pellicano Tapes Could Spell Trouble for Bill and Hillary," *Newsmax.com,* November 12, 2003.

204 "unfairly invaded the . . .": Hillary Clinton, *Living History* (New York: Simon & Schuster, 2003), p. 216.

204 "Lenzner was hired . . .": Michael Isikoff, "Clinton Team Works to Deflect Allegations on Nominee's Private Life," *Washington Post,* July 26, 1992, p. A18.

204 "Lenzner investigated Monica's . . .": "Snoop: I wasn't Hyde Dirt Digger," *New York Post,* September 18, 1998.

204   "Pellicano was reported . . .": Carl Limbacher, "Hillary's Private Eye Arrested in Reporter Intimidation Case," *Newsmax.com*, November 23, 2002.

205   "White House staffer . . .": John Podhoretz, "Oops Wrong Conspiracy," *New York Post*, September 18, 1998.

205   "Blumenthal also reportedly . . .": Ibid.

205   "A lobbyist for . . .": Dick Morris, "Fingerprints of the Secret Police: Did Clinton Aide Ann Lewis Dish Dirt on Rep Dan Burton?" *New York Post*, December 29, 1998.

205   "House Speaker Bob . . .": William Jasper, "An Irresponsible Congress," *New American*, February 15, 1999.

205   "Jane Mayer of . . .": Dick Morris, "Secret Police: Did Clinton Aide Ann Lewis Dish Dirt on Rep Dan Burton?" *New York Post*, December 29, 1998.

205   "Apparently, Kenneth Bacon . . .": "Media Ignore Top Pentagon Spokesman's File Leak Who Said Linda Tripp Had Rights?" *Media Watch*, October 5, 1998.

205   "On November 4, 2003 . . .": "Congratulations to Linda Tripp on Her Settlement Agreement," *Judicial Watch*, November 4, 2003.

206   "The charges against . . .": Hillary Clinton, *Living History* (New York: Simon & Schuster, 2003), p. 68.

207   "a whale of . . .": Ibid., p. 106.

207   "When Governor Clinton . . .": Hillary Clinton interview with Barbara Walters, *ABCnews*, June 8, 2003.

210   "I don't like . . .": Hillary Clinton, *Living History* (New York: Simon & Schuster, 2003), p. 252.

211   "Clinton . . . slugged Morris . . .": David Maraniss, *First in His Class: A Biography of Bill Clinton* (New York: Simon & Schuster, 1995), p. 455.

211   "Clinton charged up . . .": Dick Morris, *Behind the Oval Office: Getting Reelected against All Odds* (Los Angeles, CA: Renaissance Books, 1999), p. 65.

212   "She hews to . . .": Hillary Clinton, *Living History* (New York: Simon & Schuster, 2003), pp. 440–441.

212   "former Dukakis campaign . . .": Sean Hannity, Susan Estrich, and Dick Morris, "Analysis with Dick Morris," *Hannity & Colmes, Fox News,* June 4, 2003.

213   "in a better . . .": Hillary Clinton, *Living History* (New York: Simon & Schuster, 2003), p. 441.

214   "The President issued . . .": Ibid., p. 444.

215   "If all that . . .": Hillary Clinton interview with *Today Show, NBC* January 27, 1998.

215   "knew the prosecution . . .": Hillary Clinton, *Living History* (New York: Simon & Schuster, 2003), p. 465.

215   "I could hardly breathe . . .": Ibid., pp. 465–466.

215   "Hillary knew that . . .": Ann Coulter, *High Crimes and Misdemeanors: The Case against Bill Clinton* (Washington, DC: Regnery, 1998), p. 40.

215   "Evelyn Lieberman . . . had transferred . . .": Joyce Milton, *The First Partner: Hillary Rodham Clinton* (New York: William Morrow and Company, 1999), p. 5.

216   "she had had sex . . .": Ann Coulter, *High Crimes and Misdemeanors: The Case against Bill Clinton* (Washington, DC: Regnery, 1998), p. 53.

216   "*Leaves of Grass* . . .": Joyce Milton, *The First Partner: Hillary Rodham Clinton* (New York: William Morrow and Company, 1999), pp. 5–6.

216   "after our second . . .": Ibid., p. 6.

217   "Hillary turned a . . .": Gail Sheehy, *Hillary's Choice* (New York: Random House, 1999), p. 202.

217   "it doesn't make . . .": Ibid., p. 202.

217   "I do believe . . .": Hillary Clinton, *Living History* (New York: Simon & Schuster, 2003), p. 445.

217   "Looking back, I . . .": Ibid., p. 446.

218　"One can speculate . . .": Gail Sheehy, *Hillary's Choice* (New York: Random House, 1999), p. 206.

219　"I do not . . .": "Clinton Offered to Settle Lawsuit; Harassment Plaintiff's Lawyer Releases Text of May Statement," *Washington Post,* October 2, 1994, p. A6.

219　"a terrible precedent . . .": Hillary Clinton, *Living History* (New York: Simon & Schuster, 2003), p. 440.

220　"With the wisdom . . .": Ibid., p. 440.

220　"Judge Susan Webber . . .": Ibid., p. 440.

220　"Although he hated . . .": Ibid., p. 484.

220　"Then Hillary went . . .": Gail Sheehy, *Hillary's Choice* (New York: Random House, 1999), p. 204.

221　"Jennifer . . . decade long . . .": Ibid., p. 204.

221　"was working on . . .": Judy Bachrach, "The President's Private Eye," *Vanity Fair,* September 1998, p. 204.

221　"I had independently . . .": Gail Sheehy, *Hillary's Choice* (New York: Random House, 1999), p. 205.

Chapter 8: Senator Hillary

223　"Speculation that she . . .": Ibid., p. 495.

223　"I was not . . .": Ibid., p. 497.

224　"I had spoken . . .": Ibid., p. 501.

226　"My dilemma was . . .": Ibid., pp. 500–501.

226　"I want independence . . .": Lucinda Franks, "The Intimate Hillary," *Talk,* September 1999.

226　"he was anxious . . .": Hillary Clinton, *Living History* (New York: Simon & Schuster, 2003), p. 501.

229　"one of [Hillary's] . . .": Lucinda Franks, "The Intimate Hillary," *Talk,* September 1999.

229　"Clinton suffered terribly . . .": Ibid.

229 "Hillary acted like . . .": Ibid.

229 "I think she . . .": Ibid.

230 "I was cutting . . .": Ibid.

230 "We like to . . .": Ibid.

231 "she and her . . .": Ibid.

231 "doesn't she look . . .": Ibid.

231 "You could see . . .": Ibid.

232 "of 404 people . . .": Michael Kelly, "Dumb v. Dishonest," *Washington Post,* September 27, 2000, p. A23.

232 "an average rate . . .": Ibid.

232 "more than 100 . . .": Debra Rosenberg, "Many Big Donors to Hillary's Campaign Made the List for Sunday's State Dinner," *Newsweek,* September 6, 2000.

233 "Millennium Dinner at . . .": Roxanne Roberts, "Clinton's Host a Historic Fete; a Repast for the Future at the White House," *Washington Post,* January 1, 2000, p. C1.

233 "At Hillary's Table . . .": Dick Morris, "The Buying of the President," *New York Post,* January 25, 2000.

233 "At the president's . . .": Ibid.

233 "Also attending was . . .": Roxanne Roberts, "Clinton's Host a Historic Fete; a Repast for the Future at the White House," *Washington Post,* January 1, 2000, p. C1.

233 "evolved into an . . .": Ibid.

234 "The small article . . .": Candy Sagon, "Something from the Kitchen; Ann Stock and Walter Scheib Plan a White House Cookbook," *Washington Post,* November 23, 1997, p. M1.

234 "The book featured . . .": Hillary Clinton, *An Invitation to the White House* (New York: Simon & Schuster, 2000), pp. 178–181.

234 "In 1998, Capricia . . .": Ibid., p. 179.

235 "According to *U.S.* . . . ": Sheila Kaplan and Gary Cohen, "Of Perks and the Purse," *U.S. News and World Report,* January 24, 2000, p. 21.

235   "I don't think . . .": Michael Kelly, "Dumb v. Dishonest," *Washington Post,* September 27, 2000, p. A23.

235   "In 1999, alone, . . .": Sheila Kaplan and Gary Cohen, "Of Perks and the Purse," *U.S. News and World Report,* January 24, 2000, p. 21.

235   "She used federal . . .": Ibid.

236   "Hillary took a . . .": Ibid.

236   "The first lady . . .": Ibid.

236   "Late in 1999 . . .": Kemba Johnson, Kathleen McGowan, and Carl Vogel, "Not Quite Fed Up," *CityLimits.org,* December 1998, http://www.citylimits.org/content/articles/articleView.cfm?articlenumber=570 (3/14/2004).

236   "The President restored . . .": Ibid.

236   "HUD Secretary Andrew . . .": AP, "Agency to Allot NY Homeless Funds," *Evote.com,* December 22, 1999, http://www.evote.com/index.asp?Page=/news_section/1999–12/12221999Homeless.asp (3/14/2004).

236   "It's closed because . . .": Roxanne Roberts, "Clinton's Host a Historic Fete; A Repast for the Future at the White House," *Washington Post,* January 1, 2000, p. C1.

237   "a 100-year . . . we appreciate everyone . . .": Mimi Hall and Kathy Kiley, "Clintons Find New Home on Old House Lane Sign Contract for $1.7M Place in NY," *USA Today,* September 3, 1999, p. 4A.

237   "White House aides . . .": Ibid.

237   "Mr. McAuliffe did . . .": Don Van Natta Jr., "Clinton Asked Ex-Aides' Help to Buy House," *New York Times,* September 25, 1999, p. B1.

238   "It weighed very . . .": Ibid.

238   "Terry would do . . .": Ibid.

238   "leaders of several . . .": Ibid.

238   "This is a . . .": Ibid.

238   "Most people would . . .": Ibid.

238 "A million-three . . .": Ibid., p. B1.

238 "Everything that we've . . .": Adam Nagourney, "Ethics Panel Head Says Clintons Misstated Ruling."

238 "Stephen D. Potts . . .": Ibid.

239 "If the President's . . .": Ibid.

239 "only after receiving . . .": Ibid.

241 "a Marxist group . . .": Barbara Olson, *The Final Days: The Last, Desperate Abuses of Power by the Clinton White House* (Washington, DC: Regnery, 2001), pp. 16–17.

241 "New York Puerto . . .": Dan Morgan, "First Lady Opposes Puerto Rican Clemency Offer," *Washington Post,* September 5, 1999, p. A1.

242 "These are people . . .": Barbara Olson, *The Final Days: The Last, Desperate Abuses of Power by the Clinton White House* (Washington, DC: Regnery, 2001), p. 17.

242 "FBI Director Louis . . .": Ibid., p. 18.

242 "The Justice Department . . .": Ibid., p. 18.

242 "criminals, and they . . .": Ibid., p. 18.

242 "Bill Clinton offered . . .": Ibid., p. 18.

242 "no involvement in . . .": Dan Morgan, "First Lady Opposes Puerto Rican Clemency Offer," *Washington Post,* September 5, 1999, p. A1.

242 "hard to believe": Michelle Cottle, "Liberation Movement," *New Republic,* October 4, 1999, p. 20.

242 "August 9th, two . . .": Ibid.

243 "Hillary may also . . .": Ibid.

243 "the backlash against . . .": Dan Morgan, "First Lady Opposes Puerto Rican Clemency Offer," *Washington Post,* September 5, 1999, p. A1.

243 "It's been three . . .": Ibid.

243 "The Clinton family traded . . .": E-mail from Joseph Connor to author, March 21, 2004.

244   "Among her donations . . .": Andrew Goldstein, "Countdown to
       Pardon," *CNN.com*, February 19, 2001, http://www.cnn.com
       /ALLPOLITICS/time/2001/02/26/countdown.html (03/13/2004).

244   "Hasidic districts voted . . .": Barbara Olson, *The Final Days: The
       Last, Desperate Abuses of Power by the Clinton White House* (Wash-
       ington, DC: Regnery, 2001), p. 144.

245   "all four New . . .": Ibid., pp. 143–144.

245   "She'll show up . . .": "Examples of Character," http://gfreitag
       .tripod.com/Examples_of_Character.html (3/14/2004).

245   "Secret Service agents . . .": Ibid.

246   "late-night comics . . .": Hillary Clinton, *Living History* (New York:
       Simon & Schuster, 2003), p. 512.

246   "The tension mounted . . .": Joel Seigel, "Hil Letter-Perfect on
       Dave Show Visit," *New York Daily News*, January 13, 2000, p. 7.

249   "I wasn't going to . . .": Hillary Clinton, *Living History* (New York:
       Simon & Schuster, 2003), p. 520.

249   "she agreed to . . .": "Lazio, Hillary Agree to Soft Money Ban,"
       CNN, September 24, 2000.

249   "Hillary cancelled her . . . I offered condolences . . .": Hillary
       Clinton, *Living History* (New York: Simon & Schuster, 2003),
       p. 522.

250   "He set up phone . . .": Ibid., p. 522.

250   "Rick, stop with . . .": Ibid., p. 522.

252   "As noted, she . . .": U.S. Senate Roll Call Vote, 107th Congress, 1st
       Session, Vote 169, June 9, 2003 (as Asst A.G).

252   "She also opposed . . .": U.S. Sentate Roll Call Vote, 107th Con-
       gress, 1st Session, Vote 167, May 24, 2001 (as Asst A.G).

Chapter 9: The Perfect Storm

256   "Today, these two . . .": Paul Campbell, U.S. Bureau of the Census,
       "Population Projection for States by Age, Sex, Race and Hispanic

Origin: 1995 to 2025," http://www.census.gov/population/www/projections/ppl47.html (3/8/2004).

258   "A CBS-*New York Times* survey . . .": Steven Ertelt, "New Poll Shows Majority of Hispanics Pro-Life," *New York Times,* August 6, 2003.

260   "According to the Fox News . . .": Foxnews/Opinion Dynamics Survey, May 20, 2003.

262   "fund-raising committees . . . the *Buffalo News* reports . . .": Jerry Zremski, "The Senator is Pitching in for Dozens of Democratic Candidate—and Building a National Political Base," *Buffalo News,* 2003.

262   "Soft money is . . .": Glen Justice, "The Supreme Court: The Context; in New Landscape of Campaign Finance, Big Donations Flow to Groups, Not Parties," *New York Times,* December 11, 2003.

263   "Meanwhile public opinion . . .": *Meet the Press* transcript, December 7, 2003 http://www.msnbc.com/news/1002438.asp. (3/14/2004).

ACKNOWLEDGMENTS

First of all, I would like to thank my wife Eileen McGann. I am thrilled that, after all these years of working jointly with me on so many books, she has finally agreed to let me share my byline with her. This book was truly a joint effort in all senses of the word. She's a great wife and a great collaborator.

I remain very indebted to Judith Regan. The book and its title were her and Eileen's inspiration. The cover is pure Judith! She has a great brain but an even better nose, and I have learned to follow her as she picks up the scent of what people are looking for in a book.

Katie Maxwell, my niece who is a senior at Barnard, did much of the research and all of the footnoting. The fact that we still love each other is proof of her charm and that the book is published shows her ability.

Thomas Kuiper sent me massive numbers of Hillary Clinton quotes, and I am grateful for the assistance as I am for the help of Carl from the NewsMax staff.

Jennifer Suitor is a world-class publicist—the best this side of the Pacific Ocean—although she schedules her authors with a touch of sadism that matches our masochism.

Cal Morgan generaled the process and was, as always, magnificent. The ReganBooks team, including Cassie Jones, Derek Gullino, Michelle Ishay, Adrienne Makowski, and Nancy Land, all deserve thanks.

Thanks also to Katie Vecchio for proofreading over and over again.

INDEX

BOOKS BY DICK MORRIS

BECAUSE HE COULD

ISBN 0-06-078415-6 (hardcover)
ISBN 0-06-079213-2 (paperback)

In the wake of Bill Clinton's bestselling memoir *My Life*, Morris and his wife, Eileen McGann, set the record straight with a frank and perceptive deconstruction of the story Clinton tells. *Because He Could* is a fresh and probing portrait of one of the most fascinating—and polarizing—figures of our time.

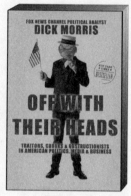

OFF WITH THEIR HEADS

Traitors, Crooks & Obstructionists in American Politics, Media & Business

ISBN 0-06-059550-7 (paperback)

Morris spotlights the many ways the public has been lied to, misled, abused, and pickpocketed.

POWER PLAYS

Win or Lose—How History's Great Political Leaders Play the Game

ISBN 0-06-000444-4 (paperback)

A riveting survey of the most dramatic political moves ever made—from the wildly effective to the utterly disastrous.

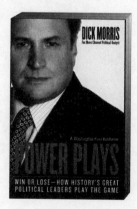

Coming Soon!

CONDI vs. HILLARY

The Next Great Presidential Race

ISBN 0-06-083913-9 (hardcover)

The race between Condoleezza Rice and Hillary Rodham Clinton in the election of 2008 would be the perfect storm of twenty-first-century politics, opening a new era in American politics . . . and leaving America's future hanging in the balance.